State and Diplomacy under Tipu Su'

Documents

edited by Irfan Habib

Indian History Congress

Tulika

Published by **Tulika Books**
35 A/1 Shahpur Jat, New Delhi 110 049, India

© Indian History Congress
First published in India in 2001
Second edition (paperback) 2002
Third edition (paperback) 2014

ISBN: 978-93-82381-48-8

Printed at Chaman Offset, Delhi 110 002

Contents

CONTENTS

Preface

In 1999, while commemorating the bicentennial year of Srirangapatnam, the Indian History Congress published a volume entitled *Confronting Colonialism: Resistance and Modernization under Haidar Ali and Tipu Sultan*. The volume contained a number of papers that had appeared in the *Proceedings* of the various sessions of the Indian History Congress and in various journals, along with an essay on Haidar Ali and Tipu Sultan by the editor, Professor Irfan Habib, serving as introduction.

It had been decided that there would be a supplementary volume, containing papers given at the special panel, 'Srirangapatnam 1799', at the 1999 session of the Congress at the University of Calicut. These paid special attention to the translation and exploration of some important documents of the time of Haidar Ali and Tipu Sultan; there were also studies of particular aspects of the history of Mysore under them. These are brought together in the present volume which too, I am happy to say, Professor Irfan Habib agreed to edit, and he contributes to it a valuable introduction.

The funds for the publication of the volume have come from the generous grant made by Infosys Technologies, Bangalore, supplemented by some other donations, originally made towards the Srirangapatnam Commemoration organized by the Indian History Congress. Our most grateful thanks are due to Mr Girish Karnad and Mr Mohammad Moienuddin, who made the entire project possible by placing our case persuasively before the donors.

This is an apt occasion also to thank most sincerely Professor K.K.N. Kurup, Vice-Chancellor, Calicut University, the host of our 1999 session, for taking so much interest in the success of our Srirangapatnam panel.

I should also like to thank the contributors for their cooperation and for waiting patiently over the two years that it has taken us to publish the volume.

Mr Muniruddin Khan has processed the entire text, while Mr Arshad Ali has maintained all the records and accounts most conscientiously.

To Tulika Books, our publishers, and to Mr Rajendra Prasad and Ms Indira Chandrasekhar personally, I am most deeply beholden, for agreeing to publish the volume, despite the delay in our submitting the press-copy to them and other lapses.

I write this preface as the outgoing Secretary of the Indian History Congress. Professor Ramakrishna Chatterji, the present Secretary, Indian History Congress, has given me utmost encouragement in completing the project which was undertaken during my term. I also gratefully record the indulgence shown to me by Professor S.P. Verma, as Treasurer of the History Congress, during the time I was Secretary.

Aligarh   SHIREEN MOOSVI
4 December 2001

Introduction

Irfan Habib

As part of the Srirangapatnam bicentennial, the Indian
History Congress published a volume, *Confronting Colonialism: Resistance and Modernization under Haidar Ali and Tipu Sultan* (Tulika,
New Delhi, 1999). The volume, which I was privileged to edit, contained a number of papers previously published in the *Proceedings of the
Indian History Congress* and in different journals, over the course of
sixty years. The editor's introduction and an article by Professor S.P.
Verma were the only fresh contributions. The present volume supplements *Confronting Colonialism* by offering fresh material, whether as
translations of documents not translated previously, or as essays on
various aspects of the history of Haidar Ali and Tipu Sultan. Only two
of the contributions are reprints, both from William Kirkpatrick's
voluminous *Select Letters of Tippoo Sultan* (London, 1811), which is
today almost as rare as a manuscript work. The other papers—translations of texts, commentaries on documents and interpretive essays—
were written for the Srirangapatnam symposium at the 60th session of
the Indian History Congress held at Calicut University in December
1999, two of them (by Dr Lafont and Dr Brittlebank) having been
presented *in absentia*.

As the title hopefully indicates, the main object of this volume
is not only to add fresh contributions to the papers collected in *Confronting Colonialism*, but also to present to the reader documentary
evidence which has possibly not yet received its due in studies on
Haidar Ali and Tipu Sultan. Not surprisingly, the neglected documentation is mainly in Persian and French. The immediate impulse of the
Anglo–Mysore Wars and the fall of Tipu Sultan led to the publication
of the translations of Tipu's revenue regulations by Crisp in 1792, of
some of his correspondence with the French (*Official Documents*

relating to the Negotiations carried on by Tippoo Sultan with the French Nation, etc. by order of the Governor General in Council, Calcutta, 1799), and of Kirkpatrick's voluminous *Select Letters* (1811).[1] Thereafter, the work of translation (or even exploration) of Persian sources has remained occasional and desultory in character. Among the relatively recent additions are the *Waqa'i'-i Manazil-i Rum*, the report of the journey of Tipu Sultan's embassy to Istanbul (Constantinople), 1786–87, the text accompanied by commentary in English by the editor, Mohibbul Hasan, himself a notable biographer of Tipu Sultan.[2] As for French, the importance of the material in that language is increasingly recognized, and we are perhaps now a long way from the earlier period of neglect. Suman Venkatesh's translation of *Correspondence of the French during the Reign of Haidar Ali and Tipu Sultan* (three volumes published from Bangalore by 1998) is one indication of the fruitfulness of the new interest. It is hoped that the present volume will mark a further stage of progress in the exploration and use of source material on Tipu in both Persian and French.

Tipu's Memoirs

The Persian material which the present volume presents begins with Tipu Sultan's own memoirs, written some time after 1792, and surviving in a defective but unique copy at the India Office Library, London (Ethe's Catalogue No. 2990). The whole of it needs to be translated; for the present, we have only some fragments translated by Kirkpatrick, placed at different parts in his *Select Letters*. Brought together here, three of these contain Tipu's recollections of the Second Mysore War (1780–84).[3] These recollections are important in that they reflect both Tipu's personality and his rather dim view of the French conduct during the war.

Tipu's personality best appears in the matter-of-fact way in which he describes the various measures he took as commander in the lifetime of his father (Haidar Ali died in December 1783) and during the late stage of the war when he was himself the ruler. There is little self-praise or vainglory here; and where, as when he exposed himself to danger in battle, one may expect him to underline his own courage, we find him modestly reticent. On the other hand, there is certainly an anxiety to explain why he treated Mathew and the English under his command after their capitulation at Bednur in 1783 in the manner that he did; and, similarly, there is certainly a considerable element of point-scoring in his long discourse on how he wished to protect the interests of the Marathas in his negotiations with the English before terminating the Second Mysore War. This is interesting in that they underline Tipu Sultan's perception of the English as his main enemy and of the Marathas as possible allies who, however, failed at every time of test. The Marathas failed most notably in 1782, by concluding the Treaty of Salbai with the English behind the back of Haidar Ali, whom, so Tipu insists, they had themselves begged to enter the war against the English.

The memoirs give the chief reasons for Tipu's dissatisfaction with the French. He was not impressed by Bussy's very defensive posture at Cuddalore, though the French general, who had once commanded immense influence over the Nizam in the 1750s, was still not as senile as Tipu thought him to be. His difficulties were compounded by the Treaty of Paris (1783), which the French made with the English, without any thought given to the interests of Mysore. This was a repeat, for Tipu, of the Treaty of Salbai, and one can understand his profound bitterness with his erstwhile allies on this score.

Briefs for Ambassadors

Tipu's memoirs, fragmentary as they are, in the translation available to us, fit well with the much longer documents that Professor Iqbal Husain has translated for this volume. These are statements of instructions (*hukmnamas*) given by Tipu in November 1785 to his ambassadors required to proceed to Turkey and then to France and England; these are supplemented by those issued in August–November 1786 for his embassy sailing directly to France. The documents are contained in a single volume at the Indian Museum, Calcutta (MS No. 1677).

The Mission to Turkey

Professor Iqbal Husain's full translation of Tipu's instructions to his envoys to Turkey provides the most authentic source for discovering Tipu's objects in dispatching the embassy, a subject on which Wilks fretted that he had no authentic information.[4] A reading of these documents should lay to rest the ghost of a 'search for legitimacy' which, since Professor Istiaq Husain Qureshi's essay 66 years ago,[5] has been accepted by practically every writer on Tipu as the embassy's real object. We read in Dr Kate Brittlebank's monograph that Tipu's ambassadors 'were *instructed* to seek the Ottoman ruler's confirmation, in his role as Caliph, of legitimacy of Tipu's claims and his rule of Mysore'.[6]

Nowhere do such instructions occur anywhere in the briefs for his ambassadors. Tipu does not even designate the Ottoman ruler as Khalifa (Caliph), or recognize his authority outside his dominions in any way whatsoever. Throughout his instructions to his ambassadors he treats the Ruler of Islambol (Istanbul) as an equal, not a superior. He is so far from having in his mind any anxiety to get a title from the Sultan, that his own ambassadors are enjoined to refer to him, as to Haidar Ali, simply as their *aqa* or master. Not once does he ask them to solicit the Porte for explicit recognition as Sultan. It should also not be forgotten that in the diplomatic environment of the eighteenth century no particular sanctity attached to any diploma from the Ottoman ruler, whom almost no one in India seriously thought of as the Caliph. I have not been able to locate the 'letters patent' or *farman* of the Ottoman Caliph, which supposedly 'gave Tipu permission to assume the title of an independent king and the right to strike coins and to have the *khutba* [Friday sermon] read in his name'.[7] Everyone seems to accept the existence of such a document (rather than of a diplomatic response by the Turkish ruler to Tipu's proposals), but no such document is extant; and when the trails are pursued, we find that the sole grounds for its existence is a news-report received by the British in June 1787 from a source remote from Constantinople, and located apparently in Hyderabad, although the embassy itself returned only in 1790.[8]

Tipu wished, through his ambassadors, to propose to Turkey that a Turkish expeditionary force be sent to India (ff. 10b–11b).[9] The explanation to be given to the Ottoman ruler of the need for this intervention was that the English had seized large territories of Hindustan and were oppressing Muslims. Again, the identification of the English as the principal enemy is manifest, although Tipu was at this time at peace with them and at war with the Marathas. As to the latter, he assured the Porte that he could look after them himself (f. 15a).

It is obvious from the instructions issued to the embassy that while a military expedition from Turkey was to be proposed, the main object of the mission was commercial. Tipu Sultan wished to hurt the trade of the English East India Company, and for this reason he had imposed a blockade of the Malabar coast under his control, a measure examined by Professor Nikhiles Guha in his paper in this volume. Such an attempt to be successful required alternative markets for the products of Mysore, and the hope was that these could be found in West Asia, especially the Ottoman empire. Given this object, Tipu's mission was partly of an exploratory nature. It was well supplied with textiles, sandalwood and pepper; and Tipu lays down strict rules as to how these goods were to be sold (ff. 50b–51a). It is probable that one reason why the route of the embassy was changed from the Red Sea (where Jedda was to be its projected port of disembarkation) to the Persian Gulf was because of the greater commercial attraction of the latter area.[10] The *Waqa'i'-i Manazil-i Rum*, already mentioned, being the report that the secretary (*munshi*) of the mission, 'Abdu'l Qadir, sent from Basra, dated 9 January 1787, is full of commercial information, with detailed statements of the prices of various goods reigning at Musqat, Bushire and Basra, the major ports of call for the mission's fleet. The *Waqa'i'* also contains detailed reports of the effort to sell the products carried by the mission.

The port of Basra, whose description is the most detailed in 'Abdu'l Qadir's report, was the prize that Tipu was seeking. He hoped that the Turkish ruler could be persuaded to lease it to him in return either for payment of a sum or in lieu of the lease of a port on the Mysore coast to Turkey. Basra could offer his fleet refuge during the fury of the monsoons; and this was important, he urged his envoys to tell the Turkish Sultan, because in order to face the English, he needed to have a good fleet. Nothing came of the proposal, and Tipu's enthusiasm too may have waned on learning that all his three ships which carried the embassy to Basra perished while they were within the Basra estuary.[11]

While commercial relations with Turkey did not prosper as Tipu had wished, it is still interesting to see what he wanted, beyond the lease of the port of Basra. This was the import of technical skills.

Tipu asked his envoys to assure the Sultan of Turkey that 'by the grace of God, innumerable muskets and cannon-pieces are manufactured in the country of the government (Mysore)'. They were to show him the muskets manufactured in Mysore and carried by men of their escort (f. 16a). Tipu's pride in the muskets produced in his workshops was not ill-placed. The report of an accident on the *Fath Shahi*

Mu'izzi, carrying the principal ambassador to Turkey (Ghulam Ali Khan), testifies to the fact that the Mysore soldiers carried flint-locks (and not the more primitive match-locks).[12]

Despite his confidence in his own manufactures, Tipu instructed the officials (Muhammad Hanif, &c.) accompanying the embassy, to buy certain specified types of guns and 'European muskets' available at the ports of Musqat and Jedda (f. 59a). The envoys to Turkey were to seek craftsmen who could 'manufacture muskets and cannon-pieces' and recruit them into Tipu's service. He wanted to have from Turkey such artisans too, as could make 'clocks (*gharial*), glass, chinaware and mirrors' (f. 16b). Of these, clocks were technologically the most significant; but it is questionable if Ottoman Turkey had any craftsmen in this art whom it could export to India.[13]

Tipu had become aware of the extensive use that was being made of coal (that is, mineral coal) as domestic and industrial fuel in . Europe, and thought that this too could be obtained from the Ottoman empire (ff. 7b–8a). Muhammad Hanif, &c., were told to obtain at Jedda or Musqat, quantities of 'stone-coal' (*sang-i angisht*), 'either free or at some price'. Tipu believed that there was 'much stone-coal' in that country (presumably, the Arabian peninsula), though on the basis of what information he thought so, is not clear. He planned to import it in large quantities as ballast on the returning ships (f. 52b). There is no reference to coal in the very detailed list of commodities procurable at Musqat when the mission's fleet anchored there in 1787, though firewood and sulphur appear on the price-list.[14] Tipu was, nevertheless, perhaps the first Indian potentate (if not the first Indian) to apprehend the value of coal and try to obtain it. If it could not be imported, he wished to have coal ores explored within his dominions. A desire was conveyed to the embassy to Istanbul and, as planned, to France, that it should procure four persons skilled in detecting the presence of coal ores for service in Mysore (f. 10b).

Another well-known object of Tipu's interest was sericulture. As Professor Iqbal Husain, the translator, duly notes, Tipu desired that from Jedda or Musqat, both 'silkworms and those who culture them' should be brought over to Mysore (f. 52b). Kirkpatrick translates a letter from Tipu at about the same time (18 November 1785), addressed to his agent at Musqat, pointing out that silkworms were cultured in Jazira-i Daraz ('Long Island') within the Persian Gulf, and asking him to procure from there both silkworms and eggs, and also 'five or six men, acquainted with the proper mode of rearing them'.[15] It seems, however, that it was from Bengal that he ultimately received a good supply of silkworms for his purpose.[16]

The fleet carrying the very large mission to Turkey suffered disaster after disaster. One ship was burnt in the Basra estuary, causing a number of deaths among those aboard. A large number of trained soldiers, especially from the elite corps, the Asadullahis, were sent with the mission to impress the Porte with their arms, discipline and military bearing. But the Turkish authorities would not permit so many to proceed to Istanbul, and a number of them then perished when the two returning ships they were aboard were destroyed by a storm not far from Basra. The remaining were further depleted by disease and cold; yet, according to a French report, a number of the Mysore sepoys were still left and, in a demonstration before the Grand Vizier, they 'went through the European exercises with great regularity and quickness'.[17]

The Turkish court, however, had no interest in Tipu Sultan's main proposal of a fight against the English and saw no particular profit in developing the kinds of commercial ties Tipu wanted, especially the lease of Basra. In terms of the specified objectives the mission was a failure, with all its expenditure in human lives and money. Yet, the vision behind it demands admiration from anyone other than the partisans of Tipu's enemies, like Wilks, who could only sneer at the enterprise and cheer its failure.[18]

The Mission to France

In the original plan, the committee of four ambassadors, Ghulam 'Ali Khan, Nurullah Khan, Lutf 'Ali Khan and Ja'far Khan, were to be the first to proceed to Istanbul, and then, hopefully with the assistance of the Turkish government, to Paris, and finally, to England. Not only were they furnished with general instructions for their conduct but they were also given specific briefs for the representations they were to make before the sovereigns of the three countries. All of these were issued on 17 November 1785. There were gifts to be presented at the courts, including one elephant at each court (with one elephant to be kept in reserve!). This was still the plan when the mission set sail aboard three ships and a galliot from Tardi on 9 March 1786. The mission remained under the impression that it had to go to France and England, even when its secretary penned his report to Tipu from Basra on 9 January 1787.[19] But the slow pace of the mission's progress persuaded Tipu that a mission sent directly to France would be more desirable; and so, some time between 15 August and 19 November 1786, Tipu decided to send a three-man embassy (Muhammad Darvesh Khan, Akbar Ali Khan and Muhammad Usman) to Paris aboard a French ship sailing from Pondicherry. Ghulam 'Ali Khan and his colleagues were ultimately asked to return home from Istanbul, although in the initial letter of instructions to Muhammad Darvesh Khan and his two co-ambassadors the expectation still was that they would be followed to Paris by Ghulam 'Ali Khan and his colleagues to continue the negotiations (f. 60a).[20]

The brief given to Darvesh Khan's mission to Paris is rather short (ff. 60b–61a), confined to the matter of the supply of muskets and guns and the recruitment of artisans. But it is to be assumed that the instructions that were given to the mission to Istanbul were also conveyed to this mission, since there is evidence that points mentioned there were in fact duly raised by Darvesh Khan's mission in France. The latter mission disembarked at Toulon on 9 June 1788 and left France, sailing from Brest, on 17 November, to arrive in India in May 1789. Fortunately, a substantial collection of the official documents concerned with this mission has been rendered into English by Dr Suman Venkatesh, so that we can now compare Tipu Sultan's proposals set out in his *hukmnamas* to both his missions, and the French responses to those proposals.

The *hukmnama* to Ghulam 'Ali Khan, &c. (in the Indian Museum MS, ff. 22b–30a) shows that Tipu expected his envoys to give a detailed account of his grievances at the unilateral French withdrawal from the war in 1783, and the conduct of Bussy both before and after the receipt of the news of the Treaty of Paris. We have already seen that these grievances recur with the same bitterness in Tipu's memoirs written later. Darvesh Khan and his colleagues apparently handed a letter to King Louis XIV with similar contents.[21]

The French response was an astonishing apology delivered on behalf of the King of France, in which Bussy was made the scapegoat:

His Imperial Majesty has given particular attention to what is written. He has seen with great regret the manner in which M. de Bussy who was asked to command the troops in India behaved during the time of the last peace. His intention should not have been to separate from such a faithful ally as Tipu Sultan without informing him about the negotiations which had begun in Europe about the cease-fire. But the distance of these places, the advanced age, the infirmity of the French General, would surely make you understand that the General had not comprehended the instructions which had been sent to him and he did not definitely adhere to them.[22]

Bussy had died on 4 August 1784, and so could the more easily be thrown to the wolves; but there was an inherent element of strength in Tipu's case against the conduct of his major ally, which could not be easily refuted or brushed aside.[23]

What was less easy for the French court to do was to respond as affirmatively to the conclusions Tipu drew from a statement of his grievances: a fresh French army should be sent to India, 10,000-strong, to be under Tipu's authority within India, for jointly driving out the English and dividing up their possessions. No separate peace was to be made with the English, even if ten years were to pass in warfare. All these were to be put in the form of a treaty, the draft of which was furnished to the French side (ff. 7b–9a).

It is not certain whether this draft was put before the French government by Tipu's ambassadors in 1788, but there was an exchange on the subject between the ambassadors and Ruffin, the French government's representative, on 19 August. The French government was overburdened by the expenditure of the late war and in the throes of a financial crisis that would lead to the Revolution of 1789. Given these constraints, the warlike proposals of Tipu Sultan were rejected with this soothing homily:

> In this moment of general peace between us and also with Tipu Sultan,[24] we cannot agree to any hostile proposition whatsoever, for [but?] we will take into consideration the steps to be taken that he could suggest to us for the future and in case of aggression against us directly. We have no wish to expand our territories in Hindustan. We will not even look on our expansion as advantageous. Our intentions are that all the local princes of this part of Asia, be in peaceful possession of their respective states and only favour our commerce.

Tipu's ambassadors had no option but to accept this position and agree to the general sentiments of friendship. But they too could not restrain themselves from stating some general truths for the benefit of the French:

> You wish to be merchants but in the existing state of affairs you cannot be so, without having a territory in Hindustan. As long as your enemies are lords there, your commerce there will be nil. Become what they are, or see to it that they are no longer so, and then you will be what you wish; and I have said enough, and you will be happy.

Having made his repartee on behalf of the ambassadors, Muhammad Usman 'went back to his usual taciturnity'.[25] He had, indeed, said enough. But the reality in France was as constraining as the opportunity in India was inviting. The war for men's minds would begin in 1789, but the war over colonies was lost and over for France.

Tipu too had by no means put all his eggs in the war-basket. Had he been confident of a French agreement over a joint war against the English, he would not have included England as the last stage in the itinerary of the embassy led by Ghulam 'Ali Khan. A major object in sending the embassy to France was to recruit craftsmen; and this did not involve warfare.

While the Istanbul embassy, also due to visit France, was asked to obtain the services of makers of 'muskets, guns, clocks, glass, mirrors, chinaware and cannon-balls' (f. 3b), the embassy directly sent to France had a much larger order (f. 61a). Tipu was proud of his ten musket factories and their products, but he wanted craftsmen making new kinds of muskets and iron cannons. He was obviously aware that muskets were all the time being improved in Europe. He therefore desired that the French king send him craftsmen capable of making new kinds of muskets and *bejars birs* (?), i.e. iron cannon-pieces (f. 61a). The reference to iron cannons suggests an anxiety to introduce cast-iron guns. Then, by way of repetition, they were to get 'clock-makers, makers of chinaware, glass- and mirror-makers and other artisans', no less than ten of each kind (f. 61a). Of special interest is an additional requirement: 'a printer (*chhapasaz*) of books', to be enticed with the advance of a proper amount (f. 61a). It is a pity that this last objective, of establishing a printing press in Mysore, could not be resolutely pursued. The French king had no particular hesitation to cooperate in the search for artisans, and a genuine effort seems to have been made to procure 'workers, useful items and seeds' for Tipu Sultan.

Arrangements were made for engaging G. Le Brun and F. Le Melloc, experts in the making of cannons and guns, and Mouriset of the royal foundries (a blacksmith 'for all the fire-arms') with a group of four under him, comprising two master-craftsmen, a carpenter and a turner.[26] Monot, an optician, and two glass-makers were also engaged, but no porcelain-makers could be induced to go to Mysore.[27] These were not anywhere near the numbers desired, viz. ten of each craft,[28] and our documents do not tell us of any success in obtaining shipwrights, as well as 'a skilled astronomer, geomancer (!) and physician' that Tipu was also seeking (f. 10b). However, even if the success in technology importation was limited, confined mainly perhaps to armaments, watches and sericulture, Tipu's efforts, in another age, would have been seen as a significant step towards industrialization.

French Policy towards Tipu

This is perhaps the best place to introduce two contributions to this volume, one by Dr Jean-Marie Lafont, on the memoirs written by Lieutenant-Colonel Russel in 1780–81, and the other by Professor Aniruddha Ray, covering the entire range of various French projects about Mysore during the period of Haidar Ali and Tipu Sultan. Russel had served with Haidar Ali and was distrustful of his ambitions, but, as Dr Lafont notes, his views did not affect the French government's decision, in 1781, to send an expeditionary force under Bussy to fight the English in alliance with Mysore. There is a very interesting sketch of Tipu's personality from Russel's pen, referring to the time when Tipu was a prince serving under his father. This is given as an appendix to Dr Lafont's paper. We see that even before the Second Mysore War, Tipu had proclaimed himself an enemy of the English: 'I want to expel them from India. I want to be a friend of the French all my life.'

Professor Ray's canvas is larger and relates to French strategies towards Mysore, which, as he shows, were governed, on the one hand, by France's own colonial interests in the Indian Ocean and, on the other, by her internal compulsions and external relations. His treatment supplements and corrects, in important respects, the narrative of S.P. Sen in his pioneer study, *The French in India*, which we have already had occasion to refer to. There were many competing interests and many voices which the French policy-makers had to consider, during a period when France itself underwent such a momentous change as the French Revolution (1789). For Tipu, France was the major hope by which Mysore could escape from the noose that Britain kept tightening around it. France's inability to deliver crucial assistance at a time of need paved the road to the tragic finale at Srirangapatnam. Professor Ray lays out for us the shifts in French aims, priorities and means during those fateful years.

The State under Tipu Sultan

The documents which Dr I.G. Khan introduces to us on Tipu Sultan's revenue administration belong to his last three or four years, 1795–98. They, therefore, belong to a period different from that of the documents translated by B. Crisp, published from Calcutta in 1792. We must remember that when the orders which Dr I.G. Khan calendars were issued, Tipu Sultan had only half his kingdom under his control, the other half having been seized by the English and their allies in 1792. More, the half that had been left to him had been devastated by the imposition of a tribute of Rs 3.30 crore, amounting to three times its annual revenue.[29] And yet there is, on the part of Tipu, the same drive and the same attention to agricultural improvement that one notices in the earlier documents. The peasants should be enjoined to work harder, given *taccavi* loans and protected from physical violence (order no 28; also no. 41). Canals, wells and dams should be repaired (order no. 11; also no. 27). Workshops of iron and steel should be established in the localities, their products to be sent to the government or sold in the market (order no. 40; also no. 57). And there should be no distillation of alcohol or cultivation of *bhang* (order no. 55a). To the end, it seems, Tipu was intent on doing whatever he thought was good for his people or would strengthen the state.

These orders provide the kind of evidence that sustains Professor Nikhiles Guha's analysis of the nature of Tipu Sultan's state and his commercial measures. Developing the thesis put forward in his *Pre-British State System in South India: Mysore 1761–99* (Calcutta, 1981), he points out that Tipu's invocation of Islam was linked to his desire to generate greater enthusiasm in his struggle against the English. He aptly quotes an English officer, Edward Moore, who observed in 1794 that Tipu's 'subjects, he [Tipu] may possibly think, will with more reverence listen to his mandates when sanctioned by religion'. At the same time, Dr Guha argues, Tipu continued the older traditions of the Mysore *raj* with donations to temples and employment of Hindu officials. It may be worthwhile to remind ourselves that another English officer, also writing in 1797, described Tipu as 'a politic and able sovereign who nourishes, not oppresses, [his] subjects'.[30]

Dr Brittlebank examines the views of Tipu Sultan that prevailed after his last stand at Srirangapatnam. One would agree that it is always important for historians to separate the subjective perception of participants in an event from the causes and consequences that we can, 'with hindsight', establish. The problem, however, lies with the hindsight, or the larger view, of historical processes that individual historians now entertain. The view of one historian may be very different from another's. This, we can see, to take China as an example, in how not only the Yi He Tuan ('Boxer') Rebellion has been treated at the hands of western and Chinese historians, but also the Opium Wars. Tipu, too, can perhaps be perceived in as many ways. But so long as the Indian people cherish some care for those who stood fast in resistance to British colonialism, the memory of Tipu should ever remain fresh and green.

At the end of the volume there is an Appendix containing a discussion of Tipu Sultan's calendars by William Kirkpatrick, taken from the introductory portion of his *Select Letters of Tippoo Sultan*. This is reprinted here because of its value as a text of reference for finding equivalents of dates given in our documents in terms of the months and years instituted by Tipu Sultan. It is important to understand that his months were lunar (or nominally lunar), while the year was solar, and conformed to the agricultural calendar.

Notes and References

[1] See bibliography in *Confronting Colonialism*, pp. 193–94. By a slip it is stated there that Kirkpatrick's *Select Letters of Tippoo Sultan* draws on the Asiatic Society, Persian MS No. 1677. These are in fact not included in the *Select Letters* at all. The *Select Letters* contain renderings of letters in Kirkpatrick's own possession, the volume of which he later presented to the India Office Library.

[2] The *Waqa'i'-i Manazil-i Rum* was published from Bombay in 1968. Mohibbul Hasan's *History of Tipu Sultan*, 2nd edn, Calcutta, 1971, is still the standard biography of Tipu.

[3] The three fragments are found in Kirkpatrick, *Select Letters*, pp. 18–21, 374–75, and Appendix B, pp. iii–xi. For three other fragments, see ibid., pp. 202–07, 325–32, 425–31.

[4] Mark Wilks, *Historical Sketches of the South of India, etc.* (original edn, London, 2 vols, 1810 and 1817), edited by Murray Hammick, II, Mysore, 1930, p. 362.

[5] Originally printed in *Journal of Indian History*, XXIV, 1945, pp. 77–84; reprinted in *Confronting Colonialism*, pp. 69–78.

[6] Kate Brittlebank, *Tipu Sultan's Search for Legitimacy: Islam and Kingship in a Hindu Domain*, Delhi, 1997, p. 70. Similar statements are made by Mohibbul Hasan in *Waqa'i'-i Manazil-i Rum*, editor's introduction, p. 1, and in *History of Tipu Sultan*, 2nd edn, pp. 128–29.

[7] Mohibbul Hasan, *History of Tipu Sultan*, 2nd edn, p. 137.

[8] The news-report from one 'Mir Muhammad Hussain' was quoted by I.H. Qureshi (in the paper reprinted in *Confronting Colonialism*, p. 76); the reporter could not possibly have had any knowledge of what was transpiring in Constantinople.

[9] Since Professor Iqbal Husain enters the folio numbers of the MS at the corresponding positions in the translation, the reader can easily trace the statement cited by its folio reference in the present volume.

[10] The decision to change the route of the journey was conveyed to the members of the embassy by a letter dated 1 March 1786 (Kirkpatrick, *Select Letters*, pp. 264–66). One reason given for the change was that the sailing season for the Red Sea had passed, and the second was that the mission would now be able to visit Basra, whose possession on lease Tipu was seeking owing to its commercial importance.

[11] The *Nabi Bakhsh* first caught fire and sank, taking the lives of 50 persons (*Waqa'i'-i Manazil-i Rum*, pp. 40–41, 59–60), and then the *Fath Shahi Mu'izzi* and the galliot *Surati* sank within the estuary as they left Basra for Musqat, when a sudden storm rose, leaving only 103 survivors out of the 400 who were aboard (ibid., pp. 98–99).

[12] A *yuzukdar* (night-guard), 'out of negligence, ignorance and enthusiasm put out his hand to press the flint-stone of the musket, and the musket immediately went off, the lead-pellet lodging in the arm of a servant of Ghulam 'Ali Khan' (*Waqa'i'-i Manazil-i Rum*, text, pp. 18–19).

[13] In 1666–77 Chardin had reported that the Turks 'lay out at least 150,000 crowns a year, to my certain knowledge' in buying watches; 'yet the Turks do not go about to learn that trade which they see so profitable' *(Sir John Chardin's Travels in Persia*, rpt of 1720 edn, II, London, 1927, p. 249). But that was, of course, over a hundred years before Tipu sent his envoys to Istanbul.

[14] *Waqa'i'-i Manazil-i Rum*, text, pp. 15–16.

[15] Kirkpatrick, *Select Letters*, p. 186.

[16] Ibid., pp. 418–19, for a letter of Tipu to the castellan (*qila'dar*) of Srirangapatnam, dated 27 September 1786.

[17] Quoted by Mohibbul Hasan (in *Waqa'i'-i Manazil-i Rum*, editor's introduction, p. 61.

[18] Mark Wilks, *Historical Sketches of South of India*, II, pp. 362–67.

[19] The information was conveyed by Tipu's ambassador to the French factors

at Basra and Baghdad, that they would be proceeding to the court of the French king (*Waqa'i-i Manazil-i Rum*, text, pp. 50–51); and the gifts intended for the king of England were cleaned and repaired at Basra (ibid., pp. 65–66).

[20] This was also stated in the letter of credentials for Darvesh Khan and his colleagues signed by Tipu and handed over at Versailles for submission to the French king on 10 August 1788 (S. Venkatesh (trans.), *The Correspondence of the French during the Reigns of Hyder Ali and Tipu Sultan*, III, Bangalore, 1998, p. 98).

[21] The French translation of a 'representation' by Tipu's ambassadors to the King of France is obviously only the first part of a longer statement, since it ends abruptly (ibid., p.196). It agrees fairly closely with the first portion (ff. 22b–23a) of the long statement Ghulam 'Ali Khan, & c., had been required to lay before the King of France, and which went on to set out Tipu's grievances (ff. 23a–29a).

[22] S. Venkatesh (trans.), *Correspondence of the French*, pp. 96–97.

[23] Not, however, for S.P. Sen, who in his *The French in India, 1705–1816*, (Calcutta, 1958, pp. 381–93), is not only hostile to Tipu throughout, but even censures his conduct in not allowing the French to intervene in his negotiations with the English, after the French themselves had quite unilaterally withdrawn from the war.

[24] The allusion obviously is to the separate peace treaties concluded between the English and the French (1783) and the English and Tipu (1784).

[25] S. Venkatesh (trans.), *Correspondence of the French*, pp. 114–15.

[26] Ibid., pp. 278–81.

[27] Ibid., pp. 210–11.

[28] Ibid., p. 210.

[29] *Confronting Colonialism*, editor's introduction, pp. xxxviii–xxxix.

[30] John Dirom, *A Narrative of the Campaign in India which Terminated the War with Tippoo Sultan in 1792*, 2nd edn, 1794, pp. 249–50.

TIPU SULTAN'S MYSORE

Mysore boundary, 1789 —··—··—
Boundary of area lost in1792 ·········

A Lost to British
B „   „ Nizam
C „   „ Marathas

0   50   100 K.M.

Faiz Habib

MARATHAS · Raichur · KRISHNA · B · Adoni · Kurnool · Cumbum · Panjim GOA · Dharwar · C TUNGABHADRA · Gooty · B · PENNER · Tadri · Cuddapah · Bednur (Nagar) · Sira · Coondapoor · Sringeri · Dod Ballapur · Hoskote · C · Chennapatan or Madras · Bangalore · Arcot · Koryal or Mangalore · SRIRANGAPATNAM · Wandiwash · COORG · Mysore · CAUVERY · A · CARNATIC · Pondicherry · Cannanore · Tellicherry · Mahe · A · Cuddalore · Porto Nova · Calicut · Farukhabad · Coimbatore · Trichinopoly · Thanjavur · Travancore Lines · Cochin · Dindigul · CEYLON · KRISHNA

xxiv

SRIRANGAPATNAM
The Last Stand 1799

CAUVERY

R

Bridge

Dungeon
Tipu fell here
Wellesley Brigade
Water Gate
Sriranga Temple
Tipu's Palace
Breach
Rajah's Palace
Mosque
Bangalore Gate
Branch of Cauvery R.
Flag Staff
Mysore Gate
Canal
Madras Army

0   250   500 Metres

Faiz Habib

Documents

War and Peace

Tipu Sultan's Account of the Last Phase
of the Second War with the English, 1783–84

Translation by William Kirkpatrick

William Kirkpatrick rendered great service to the cause of historical research by gathering together a large number of records, especially letters, of Tipu Sultan, which had fallen into private hands after the English sack of Shrirangapattana (Srirangapatnam or Seringapatam) in 1799. He published a large volume entitled *Select Letters of Tippoo Sultan to Various Public Functionaries* (London, 1811); here, he gave translations of 435 letters drawn from a register containing texts, with a considerable amount of commentary and annotation.

Kirkpatrick came into possession of 'a highly interesting manuscript, purporting to be a Memoir of Tipu Sultan, written by himself'. He goes on to describe the manuscript as follows:

This curious document was among the numerous papers discovered by Colonel Ogg. The copy with which that gentleman favoured me was entitled *Tareekhe Khodadady*, i.e. the *Khodadady* Annals, or History of the *Khodadad Sircar*. The work was, from the beginning, in an imperfect state; the narrative being brought to no later a period than the termination of the Mahrattah war, or the month of February 1787. My copy, however, has been rendered still more incomplete, by an unfortunate accident, which occasioned the destruction of several leaves of it. The original Memoir evidently formed, as far as it went, the ground-work of the more diffuse and elaborate history of Zynul Aabideen Shoostry, mentioned by Colonel Wilks, and called by its author, in allusion to his master's name, 'the Sultan of History'. I am not enabled to say, whether the copy of the fragment found by Colonel Ogg was in the actual hand-writing of the *Sultan*: but, however this may be, I venture to think, that no just doubt can be entertained of its genuineness. It was discovered in the palace of the *Sultan*, and along with other documents of unquestioned authenticity. The style and matter of it, moreover, abundantly support its claim to credit. It is written throughout in the first person; and while it states some facts which could be known only to the *Sultan*, it everywhere breathes the same over-weening spirit, which so strongly distinguishes almost every production of his pen.[1]

The manuscript was presented by Kirkpatrick in 1811 to the India Office Library, London, where it now bears Ethe's Catalogue No. 2990. It has forty-five folios of eleven lines each, and is defective at the beginning.[2] It has not been translated so far, but Kirkpatrick provides translations of three separate parts from it.

In Appendix B, pp. iii–xi, Kirkpatrick gives his translation of the first part of the Memoirs. The manuscript was found by Kirkpatrick in a defective state, being partly destroyed during the violent seizure of Tipu Sultan's archives at Srirangapatnam (Shrirangapattana). It was further damaged by a later accident.[3] As Kirkpatrick explains, it lacks, therefore, his account of his 'march from Seringapatam to Bidnore [Bednur] and of his first operations against General Mathews' (Appendix B, p. iii), and so begins rather abruptly with his siege of Bednur in 1783.

The translation continues on pp. 374–75, as part of his 'Observations' on Letter No. 336, where we have Part 2 of Tipu's account. After a break in the translation (the intervening text being summarized on pp. 375–76), the translation of Part 3 is furnished on pp. 18–21, under 'Observations' on Letter No. 8. As mentioned in the introduction, three other fragments of the Memoirs are also translated by Kirkpatrick in his *Select Letters*.

Despite his strong bias against Tipu Sultan, Kirkpatrick attempts a very literal translation—so literal, indeed, that it does not represent the original quite accurately in spirit. Many expressions and spellings too would now appear archaic. Kirkpatrick is careful to quote the original text in footnotes wherever he had doubts about his own rendering; his translation, is, however, usually found to be accurate enough in such cases.

Since Kirkpatrick's volume is now very rare, and Tipu Sultan's account of his own actions and perception of events has a value of its own, his translations of the three parts dealing with the Second Mysore War are put together here. Not much liberty has been taken with

Kirkpatrick's translation, except for modernizing the spellings of some words, putting in some words which seem to represent the Persian original better, and removing certain linguistic obscurities. The quotations in Persian writing have not been reproduced, but Kirkpatrick's own footnotes have been largely retained. Some statements of Kirkpatrick obviously display his bias against Tipu Sultan, as, for example, in footnote 13 below. My own comments in both the main text and the footnotes are within square brackets.

It may be noted that Tipu Sultan, who must have composed this account some time after the Treaty of Mangalore, concluded in March 1784,[4] wrote it as a private document and so is uninhibited in his expressions, which are here rendered more or less exactly as in the original. In the translated portions, there occur no dates; some essential dates are, therefore, furnished within square brackets.

Irfan Habib

TRANSLATION

Part 1

A discharge of artillery and musketry succeeded, which occasioned the loss of a few of those who looked on.[5] Then the troops of the *Usud-Ilhye* [Asadullahi],[6] and the French people, advancing on each side of the road, gave another discharge of musketry. Immediately on hearing this discharge, I (being then seated at the distance of a hundred yards) advanced rapidly with a division, when about sixty of the English people were sent to hell. The rest being pursued left behind them the two guns they had previously seized on: and thus the aforesaid English (*Nazarenes*)[7] were driven back, discomfited and disheartened, to [the position occupied by] their worthless leader, who thereupon, with all his forces, sought [refuge in] the fort and batteries [of Bednur]. Writings of the said worthless leader were found in the pockets of four of the English *sirdars* [or officers] who were among the slain.[8] On this day about three hundred English were made prisoners and twenty guns taken. On the second, or following day, I myself, taking two thousand light troops with me, attacked and gained possession of a large powder-magazine at some distance from the fort, and of a magazine of grain close to it. Six hours after the capture of these two places, the enemy sent about four thousand men to attack us. This force advancing by a concealed route [or secretly], an action ensued between them and the *Usud-Ilhye* [Asadullahi] army, in which both parties, passing from the fire of musketry, fought with the bayonet and sword. On this occasion, also, about two hundred of these good-for-nothing people were sent to hell. A few persons, too, of the army of the *Ahmedy Sircar* tasted the sherbet of martyrdom; and one *Risaladar*, after being wounded, was carried off by the English.

The third day I had all the powder and grain removed from the said magazines, and lodged in a place of safety. On the same day, the English set fire to the palace of the *Rajah*, and to ten or twelve other noble buildings; keeping up, also, such a fire [from their guns], that there was not a span's space of the wall [of the other town] which was not reached by their shot. On the fourth day, carrying on my approaches in front of the *Darul Imaret*,[9] and in front of the mosque, and by two other sides, I erected batteries close to the fort, in which I placed some large guns, which I had caused to be removed from the walls of the city.

The English had conveyed into the fort, from the different magazines [of the city], about fifty thousand shot, and a vast quantity of powder. The remainder, consisting of about two hundred thousand shot, one hundred thousand *utls* of lead, and five hundred thousand *utls*[10] of powder, besides an innumerable quantity of other stores, fell into our hands. Having next fixed on a high spot, I caused batteries to be constructed and mounted with guns, at sight of which the faithless English[11] opened a very heavy fire. When the said English became tired [of firing], the batteries of the *Usud-Ilhye* opened their fire, discharging from four to five thousand shot; and in this manner did the firing continue, on the part of the *Usud-Ilhye Sircar*, for five or six days. As to the English, they did not fire a single shot from the fort on the second day. What fire they kept up was on the first day: the reason of which was this. The fire from without was so hot, that no creature within the fort dared approach their guns [for the purpose of working them], while General Mathews (the name of their worthless leader) causing a ....[12] to be made, crept or slunk into the same. There was not, in short, a span's space throughout the fort, which the shot of the *Usud-Ilhye* guns did not reach, or where the blood of the English was not spilt.

On the fifth day the English, during a storm of rain, rushed from a concealed place, and attacked our entrenchments: but the

Ahmedy troops being on their guard, the infidels were repulsed at the point of the sword and bayonet, many of them being seized by the legs, and in that condition thrown by the people of the *Sircar* into the trenches. The rest, leaving their wounded behind them, fled in confusion into the fort.

After this, I pushed on my approaches before the gate of the fort, and on every other side, still nearer; and caused such a fire of musketry to be kept up, that not a single man of the English, within the fort, dared ascend the walls, or come near their guns. In this manner did the English altogether make three sallies, in considerable force; but were each time repulsed with great loss, and compelled to slink back, like mice, into the fort. Thus did hostilities continue during ten days. On the eleventh day the English begged for quarter, and sent me the draft of terms of capitulation, consisting of the seven following articles:

'Article 1. Neither the troops of the *Sircar* of the *Usud-Ilhye*, nor the inhabitants [*ryots*] of the country of the *Sircar*, shall, after we evacuate the fort, spit in our faces,[13] or abuse us, or wound us.

Article 2. Let our private property be left to us; and let guns, muskets, money, goods, military stores, &c. be taken by the *Sircar*.

Article 3. Whatever money, goods, or cattle, belonging to the *Sircar*, may be in our possession, we will deliver up the same: and if we should take with us to the value of a *daum* or *dirm*[14] of money or goods; and if, upon search by the people of the *Sircar*, any thing of the kind should be found upon us, we consent to be considered criminal. Inflict [in that case] whatever punishment you please upon us.

Article 5. Let some ships of the *Sircar* be lent to us [for conveying us home]: and let us be favoured with grain, and other articles of provision, by the *Sircar*, at a fixed price. After we arrive at our own place, the amount of the price of the same shall be sent.

Article 6. Ships to be furnished for the conveyance of whatever number of men shall [choose to] embark. But those who may not consent [or like] to embark on board of ship, shall be dispatched by land to *Bombay*, under an escort.

Article 7. Two *Sirdars* [i.e. officers of rank] of the *Sircar* shall remain with us, as hostages, until our embarkation; and two English *Sirdars* to remain with the *Sircar*. Whenever the *Sirdars* of the *Sircar* shall return to the Presence [i.e. Tipu's headquarters], the two *English Sirdars* shall be dispatched [or sent back to us].'

I agreed to these proposals, and, according to the request of the English, caused two treaties, one in Persian, and the other in English, to be drawn up: to which were affixed my seal and signature, and, in like manner, the seal and signature of the English. One of the treaties was kept of the *Sircar*, and the other was given to the English. The following morning the English, preparing [or assembling] all their people within the fort, loaded such parts of the *Tosheh-khaneh* [storehouse] of the *Sircar* as consisted of specie, on mules, horses, and bullocks, bearing the mark[15] of the *Sircar*, and distributed the rest of the articles amongst their people; after which they came out of the fort [28 April 1783]. On passing the gate, the worthless chief of the English first, drawing his sword, delivered up the same with his own hand: after which, all the rest, amounting to about two thousand two hundred English people, and ten thousand infantry, native troops, grounded their arms, and proceeded to the encampment assigned them without the city. The next day, sending for Mathews (the name of their worthless leader) and their other worthless commanders, I demanded of them, whether the treaty which they had executed the preceding day was right [or valid] or not right. To this they all answered, that on that point there was not any doubt, and that the treaty was right [or valid]. Hereupon I sent to them about twenty principal men and *Sirdars* of the *Sircar*, through whom I thus interrogated them:

'What is the reason that, contrary to the treaty, you have taken with you the money and goods [of the *Sircar*], and also the prisoners made by you in the *Sircar's* country, dressing them up in your own apparel: What is the reason that you have loaded cattle, bearing the mark of the *Sircar*, with specie, and carried the same away? Finally, why, at the time of your evacuating the fort, did you distribute among your people the *Tosheh-khaneh* of the *Sircar*?'

Their answer [to these demands] was, 'that they had no knowledge of the matter; and that if the *Sircar* had any suspicions, and did not put trust in their declaration, a search might be ordered by the *Sircar*'. To this I replied, through the *Sirdars*, 'that it would be best for them to issue positive orders to their people to deliver up to the *Sircar* whatever coined money of the *Sircar*, captives made in the territories of the *Sircar*, or cattle, goods, &c. they had taken with them'. In reply to this they declared, 'that neither themselves, nor any of their people, had a single *daum* or *dirm* [farthing], or retained a single hair of any inhabitant of this country'; proposing, at the same time, that a guard of the *Sircar* should be placed over them, and that a search should be made, and [everything] taken [that might be found]. After much altercation on their part, the *Sirdars* of the *Usud-Ilhye* took from them, and brought [to me] a writing to the above effect. Hereupon I dismissed the accursed, worthless *Sirdars:* and on the second [or following] day [1 May 1783], having surrounded them with guards, I caused them to march from the encampment they then occupied to the vicinity of another spot [which had been appropriated by them] as a burying ground. The *Sirdars* of the *Sircar*, placing themselves in the road, examined them, one by one, as they passed. The accursed ones were, in consequence, found to have concealed in every seam of their clothes, *Hydery hoons* [*pagodas*] and jewels. They had also made holes in sheep's heads, which they had filled with *pagodas*.[16] Some had concealed *huns* (*pagodas*) in loaves of bread; others within hookah pipes, and hookah bottoms; while several had also concealed the *huns* in their privy parts:[17] all of which were detected by sweepers, and other *Samries*, appointed for the purpose by the *Sircar*.[18] Many young people, also, male and female, natives of the country of the *Sircar*, were found disguised in the dress [of the English]. These captives, of their own accord, set up a loud cry, [by which means] about five hundred were discovered. The search being over, I had the worthless [English] *Sirdars* placed separately, the [ordinary] English people separately, and the other infidels [Indian Christians] separately; and as they had not acted conformably with their written engagements, I made all of them prisoners, and distributed them throughout the country. During the investigation, ten or twelve Musulman women (*Syeds* and *Shaikhs*) who had been made captives, or slaves, by the infidel English, at *Surat* and in *Bengal*, were found among their people. These persons being likewise separated from the English, and restored to their freedom, were permitted to depart.

After this, passing the *Ghauts*, I proceeded, by five or six days' marches, to fort *Kurial-bunder* [Mangalore], which is an excellent fortress, erected by[19] the *Ahmedy Sircar*, and on which, in the course of five and twenty years, about twenty *lacks* of *rupees* have been expended. An ungrateful rogue who had been honoured with the government of it, had invited the English, and delivered it up to them. Here I arrived; and on the second [or following] day, after crossing another *Ghaut* [or pass] situated two *coss* on this side of the said fort, encamped near the city [20 May 1783]. The worthless English, who commanded in the

9

fort, had erected a battery of heavy guns on an eminence near the fort, in which were placed about three hundred English and a thousand other troops. After I had taken up my position, I dispatched a *Kushoon* to occupy the town. This division, passing the outer-wall, was attacked by a body of English, posted there by the enemy: between whom and my people a sharp conflict was maintained till evening. Having, during the same day, collected the necessary materials for the purpose, I erected a battery in the night, opposite to that of the English, in which I placed fifteen guns: and sending a storming party of two *Kushoons*, I posted them in a hollow, where they remained till the hour of morning prayer; when, after firing a volley [from our battery], and crying out '*Allah yar*',[20] they rushed forward, and with great slaughter drove the faithless English from the eminence they occupied; taking also many prisoners, and pursuing the fugitives to the very gates of the fort, in front of which my people maintained themselves, till such time as, with the divine assistance, I was enabled to entrench them. In the course of the two next days, everything being prepared for the purpose, I invested the place, and mounted two batteries. A very hot fire was kept up on both sides the first day. On the second day the gunners of the *Hydery* army served the batteries in such a manner, that ten guns of the fort were dismounted and shattered to pieces, and a great number of the English sent to hell. In the end, the English abandoned all their guns, and were no longer able to appear on the walls; while I had two or three other batteries erected, in which placing six mortars, I caused large stones to be thrown from them. Hereupon the faithless English dug trenches within the fort, into which they slunk [for shelter].

In this conjuncture the rains of that country, which continue for six months, set in. At the end of two months, I had carried my approaches, notwithstanding the violence of the rains, to the ditch of the fort; in the course of which time the besieged had made two sallies, at the hour of midnight. On one of these occasions I happened to be seated near the trenches, in a house in which I had taken up my residence, when hearing a more continued report of musketry than usual, I hastened, in the midst of the rain and darkness of the night, to the support of the people in the trenches; and said to the *Sirdars* of the *Usud-Ilhye* army, 'that, with the divine aid, I would the following day, when the sun was in the meridian [or at twelve o'clock] cut off the heads of the infidels within their own ditch and batteries, by the hands of my [ordinary] foot troops (*Ehsham*);[21] and, in this manner, retaliate their *thief-like* action of coming against us in the night.' Accordingly, under God's assistance, and the protection of our Prophet, I formed a party of thirty *Ehsham* soldiers[22] and twenty other persons of approved courage;[23] which dividing into two bodies, I sent one of them, consisting of twenty-five men, in noon-day, against the gate-battery, and the other twenty-five men into the ditch; where each party falling upon the faithless infidels, they cut off the heads of about forty of those impure-minded [people]. Such as escaped the edge of the sword, falling into the ditch and other places, fled like chickens, and crept [for concealment] into the nearest holes. The *Usud-Ilhye* men, resembling lions, returned in safety with the prisoners they had made. In fine, the English were reduced to such straits by our fire, that they no sooner saw one of the *Hydery* people lift a musket to his shoulder, than they would take off their hats, and bow to him like an ape.[24]

One day the English, at break of day, attacked and penetrated into the trenches at the edge of the ditch. I was seated, at the time, in my quarters, having just performed my customary exercises,[25] when hearing the noise of musketry and of men, I took a company of *Usud-Ilhyes*, and ran on foot to the trenches, where I found the English standing. The *Usud-Ilhye* people, instantly attacking them with sword and bayonet, sent several of them to hell, and made some of them prisoners. The remnant of the sword took to flight. In short, during three months, such was the slaughter *on both sides,* that the trenches exhibited nothing but a mixture of mud and clay with the blood and flesh of men. The toes of many were completely rotted, in consequence of the excessive rains, and owing to the mire [in the midst of which they were constantly forced to stand]. Often of a dark night, and [wading] through the floods occasioned by the heavy rain and wind (which here always exceed anything known in other parts of our kingdom), I say, often during this time, have I, both by night and day, gone the rounds, to see that the necessary works were properly carried on, and that the *Ahmedy* people were duly watchful. In consequence, it happened that two or three *Sirdars*, and others, fell, in the darkness of the night, into wells, which were then quite full, and became martyrs, without anyone's knowing of the accident. Moreover, at this time, the water lay on the ground knee-deep.

Part 2

Carrying on a mine by a double shaft to the foot of the wall, I only waited the proper moment for springing it. I had also erected a battery opposite to the gate, and on the edge of the ditch, in so elevated a situation, that not being able to stand the fire of musketry and cannon, which was kept up from it, not a single Englishman dared to appear on the walls or bastions of the fort. Thus circumstanced, the English demanded a capitulation, and were disputing respecting the article of delivering up their arms, when letters reached me from *Cuddalore*, written by the pseudo-commander[26] of the French [Bussy], and by Meer Moaayenuddeen [Mu'inuddin], whom I had left at the head of a division of my army to assist the aforesaid pseudo-commander [Bussy]. These dispatches purported, that in a single [or in the only] action which had taken place between the French and English before the fort of *Cuddalore*, the former, to the amount of five thousand men, had been defeated, with the loss of fifty guns; in consequence of which they had been compelled to flee, and shut themselves up within the fort: that the army of the *Sircar*, though placed at the disposal of the French for their assistance, had not been required to join them upon this occasion, but were left *standing* four or five *coss* in the rear[27] of the English: that the second day following this defeat, the English had sent into the fort of *Cuddalore* a letter of peace[28] from the French King (*Rajah*): that Bussy, the pseudo-commander of the French, who was very old (being eighty or ninety years of age),[29] and being in his dotage, had lost his wits (at least, two-thirds of them),[30] immediately at sight of his King's [*Rajah's*] letter of peace complied with its contents: and that, finally, the two *accursed* ones [the English and the French] had discontinued hostilities, and 'concluded an accommodation'.

These advices were accompanied by an order from the French pseudo-commander to Cossigny,[31] who was, at this time, at the head of three hundred French Europeans (*fringies*), serving immediately with myself, directing him and his party to leave me, and repair to [*Cuddalore*]. At the same time, several Frenchmen, who had served during twenty years with the *Usud-Ilhye* army, quitting me without any notice, at the instigation [or hint] of the accursed pseudo-commander, set out with the rest. It was to no purpose that I remonstrated on the occasion with Cossigny, and the faithless set so long in the employ of the *Sircar*. Nay, they were ripe for disloyalty.[32] No doubt, there would have been but little difficulty in putting Cossigny and his companions to death; but, inasmuch as they had eaten [my] salt, I did not think proper to act by them[33] in that manner.

Two days after this, the aforesaid Frenchmen, procuring passports from the English, and supplying themselves with some few necessaries, set out from *Kurial* [Mangalore] for *Mahe*, a sea-port belonging to the French, which they reached in five or six days. They left behind them in their camp about a hundred sick, whom I furnished with provisions, and embarked on a ship, which conveyed them to the place of those accursed ones (i.e. *Mahe*).

[The *Sultan* then proceeds to state, that disregarding the ungrateful and perfidious conduct of the French, he determined to add to the obligations they already owed him, by consenting, at the instance of their *worthless* commander, Bussy, to make peace with the English: and that, in consequence hereof, he discontinued the war in the *Carnatic*, and relinquished his design upon *Mangalore*, at the moment that he was about to reduce the place; contrary to the advice of his *Sirdars*, who strongly urged him (to prosecute the siege and) to put the garrison to the sword.[34]]

Part 3

Previously to the resolution of making war against the English (i.e. before the commencement of hostilities against the English by Hyder Ali Khan) the Mahrattahs being reduced to great straits, and defeated by the English, had [actually] filled their houses with straw, and prepared to burn the city of *Poonah*. In this situation they dispatched four of their principal and confidential people to our late father, with letters, accompanied by oaths and deceitful engagements, soliciting the grant of a fort within our dominions, wherein they might lodge their chief (more worthless, in truth, than a groom).[35] Accordingly these trusty persons (who, in fact, were not to be trusted), arriving in the presence of our deceased father (whose place is in Paradise), represented, that being broken down [or discomfited] by the English, they were on the point of abandoning their country, within eight *coss* of [the capital of] which the English were arrived: that, in these circumstances, they could look for help to no one but his Highness; that their master was a child, the preservation of whose life, honour, country, and wealth, by the *Usud-Ilhye*[36] state, would confer an obligation, which would continue to be acknowledged, as long as any of the Madho Raos existed; and, finally, imploring his Highness to consider their chief in the light of a son. These representations were seconded, on the part of Nizam Ali Khan,[37] whose country had also been threatened by the English, and whom the Mahrattahs had prevailed on, by promises and engagements, to espouse their cause, and to interest himself in their favour (with our late father); in consequence of which he, accordingly (through the Mahrattah *Vakeels*), made certain proposals, ratified on the *Koran*, to his Highness, our father. Hereupon our father (who reposes in Paradise) agreed to their propositions, and resolved on war with the English, notwithstanding the opposition made to the measure by the chiefs of the state, who represented that the war would prove arduous and tedious; that there was no necessity for his drawing the misfortunes of another's upon himself; that these two impure ones (namely Madho Rao and Nizam Ali) were both of spurious origin, and neither their words nor actions entitled to the least credit or faith. Our illustrious father replied, 'that it was a traditional saying of the Prophet: "Verily only by deeds, and not by thoughts, [shall ye judge]." We lay them under this obligation: if they have any evil designs in their hearts, the Almighty will requite them': and, so saying, he prepared for war.

It was further stipulated by the treaty concluded [on this occasion] between *these two bastards* and the *Hydery* state, that no peace should be entered into with the English, except with the knowledge of all three. Accordingly, while Sadlier[38] was still on his way, we wrote to the chiefs who accompanied him, desiring that his progress might be retarded, by amusements and entertainments at every stage. In the interim, we wrote ten or twelve letters to Madho Rao, the chief of the Mahrattahs, stating, that though he had, upwards of a year ago, and during the life-time of our illustrious father (who reposes in Paradise), secretly, and without our knowledge, concluded a separate peace with the English, yet he had not, to that moment, made any communication on the subject to us. 'It is well [we proceeded]: our pleasure is yours. The confidential agents of the English are on the way from their own country to our Presence, to solicit peace: if such be your pleasure, signify your demands to us by letter, that we may treat for you at the same time that we treat for ourselves. If on the other hand, you should have actually concluded a separate peace without our knowledge, let us be informed thereof, in order that we may set about a peace for the *Hydery Sircar*. To no one of our letters was any answer sent: neither did they write a word to their own *Vakeel*, residing with us, though he was a kinsman of theirs [i.e. of the *Paishwas*].[39]

In this manner did we, for six months, contrive to put off the arrival of the English ambassador;[40] at the end of which we wrote to the Mahrattah *Vakeel* at our court to this effect: We have, by different means, managed to detain the English ambassador six months on the road; in which period we have written about fifteen letters, on the subject of peace, to your master. You, also, have repeatedly written; but to neither has any answer been given. Now that the English ambassador is at hand, what would you advise to be done? Let us know your opinion. To this the Mahrattah *Vakeel*, who was among the nearest of [the] relatives [of the *Paishwa*], replied by letter: that his master was an infant; that his ministers, &c. were bastards, on whose words and actions no reliance was to be placed; and that six months had already passed, in expectation [of hearing from thence]. How much longer [continued he] are you to wait? Conclude your peace with the English; and, dismissing me, let me proceed to those good-for-nothing fellows,[41] in order that I may be enabled to deal with them personally, either by reproaches or a sound bastinade; and, by this means, bring forward some person, who shall prevent, for the future, the recurrence of such shameful conduct.

After this, we protracted the negotiations for peace with the English for two months longer, during which time we again wrote [to *Poonah*], but without any better success than before: whereupon we proceeded to conclude the treaty with the English, &c. [The Treaty of Mangalore was signed on 11 March 1784.]

Notes and References

[1] William Kirkpatrick, *Select Letters of Tippoo Sultan*, Preface, pp. xvii–xviii.

[2] Hermann Ethe, *Catalogue of Persian Manuscripts in the Library of the India Office*, I, Oxford, 1903, p. 1624.

[3] Ethe, ibid., says that a note on the fly-leaf by Kirkpatrick mentions that 'the first three pages [were] accidentally destroyed since the MS came into my possession', and that these 'were occupied chiefly with an account of the Sultan's ancestors'.

[4] Kirkpatrick believes (*Selected Letters*, p. xxxii) that the Memoirs were actually written after the Treaty of Srirangapatnam (1792).

[5] Original 'beholders of the spectacle or diversion'. By this expression the

15

writer probably meant to convey the idea that the resistance made by the English, on this occasion, was trifling.

6 This term seems to imply, throughout these Memoirs, not the particular body composed of converts to the Mahommedan faith, elsewhere called *Usud-Ilhyes*, but the troops in general.

7 [The term in the original, *nasrani*, means Christian; Kirkpatrick's rendering of it as 'Nazarene' is literal, but has a very archaic sound in English, which it lacks in Persian. In our reproduction of Kirkpatrick's translation, it is rendered as 'English' or 'French' according to the context, suiting Tipu's own intentions.]

8 Tippoo would not appear to have derived any information from the intercepted letters of the English. Great numbers of dispatches, to and from English officers in command, were found at *Seringapatam*, the seals of which had never been broken. Either he had no persons about him who were capable of reading and explaining their contents, or, if he had, he did not choose to trust them. Whether he ever endeavoured to obtain a translation of any of these letters, by means of his English prisoners, is unknown: but it is probable that if he had fallen on this expedient, and had found it to answer, so many of them would not have remained unopened to the day of his death.

9 i.e. 'the house, or place, of nobility'. Probably, the principal edifice in the fort.

10 I have elsewhere supposed that by the word *utl*, a *maund* (or 82 lbs) was meant; but either a much smaller weight was intended by that term, or there must be some error in the numbers here given, since these carry the quantities of lead and powder beyond credibility. Perhaps for *utl* we should read *rutl*, a weight equal to eighteen ounces avoirdupois; or, possibly, by an *utl* might be meant not the *Bengal Bazar maund*, of forty *seers*, or eighty pounds avoirdupois, but the *Macha maund* of two *rutls* and three quarters, or three pounds avoirdupois: I inclined, on the whole, to the latter explanation.

11 [Kirkpatrick renders *be-din* as 'without religion', which is literally correct, but idiomatically, 'faithless' seems a better rendering.]

12 The word which I have left untranslated is not legible: at least I can make nothing of it.

13 Of this strange stipulation it may be sufficient to observe, that it is much more credible that it should be an exaggeration or mis-statement (not to say an absolute invention) of the *Sultan*, than that it should have actually proceeded from General Mathews. We have abundant proofs, in the course of this volume, that the *Sultan's* regard to truth was far from being very strict: and perhaps there was no occasion on which he was so likely to deviate from it as in speaking of the English.

14 The lowest denomination of money.

15 The mark here alluded to probably consisted either of the tiger stripe or the letter *h* (the initial letter in Hyder), both of which were employed by the *Sultan* for such purposes.

[16] This is a doubtful passage [but Kirkpatrick's translation seems accurate].

[17] [Translation revised in accordance with text quoted in footnote by Kirkpatrick.]

[18] He means to say, that the outcastes only were employed in this service, as any others would have been defiled by it.

[19] Original literally '*newly* erected'; which, however, not agreeing very well with the period mentioned immediately after, I have, in my translation, omitted the adverb. The *Sultan* meant by the expression, not (as might be supposed) that the fortress in question had been *recently* built by himself, but since the acquisition of *Canara* by his father.

[20] 'God is our friend.'

[21] Meaning, I suppose, as if in contempt of his enemy, that his irregular infantry would be sufficient for the purpose.

[22] The *Ehsham* were sometimes employed for the purposes of parade, constituting a sort of guards. They were most commonly, I believe, stationed in garrison, but occasionally acted with the army in the field.

[23] Literally, I believe, 'manly man', a respectable person.

[24] This representation is, no doubt, founded on the practice, not uncommon with soldiers at sieges, of *bobbing*, as it is called (i.e. dropping the head) to avoid shot or shells: and as a hat presents rather a conspicuous object to a marksman, it may be easily conceived that this might have been occasionally taken off with the same view.

[25] Original *warzish.*

[26] Original *na-sardar*, 'no-commander'. [Kirkpatrick's rendering is 'worthless commander'.]

[27] *Pichhari*, a Hindivy word signifying 'the rear'.

[28] Original *khat-i sulh.* Probably orders for the cessation of hostilities, and a copy of the treaty of peace between the two nations in Europe.

[29] [Bussy, born in 1718, was actually 65 years old at the time. He died at Pondicherry in January 1785.]

[30] The perplexity of the original, in this place, is such, as to make it very difficult, if not impossible, to give a close translation of it. [From the text quoted here, Kirkpatrick's translation appears accurate. *Kam* in the text should be read *gum.*]

[31] So I read the name given in the manuscript.

[32] [Kirkpatrick renders *haram-namaki* here as 'sedition [or treachery]', but both words are too strong.]

[33] This passage is likewise obscure in the original. I suspect the text to be corrupted.

[34] Kirkpatrick's summary of further contents.

[35] In the original the word *Syse* (or horse-keeper) is introduced for the sake of a jingle with the word *Ryse* (a chief or leader).

[36] The *Sultan* gave various denominations to his government or state. It was sometimes, as in this place, the *Usud-Ilhye Sircar:* at others, the *Hydery,* the *Ahmedy,* and the *Khodadad Sircar.*

[37] Called caustically, in the original, Hujjam Nully Khan. [See Kirkpatrick's

own explanation in his *Select Letters*, p. 392: *hajjam* meaning 'barber'. He should have added that *nali* means 'tube', and this was probably considered appropriate here because barbers used to perform blood-letting through a sucking tube.]

38 [Anthony Sadlier, one of the two English commissioners appointed on 31 October 1783 to proceed from Madras to Mangalore to negotiate with Tipu Sultan.]

39 This *Vakeel* was probably one of the Rasta family.

40 [Sadlier reached Mangalore on 4 February 1784, taking three months, not six, to reach his destination.]

41 *Nabakaran* in the original.

The Diplomatic Vision of Tipu Sultan

Briefs for Embassies to Turkey and France, 1785–86

Translation by Iqbal Husain

PREFATORY NOTE

From the very early period of his reign, Tipu Sultan was active in issuing detailed instructions (*Hukmnamas*) to his officers and other functionaries. Many of these are available in the original and preserved in the Commonwealth Library (formerly the India Office), London;[1] the Asiatic Society Bengal, Calcutta;[2] and the Salar Jang Museum, Hyderabad. These *Hukmnamas* contain a wide range of instructions concerning judicial, civil, military, commercial and diplomatic matters. William Kirkpatrick has calendared (often with extensive translations) a large number of Tipu Sultan's letters, with very informative commentary, published in 1811.[3] One volume, which he regretted not having made copies of and so could not include in his collection, was the one that is presented here in translation.[4] The volume ultimately made its way to the Asiatic Society, Calcutta, as MS No. 1677. Professor Mohibbul Hasan does refer to this volume in the bibliography of his *History of Tipu Sultan*, but he does not actually discuss its contents. It will be seen that it throws much light on Tipu Sultan's vision of diplomacy and concern for promoting overseas trade and commerce, as early in his reign as 1785.

The first of Tipu Sultan's *Hukmnamas* (ff. 26–27b) in the volume is addressed to Sayyid Ghulam 'Ali Khan, Sayyid Nurullah Khan, Lutf 'Ali Khan and Ja'far Khan,[5] who were selected to form the embassy to Turkey, and were required to proceed from there to France and England. They were instructed first to go to Nagar (modern Bednur) and, after collecting presents and other merchandise, to proceed to Tadri[6] for their voyage to Constantinople.

The *Hukmnama* in the first part contains instructions to be

19

followed while negotiating with the Sultan of Turkey (Rum), his Vazir, ministers and other *amirs* (nobles); the second part gives instructions to be followed when the mission proceeded further and visited the courts of France and England. Here are also given letters of authority to the ambassadors for use at the Turkish Sultan's court.

Tipu Sultan designates the Ottoman ruler as *Khundkar* or Sultan, and the kings of France and England as *Rajas*. This nomenclature he appears to have followed in all his subsequent correspondence.[7] It is significant that he does not give the title of *Khalifa* to the Ottoman ruler. At one place, he is designated the *Padshah-i Ahl-i Islam*, or the King of Muslims, but without any indication of his right to allegiance from all Muslims. In fact, Tipu wants himself to be treated throughout as equal to the Ottoman ruler as well as to the French and English kings.[8]

According to the programme set for the mission, it was to begin its voyage from Tadri. It set sail on 9 March 1786[9] on four ships, the *Fakhru'l Marakib, Nabi Bakhsh, Fat'h Shahi Mu'izzi* and the galliot, the *Surati*. The ships were originally to sail to Jedda, as will be seen from the instructions translated here, but the route was changed and the ships sailed for Musqat, to proceed thence to Basra.[10]

Tipu Sultan's stringent instructions were that the members of the embassy should work in consultation with each other. The details of this voyage, as given in the *Waqa'i' Manazil-i Rum*, show that the members did not, however, work in unison and constantly quarrelled with each other on one issue or another.

Tipu Sultan's embassy to Constantinople ('Islambol'), which was initially directed to proceed thence to France, reveals his anxiety to promote diplomatic relations with Turkey and France so as to secure both commercial benefits and military assistance. Tipu Sultan used the traditional device to mobilize the support and goodwill of the rulers of Turkey and France, through presents consisting of valuable jewellery, robes of honour, perfumes, etc. Even four elephants were sent (all of which, alas, died on the initial voyage), with the obvious design to overawe the courts.

For the ambassadors of the mission, Tipu Sultan prepared briefs to be followed by them while negotiating with Turkey, France and England. The ambassadors were required to follow the brief in letter and in spirit. Deviations were only allowed if they were in the interest of the kingdom of Mysore. For initiating negotiations, Tipu

First page of Instructions to Ambassadors sent to the Court of Constantinople

Sultan instructed the ambassadors to select one among themselves as their spokesman; the others were only to interrupt if the former deviated from the brief. The Sultan was obviously anxious that his ambassadors should strictly carry out his instructions during the negotiations with the representatives of the courts to be visited. Considering that the British representatives in Constantinople were presumably anxious to know the details of the negotiations of his ambassadors with the Turkish ruler and his representatives, Tipu Sultan instructed them to maintain strict secrecy, not only from the British but also from the French. Tipu Sultan's aversion to the English needs no explanation. With regard to the French, one must remember that he had not been happy with the conclusion of the Treaty of Paris in 1783 between England and France.[11]

As an independent ruler, Tipu Sultan treated the Sultan of Turkey as an equal. It would be rather naive to suggest that the embassy to Turkey was to secure for him any authority from the Sultan of Turkey so as to provide him with a mantle of legitimacy. No request for any specific act of recognition from Constantinople is at all contemplated in these instructions. The French sources confirm that Tipu Sultan assumed the title of 'Nawab Tipu Sultan Bahadur' on the very day of his accession to the throne in 1782.[12] This fact is also corroborated by the *Hukmnamas,* and there is not a single word to suggest that Tipu Sultan was keen to obtain confirmation of these titles from the Ottoman court.

The instructions translated here bring out Tipu's interest in securing the port of Basra and its adjoining country in *ijara* (farm) (ff. 4b–5a). His concern in this regard becomes clear from his *Hukmnama* issued on 14 Muharram 1200 Hijri/17 November 1785 (ff. 15b–16a). His ambassadors were to explain to the Sultan of Turkey that due to heavy rains and the rough condition of the open sea, the ships could not be left on the shore. In exchange, any port of the government of Mysore that the Turkish Sultan desired would be made available to his government. Tipu's instructions required his envoys to send him the Sultan of Turkey's letter approving the lease of Basra to the Mysore government. Colonel Wilks appears to have derived information from the English factors at Constantinople as well as from Kirkpatrick, about the negotiations that took place between Sayyid Ghulam 'Ali and the Vazir of Turkey. He says that the proposal greatly annoyed the interpreter, who warned him against making such a proposal. Our

Hukmnama shows that Tipu was not making a one-sided proposal: he wished to obtain Basra in *ijara* in exchange for any of his own ports to be ceded on similar terms to the Sultan of Turkey.

Tipu Sultan was interested in securing experts and experienced artisans for manufacturing muskets, guns, clocks, glass and chinaware. He also desired to have astronomers, geomancers, physicians and experts in identifying mines of sulphur, silver, gold and coal. He desired that the Sultan of Turkey and King of France be requested to assist the ambassadors in securing their services. His interest in securing European artisans for making guns, match-locks, etc., was with the object of modernizing his own army and to compete with the Europeans, especially the English. He clearly considered that the English ascendancy in this country was due to their advanced technology in these fields.

Tipu Sultan's interest in undertaking the construction of a canal from the river Euphrates to the holy city of Najaf at his own expense is also of some interest in that he probably felt that Mysore had the necessary expertise for the purpose. His ambassadors were to seek permission of the Sultan of Turkey and obtain a letter from him instructing the local officials (*ta'alluqadars*) of the area to extend all support to complete the proposed construction of the canal. Wilks notices this peculiar request and records the Ottoman Vazir's reaction: 'the Vizieer smiled, spoke Turkish to the Reis Effendis, stating (as understood) that if the things were proper, it would be effected without the aid of the mighty Tippo Sultan'. The Vazir, however, in his formal response, merely asked Sayyid Ghulam 'Ali to negotiate with Sulaiman Pasha, the Governor of Basra.[13]

II

The second part of the first *Hukmnama* contains the letters of authority issued to the ambassadors, empowering them to negotiate with the Sultan of Turkey and the King of France. The portion dealing with France should be read with the much longer *Hukmnama* (ff. 22b–30a) laying down the brief to the ambassadors for negotiating with the French court. The latter document offers a detailed statement of the causes of Tipu Sultan's dissatisfaction with the French conduct of the war under Bussy, and the circumstances that led the French to withdraw from the war once the terms of the Treaty of Paris of 20 January 1783 became known to them in India. It is important to have

Tipu's own version of the events which, though marked by exaggeration here and there, by and large keeps to the facts. It is clear that he was not happy with the Treaty of Mangalore, 1784, that he had made with the English. He sought an agreement with the French for a military alliance, urging that it should contain the condition that until the fort of Chennapattan (Madras) together with the Carnatic and other ports were occupied, the two contracting rulers would not make peace with the English.

Tipu asked his ambassadors to Constantinople to suggest to the Ottoman Sultan that he should send Turkish troops to Mysore to fight the English. But it was probably to France that the appeal was more seriously made. Tipu sought a body of 10,000 French soldiers with veteran high-ranking commanders, and offered to pay all the expenses for their food, voyage, etc. He also offered to extend all facilities to them, such as supplies of tents, gun-powder and cannon-balls, and oxen for drawing guns. Tipu however insisted that the French commanders with their troops should be under his authority in all matters of war strategy, march and halt (ff. 7b–8a). It is clear that even if the French had been willing to send troops, Tipu's insistence on keeping the sole supreme command in his own hands would have become a matter of dispute.

Tipu Sultan was desperately trying to secure a French alliance. To induce the French to accept his plan, he suggested that after the conquest of the Carnatic and Madras, 'whatever is attached of old, as *jagir* to the fort of Pondicherry together with the fort of Chennapattan (Madras) and other ports on the same sea-coast would be given to the French Commander for the king of France' (f. 8b).

Tipu Sultan dreamt big. The overthrow of the English bastion, Calcutta, and the Presidency of Bombay could also have been on the cards after the conquest of the Carnatic. He gave tempting proposals to the French: 'All the ports together with the old territory attached to them shall be entrusted to the French and (all) other places together with the country shall be handed over to the servants of this Government' (ff. 8b–9a).

Tipu was also keen to replenish his armoury by acquiring the latest arms, especially French and German guns (f. 10b).

Apparently, Tipu Sultan was so anxious that an agreement be made with France, that he decided to have an embassy led by Muhammad Darvesh Khan sent directly to France via Pondicherry on a

French ship. The Statement of Instructions to this embassy is given on ff. 60b–63b. It was still, however, expected that the embassy led by Ghulam 'Ali Khan would also proceed from Constantinople to Paris, and so this letter does not contain the details that the instructions to the embassy led by Ghulam 'Ali Khan contain. The date of the *Hukm-nama* to Darvesh Khan and his colleagues is lost, but it was written between 15 August and 19 November 1786. Members of this embassy embarked from Pondicherry on 19 July 1787 and disembarked at Brest in September 1787.

III

Tipu Sultan's interest in promoting overseas trade is well known. This consideration led him to impose a monopoly over sea-trade. The European settlements on the Malabar coast suffered heavily as a consequence.[14] Dutch sources confirm that the presence of Tipu Sultan in Malabar dislocated their trade.[15] English trade too appears to have suffered greatly and the English were even planning to wind up the Tellicherry Factory.[16] Tipu Sultan, however, lifted the ban for Armenian merchants; and the goods brought by them to Mysore ports were exempt from duty. They were also free to buy and sell merchandise in the kingdom of Mysore and enjoyed full freedom of movement.[17] His embassy to Turkey aimed at promoting trade across the Arabian Sea, both through the Gulf and the Red Sea. The four ships which carried the mission were laden with merchandise, rich presents for the Sultan of Turkey, the kings of France and England and their nobles.[18] The total value of the goods in the ships is estimated at over Rs 20 lakh.[19] The staff to man the ships consisted of about 900 men and various functionaries.[20]

According to the first *Hukmnama*, the sale of merchandise and presentation of gifts and offerings to the Sultan of Turkey and the kings of France and England and their officers were to be made as per instructions. Tipu Sultan decreed that if the ambassadors could not succeed in meeting the Sultan of Turkey or the kings of France and England, the presents assigned for them were to be sold and money obtained.

Tipu Sultan kept himself up-to-date with regard to market trends in the Gulf region. This was possible for him as his own ships and French ships, as well as the ships of the Imam of Musqat, plied frequently between Mangalore and Musqat. Tipu Sultan also maintained a brisk correspondence with his agent there.[21]

The documents translated here show that from the very beginning of his reign, Tipu Sultan was anxious to develop the economy of Mysore. Although Mysore had forests and could still produce cheap charcoal, Tipu not only obtained information about the industrial use of coal, but wanted to import it and also bring in expertise to exploit local ores. This, he expected from the Turkish dominions (f. 7a–b), and thought that coal could be brought from Jedda on ships in the form of ballast (f. 52b). From France he sought experts to help in exploring coal ores in Mysore (f. 10b).

Equally interesting are Tipu Sultan's instructions to his officers to look for silkworms and experts in sericulture, and to bring them from Jedda to Mysore (f. 52b).[22]

His interest in the mechanical arts naturally included firearms manufacture, but was not confined to it. In our documents we see him equally anxious to show off the muskets that Mysore could already produce in its 'ten musket factories', and to import European and Ottoman experts in their manufacture (ff. 10b, 11b, 61b). He was also looking for a printer, clock-makers, glass-makers, etc., whom he enjoined his direct embassy to France to try and bring on its return journey (f. 61b).[23]

Tipu Sultan combined vision with a sense of thrift. He required his ambassadors and other officers to enforce economy in hiring ships, camels, etc., and always to keep in mind savings in expenses and profits for the government. He strictly forbade the members of the embassy and others aboard the ships from carrying on private trade. He ordered that not a single *than* (package) of unstitched cloth and other merchandise of private parties should be allowed to be carried on government ships or on ships hired by the government.

According to the first *Hukmnama,* the ambassadors were to maintain a daily account of income and expenditure, which was to be signed and sealed by each of the ambassadors, kept in safe custody and presented to the Sultan, on their return to Mysore.

Tipu Sultan, realizing that France would be a cold country, gave instructions to the envoys to provide woollen clothes to the Asadullahis and others out of government money, so as to enable them to protect themselves from the weather.

The details of trade and commerce under Tipu Sultan have been a matter of considerable interest for modern historians. Tipu

26

Sultan was undoubtedly far removed from the class of other Indian potentates both in his global views and his anxiety to promote commerce under state auspices. It was a tragedy that his ambitious project for overseas trade in the 1780s could not succeed. At a late stage, he decided to restrict the mission of Ghulam Ali Khan and others to Turkey alone, and sent a separate mission to France. No one, in the event, was sent to England. But even the mission to Turkey, routed now through the Gulf, proved an expensive misadventure. All the elephants died on the voyage. While the *Fakhru'l Marakib* remained at Musqat, the other three ships made their way to Basra, only to be destroyed there: one by fire, the other two in a storm. The ambassadors returned in 1790 with only a few survivors out of the 900 men that had been sent. The loss of life and money was enormous. Wilks writes, 'that the only value received in return was a *firmaun* from the Sultan of Room [Turkey], and sixty-five half quires of journal, worth at the highest estimations of the two articles, in rarity and waste paper, about five rupees'.[24] The judgement of present historians, one is sure, would be far more generous.

TRANSLATION

(f. 2b)

Statement of Instructions (*Hukmnama*[25]) addressed to Sayyid Ghulam 'Ali Khan,[26] Sayyid Nurullah Khan,[27] Lutf 'Ali Khan[28] and Ja'far Khan[29]

First you should proceed to Nagar[30] and from there collect the merchandise including three silver canopies ('*anbari*), two palanquins, and other materials, according to the list *(yad-dasht)*, and then proceed to Tadri.[31] From Nagar, Nurullah Khan should be asked to go to Khwushhalpur, to bring with him two ships from there. From the port of Koriyal (Mangalore), the '*amaldar* (administrator) would dispatch one *ghurab* (galliot). You should put on board the ship *Fakhru'l Marakib* the entire articles of merchandise, presents, and other baggage accompanying you, and the two elephants, all the three silver canopies and two palanquins and the *Asadu'llahis*[32] and the *sazawals*[33] of the *jaish*.[34] Two elephants, together with fodder for elephants, in the quantity required for each animal, should [each] be loaded on each of the

27

other two ships. Faqir Muhammad Haidarabadi[35] is coming with his own contingent *(risala)*. That should be put aboard one small ship. On the other new ship, the *jauqdar*[36] together with the *sardar* (commandant) of the ships should be put aboard. You should have four servants each, accompanying you on the big ship *(Fakhru'l Marakib)*. The remaining servants (f. 3a), porters (*kahars*), etc., should be put on the *ghurab* (and) on the other two ships. By the Grace of Almighty God, after reaching Jeddah, Faqir Muhammad *risaldar,* Muhammad Hanif, Muhammad Shafi', etc., should be left there for selling the merchandise. You four, according to the statement *(yad-dasht)* separately given, together with the four elephants and the other commodities, should proceed to Islambol (Istanbul),[37] by way of Egypt. There, according to the separate Statement of Instructions, you should enter into negotiations (lit. 'queries and answers') with the Ruler of Turkey (*Qaisar-i Rum*), and put into execution whatever is required for the benefit, welfare, good repute and credit of this Government. You should give the presents to the Ruler of Turkey, and the ministers and nobles of the said [Ottoman] Ruler (*Khundkar*),[38] viz. the elephants, canopies, robes of honour, etc., according to the list separately given, and proceed with the negotiations. You should not divulge to anyone the matters of negotiations between you four and the [Ottoman] Emperor and his ministers. Of course, there will be English and French *Vakils* (representatives) there. It is necessary to keep everything secret from them and others. Whatever questions and answers are to be made [in negotiations with the Ottoman Ruler and ministers], should be written down on paper a day in advance at your own place, with all of you sitting together and with absolute unanimity, and your seals and signatures are to be affixed thereto.

Questions and answers are to be given in accordance with that (memorandum). There should not be a single word put in extra or less, in departure from what is written. In case the people of Turkey (*Rum*) and either of the European (*Farang*) powers raise issues outside your settled brief, you should write it down in detail in front of the person raising the issue. You should tell them: 'We will go to our place and then after considering it, reply to you.' Apart from the proposal written down at your house (in advance) (f. 3b), if any one of you gives even one [different] word in answer, he would be an offender against this Government. You should write down whatever answer he has given with date in your note-book and bring it with you to this

Court (on your return). Whatever is proposed for negotiations should be written down on a piece of paper. There should be one of you designated by you, who should be the spokesman to speak according to that paper; the other three persons would remain seated silently and listen to him; in case in his speech he deviates through addition or omission, you should immediately remind him of the written brief. Four copies of the memorandum of the proposed questions and answers, settled among the four of you, should be transcribed by the two Persian-writing *munshis* (secretaries) accompanying you, and kept by you in front of yourselves. The (original) paper containing the brief, duly signed, should be placed in a box and sealed and kept in safe custody in the Government *toshakhana*.

The particulars of every stage of journey and (leading) members of each of the three States [Turkey, France and England], with indications of status of the said (leading) members and description of their affairs as discovered (by you) and the industries and rarities of each city and territory and the account of the affairs of the cities, should be written down in front of each of you, in the hand of both the said *munshis* and by the Persian-writing *mutasaddi* (official), each in a separate book. Requests should be made in the proper and necessary manner to the Sultan of Turkey (*Rum*) and the King (*Raja*) of France, for obtaining artisans expert in the manufacture of muskets, guns, clocks, glass, mirrors, chinaware, and cannon-balls (*golha-i-gazand*), and for such other craftsmen as may be there. You should engage [and bring back with you] such numerous artisans. Apart from them, you should give advances (*musa'ada*) to [other] artisans of the said categories, obtaining from them bonds of agreement to come to this Court, which you should bring with you (f. 4a).

After your reaching Islambol, if the *Vakils* of France or the English come to your house to meet you, you should meet them and according to their personal status and ability, present each of them with cloth, etc. After you have spoken to them in friendly terms, you should give them leave to go. The treasury of the Government that has been put in the charge of Sayyid Nurullah Khan and Ja'far Khan, for meeting expenses of the men (of the mission)—out of this, with all four of you sitting together, and inspecting the presence of all those accompanying you, disbursements of salaries should be made according to the verification directly by hand, personally, to them. For the task of counting, keeping and paying, 'Abdu'r Rahman *Khidmatgar* (servant), Kamal *Chela* and another *chela*, Abdu'r Rahman, together with *kullars*,[39] have been deputed. The Government treasury should be kept sealed with the seals of Sayyid Ghulam 'Ali Khan, Shah Nurullah Khan and Ja'far Khan. Whatever articles are expended in the Courts of the said Rulers, in a suitable quantity, the remainder should be sold for money. Four elephants have been sent to accompany you. Of them, one is to be presented to the Ruler of Turkey, one to the King (*Raja*) of France and the third to the King (*Raja*) of the English. And one elephant which would remain should be sold at the time of your return and money obtained thereby. Whatever money is spent according to the verified record, should be written in the daily cash book (*roznamcha*) by the *mutasaddis* (officials) deputed with you. That, with seals and signatures of all four of you, should be kept with the *mutasaddi*. The robes, etc., and cash, which is spent in *in'ams* to the men of the above-mentioned Rulers, the monthly income–expenditure account thereof (f. 4b) should be written, and on that too your seals and signatures should be affixed, to be kept safely. In case anyone applies for an advance of money against his salary, it should not be given. Only after completion of the certified period, should the money be disbursed.

At the time of departure and arrival, except for the Government merchandise, the stitched robes of [the four of] you and of the men accompanying you, if anyone carries or brings aboard the ships, those of the Government as well as those hired, one *than* (of cloth) or any article of trade, you would be held accountable for it to Government.

The ships ply up to Jeddah. From there, according to the requirement, vessels may be hired on reasonable rates at Government expense for the further voyage. If you go by the land route, [and] if you think that it is not possible for the Asadullahis or *Sazawals* of the *jaish* to travel by foot or if they fall ill, the amount of hire should be disbursed from the Government [treasury], asses or camels hired and they be seated thereon, so that they may be taken on the journey in your company, till they get well.

First, you go to the Ruler of Turkey and from there to the King of France and thereafter to the King of the English. From there you should board a hired ship and come by sea to the port of Koryal (Mangalore). Whether you get the opportunity of going to the Christian kings, or not, you should return by the sea route aboard hired ships

(f. 5a). Whatever is the hire of the ships, keeping in view due economy required by the Government, should be paid out of Government (money). On journey by land no halts should be made at less than five *kurohs* [about 18 km]. The details of the daily movement and halt on the land route should be written by the *munshis* and *mutasaddis* in the note-book to be brought to this Court. Whenever you happen to visit the above-mentioned Kings [of France and England], and the Sultan of Turkey and their great men, and they give presents from themselves to you and the Government, these should be recorded in detail in the account book thereof, this to be kept with your seals and signatures affixed thereon.

Whenever you appear before the Sultan of Turkey, you should obtain from him on farm (*ijara*) the place (*makan*) of Basra along with its adjoining country.[40] Send to this Court a report of this matter and negotiations thereon together with letters of the said Sultan accepting (our) farm of Basra, through two men and two clever *harkaras* (messengers), to be sent *via* Basra. An order (*takid*) of the said Sultan addressed to the authorities (*ta'alluqadaran*) of Basra in regard to the said persons being put aboard ships should be obtained and given to the said persons when they are sent off (f. 5a), so that there is no delay in their arrival. In the same manner, after the negotiations with the Sultan of Turkey and the King of France, a detailed account of the same should be sent to this Court, each through two men and two *harkaras* in the manner specified above. After negotiations with the King of the English, you would be coming yourselves; and so there would then be no need of sending any men and *harkaras* to this Court.

After the matter is put before the Sultan of Turkey, and permission (*parwanagi*) taken (from him) for bringing a canal to Najaf-i-Ashraf in front of the mausoleum of Hazarat *Amiru'l Mominin* ('Ali), they should obtain his instructions (*tawakid*) addressed to the authorities (*ta'alluqadars*) of that area for assistance and the supply of labourers, etc., for undertaking the work, [copies of?] which should be sent to this Court. After the said instructions are received, some men with money will be sent to the said place [for constructing the canal].

Cloth, black pepper, and sandalwood meant for sale have been given into the charge of Muhammad Hanif, etc. This should be sold for profit, and the money realized should be brought (f. 6a) to the designated place and used for disbursal of the salaries of the people deputed with you, according to the certificate (*tasdiq*).

With reference to Murad Khan and Shamsu'ddin, [of whom the former] is the commander (*sardar*) of the ships: First (?), Murad Khan along with soldiers (*jawans*) of two or three *yazuks* (watch-parties) would be on board the ship *Fakhru'l Marakib*. All the four ships are under his command. At the time of your departure, every one of you four persons, and the said person (Murad Khan) should with unanimity perform all the work that needs to be done.

For the time you appear before the Kings of France and English, two separate written statements of instructions (*Hukmnamas*) have been written for negotiations to be conducted with each of them [ff. 22b–30a and ff. 33–35a]. You should conduct the negotiations according to what is expedient for this Government and is suggested by loyalty to your salt.

For the giving of robes of honour (*khil'ats*) and elephants, etc., a separate statement of instructions (*Hukmnama*) has been written. According to that whatever, less or more, appears suitable should be given.

Similarly, for the ministers of all the three Rulers, proceed on the basis of the maxim, 'Decide the case relating to land while standing on that land', and whatever in robes, etc., (f. 6b) appears suitable [to the status of each] should be given.

If any of the three said Rulers enquire as to what goods are deemed better and may be acceptable as presents in your country, you should answer that by the Grace of God everything is available there, but better craftsmen and gifts of muskets and guns, glass, clocks, chinaware, are in demand, and may be given to us to be carried home.

If you happen to visit the Ruler of Turkey at the time of your return (from France and England), you should come after presenting to him the elephant without a canopy that would have still remained with you. In case you do not happen to go there, you should sell it according to the instructions given above.

If the said [Ottoman] Ruler (*Khundkar*) tells you that he is sending one of his nobles for negotiations with your master and one or two among you should take the said persons to your master, you should reply that 'there are other intelligent persons like us [in our party], one or two persons (f. 7a) among them are ready [to go]. Please grant leave to your (designated) noble; we will send them (i.e. those of our party) along with other persons to accompany them.' If the above-mentioned Ruler (*Khundkar*) sends one or two of his trusted ones, you, from your side, should assign Shukrullah Khan, and/or other intelligent persons along with one *chobdar* (mace-bearer), four rocket (*ban*) men,[41] two *harkaras* (messengers), and one servant to serve as escort, and arranging their conveyance and [voyage aboard ships] send them to this Court.

Those who are unbelievers among the *Sazawals* of the *jaish* may all be persuaded, after their boarding the ships, to convert to Islam, making them agree to this by offering them thirty or forty rupees. They are thereafter to be enrolled among the Asadullahis.

After speaking about it to the said Sultan (of Turkey), you should obtain a view of their military arrangements and bring a detailed report on these with you.

For the two said Kings (*Rajas*) (of France and England), *khil'ats* etc., have been given; if perchance, you do not have the opportunity of going to any of them, you should sell the *khil'ats*, etc., for money.

In that country (Turkey), there is plenty of stone-coal[42] (f. 7b). The stone-coal may be obtained free or at a price in exchange for the *nilam* stone and sand, which is put aboard ships as ballast; and the stone-coal should be put aboard ships at the time of your return.

As many Turks and Mughal soldiers (*jawans*) as may be available should be engaged by making advances (*musa'adat*) of Rupees 10 to 11 to the *jawans* per head, and Rupees 50 to 60 to their captains (*sardars*) per head, and they be sent with Muhammad Hanif so that he may bring them to this Court.

Copy of the Letter of Authority (*Munshur-i Mukhtari*) [for Concluding a Treaty with the King of France]

By the will of God, authority is hereby given in regard to the obtaining and giving of written agreement, comprising five clauses, from and to the King (*Raja*) of France, as detailed below, so that till the Sun and Moon endure, the bond of friendship and unity between this Government and the King of France should prosper day by day.

Clause I: To wage war against the English, agreement is made that until the taking of the fort of Chennapatan (Madras) along with the country of Carnatic ('Karnatak'), the other ports and Mumbai (Bombay) and Bengal (f. 8a), together with its dependencies, the two (contracting) rulers (*sardars*) will not make peace with the English. If this matter prolongs for ten years, peace should still not be concluded, however much during this period the English should show submissiveness and entreaty, and give satisfactory assurance of acceptance of terms. Peace with them should not be made until the said forts and places are (actually) taken over.

Clause II: Ten thousand Europeans ('hat-wearers') with war-tried high commanders should be despatched (from France). If they arrive at Pondicherry ('Phulchari') or Calicut ('Kalikot') or elsewhere in any part of the country of this Government, then, after having assisted them to land, this Government would provide them oxen for drawing artillery pieces and grain for food, according to need, together with tents, gun-powder, and cannon balls.

Clause III: The French Commanders, with their army, should be under the authority of this Government in all matters of war strategy (maslihat-i jang), march and halt. If anyone commits an offence, he shall be punished in justice according to his offence (f. 8b). The servants of this Government and the French would be under one authority, and must recognize the same, single master.

Clause IV: After the conquest of the entire country of Carnatic and the fort of Chennapattan (Madras), whatever is attached of old as jagir to the fort of Pondicherry, that, together with the port of Chennapattan and the country attached to it of old, and, in addition, other ports on the sea-coast of that side, should be given over to the French Commander for the King of France. The fort of Trichinapalli, Thanjavur, etc., in the country of Carnatic, which has been in the possession of Muslims from olden days, would be given over to the custody of the servants of this Government.

Clause V: After the conquest of Chennapattan, the army of this Government, along with the French army, shall be sent with [necessary] material, by the land route and by sea, to conquer Bombay ('Mumbai') and Calcutta. After the conquest of the places of the said territory (f. 9a), all the ports, together with the territory attached to them as of old, shall be entrusted to the French, and (all) other places, together with the country, shall be handed over to the servants of this Government.

The agreement with the French should be written in the hand of the munshi (secretary) of the said King, with the seal and signature of the said King and signatures of his ministers, etc., and leading men. This should be obtained and kept in your possession. In case you think it proper, the seals and signatures of the other chief French officers may be obtained [on it] for strengthening the agreement. The written agreement that you give should be written on a separate paper by your own *munshi*. After all of you four have scrutinized it carefully, it should be handed over [to the French] with the signatures and seals thereon of all of you four chief officers; and this matter should be kept very secret. If the French King says, 'We are ourselves giving an agreement, in accordance with the above. But you are only servants, there is nothing here written by your master. How much credit can be given to your writing (only)?', you (f. 9b) should answer: 'We possess the written authority from our master. At present, we are giving a written agreement ourselves, and in it we are recording [our assurance] that we shall get our master's writing and submit it to you. And if the writing of our master is not obtained, the written text of ours shall stand void. Just now you may please give your agreement according to the above written text, and we will in your presence give a copy of it together with our own letters, along with a *harkara* and two men of our own. It (the agreement) along with the letters may be sent on a small ship to our master so that the required written agreement (signed by our master) may be obtained from there and given to you. God willing, these will come, and till these come, we will remain here.' Besides these, whatever oral and written negotiations take place, copies (of the record thereof) should be sent, along with the two men (aforesaid), to this Court (f. 10a), on the ship of the French King, so that a reply thereto will reach you expeditiously.

It is very cold there. You should buy woollen clothes (*namd*), etc. from Government money and distribute them among the Asadullahis to protect them from cold. For distribution as presents among the high officers (at the French Court), etc., bed (covers), fans, children's toys and twenty palm-leaf *tajhauris tadpatri* have been given over to your charge, according to a separate memorandum (*yad-dasht*). To each one whatever is deemed proper should be given. Whatever remains should be sold and money obtained.

Twelve eunuchs of nine or ten years, of the Abyssinian race or any other, should be purchased and brought back. In case they are available in Jedda or (elsewhere) on the way, they should be bought and sent to Muhammad Hanif, for him (f. 10b) to send them to this Court. Whatever expenditure is incurred in the purchase of the said eunuchs, should be paid out of the Government money.

Good carpenters and ironsmiths, for construction of ships, and other craftsmen that are not available in this country, should be brought from the country of Turkey (*Rum*) and of the French King. Similarly a skilful astronomer, geomancer and physician should also be brought.

Five or six fair-faced (slave) girls from amongst Turks, Arabs or Mughals, should also be brought, after paying whatever amount has to be expended [in making their purchase].

French, German ('Aleman') and English muskets should be purchased and brought, in whatever quantity these are available.

The services of four expert persons as are skilled in recognizing the presence of (ores of) stone-coal should be obtained and they should be brought with you.

Shukrullah *Chela* has been appointed to write the entire account of the *toshakhana* (stores). These should be got written by the hand of the said *Chela*.

Copy of the Letter of Authority (for Embassy to the Sultan of Turkey)

By the will of God, in the matter of giving the written text of an agreement, comprising five clauses, to the Sultan of Turkey (*Rum*), as detailed (f. 11a) below, an order of authority (*hukm-i mukhtari*) has been given to you:

Clause I: As long as the Sun and Moon endure, may the bond of friendship and amity between this Government and the Sultan of Turkey prosper day by day.

Clause II: Basra, along with its territory, shall be given in farm (*ijara*) to the servants of this Government. The amount of farm shall be paid to the government of the Sultan of Turkey.

Clause III: Any port which the Sultan of Turkey desires to have in the territory of this Government, shall be given by this Government, along with the territory attached to that [port], to the servants of the Sultan of Turkey, on farm. May the exchange of communications and the coming and going of ships to and fro among Muslim people continue to the end of time so that the Muhammadan (*Ahmadi*) religion may daily prosper.

Clause IV: Whatever be the size of the army the Sultan of Turkey would send, the expenses thereof shall be borne by this Government. Whenever the Sultan of Turkey asks for [the return of] his army, it would be put aboard ships and sent back (by this Government), paying the expenses.

To the degree that the terms of settlement (lit. questions and answers) written above are accepted by the Sultan of Turkey, an agreement should be obtained (from him). Thereafter you should give your written agreement; and both the agreements [i.e. the one given by the Sultan of Turkey, and the other by Tipu Sultan's emissaries] should be copied (f. 11b) and sent to this Court, so that a written text, drawn up in accordance with it (the said terms of agreement) be impressed with (our) seal and sent (back to the Ottoman Court).

Clause V: Though there are numerous artisans capable of making muskets and guns under this Government, still some artisans able to manufacture muskets, guns, *qimara* (gun-pellet ?), etc., and other craftsmen should be sent to us. The artisans of all kinds from this country as are desired by the Sultan of Turkey—such craftsmen will be immediately sent by ship along with their families.

Arrange to obtain (the services) of two persons there who are expert in identifying the mines of sulphur, and bring them with you.

A sum of 50,000 *hun Bahaduri*[43] obtained from the sale of goods is to be given by Muhammad Hanif, Murad Khan, Ziyauddin and Shamsuddin, to meet the expenses of men accompanying you. You should give your receipt and take the said money. Then, according to the certificate separately given in the note-book, after the lapse of thirty-six days, it should be disbursed personally in the presence of all. The pay-draft (*parwana-i tankhwah*), with seal and signature, for the said 50,000 *huns* is being separately given to you, drawn against the names of Muhammad Hanif, Murad Khan, etc. You should pass on the said draft to the said persons and obtain the specified amount from them. For the men going to Turkey, apart from the monthly pay, an additional allowance for diet (*khwurak*) has been ordered. From the time they board the ship (f. 12a), a ration (*bhatta*) of rice, etc., has also been ordered. During the period they receive the ration aboard ship, their diet-money(*khwuraki*) need not be paid. When the ration is stopped, from then on the diet money should be given. Otherwise, the deduction (for payments) will not be allowed.

Two hundred candies of *Mehrakasish* (?) together with experts in identifying gold and silver ores should also be brought along with you.

Written on Eleventh Haidari of the Jalu Year, corresponding to Thursday 14th Muharram, 12(00) Hijri [17 November 1785], camp Zafarabad (Gurumoconda).

[Further notes:]

(1) Bir (?) and Panjarsi (?) guns, capable of firing balls of different kinds, weighing from forty-two *ratl* to six *ratl:* twenty-four such guns should be purchased and brought. If some larger or smaller number thereof is obtained, it does not matter.

(2) Amount for three years' pay of men accompanying you, set at thirty months, numbering 297 men, and four elephants, according to the separate book of certification: 40,500 great *huns* (f. 12b). Besides this, 24,000 great *huns* are assigned for the purchase of the commodities desired, etc. The total of 65,000 *huns Bahaduri* has been paid to Muhammad Hanif, Murad Khan, etc. A written statement has been given. (The four of) you should give your receipt and obtain the amount.

(3) One copy of the *Fathu'l Mujahidin* has been given. The *Asadullahi* soldiers (*jawans*) and *Sazawal-i jaish* should be made to act in conformity with its regulations.

(4) One fresh *kotal* (?), in addition to jackets (*angarkaha-i malbus*), should be given to each of the *Asadullahi* soldiers and *Sazawals*. When they go before any high officer (of the Ottoman Court), they should be made to wear the said *kotal* (?) jackets.

(5) One tent for holding the office (*kachehri*), two lamps, and two carpets (*shatranji*) have been sent with you. Whenever the occasion comes of travelling by land, you should buy a camel for Rupees 34 and load them on it for further carriage.

(6) Whenever you have occasion to arrive at an important place, etc. (f. 13a), have the office-tent set up and keep the Government (gold) cloth, along with a *yuzuk* of soldiers there, for security. Whatever Government business has to be decided, all the four should settle it in agreement sitting together in the tent. No one should take residence in the tent; and apart from Government business nothing else should be discussed in the tent.

(7) A sum of 100 *ashrafis*, 200 *Sultani huns* and 500 silver *Haidaris* have been given to your charge for being given (as presents) to the Sultan of Turkey and the high nobles there. You should offer it on the occasion of your attending on the Sultan and the high nobles, as appears suitable.

(8) Three silver-plated '*ammaris* (canopies) have been put in the charge of the *chobdars* (mace-bearers). They are to be instructed to keep them clean and carry them with them. Each of the three '*ammaris* has an umbrella (f. 13b), two silver stands together with capitals (*kalas*), *sari*, *jhol*, etc. The articles appertaining to elephants have been given over in good order. Similarly, the *thup* (?) and tree on account of the two palanquins, together with umbrella, pillow, quilt, etc., according to a separate note (*yad-dasht*) in the custody of the Superintendent of Stores (*Darogha-i-Toshakhana*) of Pattan, should be kept with you. When you present (the elephants and palanquins), all these articles and the '*ammari* should be given (along with them) in good order.

(9) You should remain informed of the diet of *Asadullahi* and *Sazawal* personnel. If any of them falls ill, have medicine given to him.

(10) Apart from two companies (*jauq*) of *Asadullahis* and *Sazawals*, two *kandlas*[44] have been given from the Government. On land, the *kandlas* should be set up and dismantled. On the journey, a camel should be hired at the appointed rate, such as can carry the load of the two *kandlas*. For the conveyance of the palanquins, gold-cloth, etc., camels on hire along with labourers should be engaged. Paying the hire, the goods accompanying you should be carried in all safety.

(f. 1b)

Fresh Instructions[45]

On the way, whether in the country of Arabia or Iran ('Ajam) or Turkey ('Rum'), whenever you find shrines of saints and Prophets, you should go there, and taking a sheet (*ghilaf*), [other] offerings and sweetmeats, recite the funeral prayer (*fatiha*) and distribute an appropriate amount of money in alms. You should enquire from the Sharif of Mecca and the Sultan of Turkey and then report to this Court as to what offering is acceptable and long-surviving, at Mecca, at Medina, at the Shrine of the Prophet ('*Saint of Saints*'), at Najaf, at Karbala, and at the Shrine of Imam Riza, and whether or not if silver door-frames are sent these will be installed at the said places, and whether if in front of these shrines, a large hospice (*sarai*) is built and a hall on the upper floor (*diwan-i balakhana*), with a drum-house (*naqqar-khana*) added, this may be better or not. Written on Eleventh Haidari, Jalu Year, corresponding to 14th Muharram, Thursday, 12[00] Hijri [17 November 1785].[46]

(f.14b)

Statement of Instructions (*Hukmnama*) for Negotiations with the Ruler (*Khundkar*) of Turkey (*Rum*)

You should, reaching Jeddah, proceed to Islambol (Istanbul), and present to the Ruler of Turkey one elephant with silver canopy, one roofed palanquin, one finger-ornament (*sarpanj*), one astrolabe (*falaki*), a bejewelled medallion, twenty-one embroidered robes, etc., and also give robes to the Ruler's ministers in accordance with the separate memorandum (*yad-dasht*).

You should say that the country of Bengal, which has revenues of twenty crore of rupees, the country of Carnatic with revenues of three crore of rupees, and the country of Surat, Gujarat, etc., with three crore of rupees [f. 15a], in total rupees twenty-six crores, which belonged to the Emperor of Hindustan, has been seized by the English, by use of collusion with and [inciting] treachery of the governors of these territories. Twenty-five to thirty years have passed since then. They have invited many Muslims to join infidelity and have converted them to their own religion. They have made Muslim women and children into their slaves; they have destroyed mosques and tombs of Muslims and built their own churches (lit. idol houses). When the dominance of infidelity reached its acme, the ardour for Islam was enflamed, and our master [Haidar Ali] launched an attack on the faithless Christians, sent thousands of them to the lowest hell, and made many of them captives and prisoners. After two years he gave crores [of rupees] in help and lakhs [of men] in reinforcement to the French, who had been expelled from the country of Hindustan at the hands of the English, and summoned them from the port of Mauritius, which is an island of the ocean, and gave them their old places [f. 15b], namely, the ports of Pondicherry (Phulchari) and Mahe, after establishing them there. Finally, he conducted a great war for four years, and for the sake of the strength of the Muhammadan (*Ahmadi*) faith, thousands of high commanders and lakhs of soldiers tasted martyrdom in the four years of war with the infidels [the English]. The faithless Christians became helpless and sent their high representatives to our master and sought peace with expressions of helplessness and importunity; and the French mediated on their behalf. There was no option but to accept peace. Other factors also came about to make the conclusion of peace expedient. The Marathas, owing to their sympathy for infidelity, had become allies of the English, Owing to this, concluding peace with the English, [our present master, Tipu] is engaged in destroying and suppressing the Marathas, and by God's aid, they shall receive a satisfactory chastisement. By His grace, this Government has large forces on land. For the destruction and suppression of the Christians, ships are needed.

By God's grace this Government has large resources for building ships and there are many safe havens for ships under this Government. But owing to the six months of the rainy season (f. 16a), the ships cannot remain at sea owing to storms. Therefore, our master wishes that if he [the Ruler of Turkey] gives the port of Basra on farm (*ijara*), the fixed amount would be paid to the [Ottoman] Ruler's government, and [our master] would keep his ships in the safe haven of the said place. He also has the intention to keep constantly open the exchange of communications and voyages of ships between the people of Islam till the end of time, so that the strength of the religion of Prophet Muhammad (Peace be upon him!) grows every day.

In return for it [Basra], any of the ports of this Government that is chosen [by the Ottoman Ruler] will be given over to the servants of the [Ottoman] ruler. Merchants, etc., will then travel to and fro taking the fine commodities and goods of this country to the country of Turkey (*Rum*), and bringing the rarities of the country of Turkey to this country.

[Our master] has sent us to report the situation in this country to the [Ottoman] Ruler and the King of France. It is hoped that he [the Ottoman Ruler] would write a letter (*takid*) to the King of France and the King of English and send us along with his trusted officials so that we should go to both the Kings and report to them of the breach of promise made by their people and enter into negotiations with them. If opportunity arises (f. 16b) we will present ourselves to the august presence [of the Ottoman Ruler], and report all the facts. If we have to return by the sea route to our country, we will submit [to the Ottoman Ruler] our report of the negotiations with both the Kings [of France and England] with trustworthy persons capable of giving information, and then start on our return voyage to our own country.

Further, our master has resolved upon bringing a sweet-water canal from the Euphrates to Najaf Ashraf in front of the sacred tomb of His Holiness the Commander of the Faithful 'Ali' (Peace be upon him!), for public welfare. The person in authority (*ta'aluqadar*) of

41

Najaf may be told [by the Ottoman Court] that high officers of this Government are going to come. They should be given permission (*par-wanagi*) for excavating the canal. They would give the required amount of money, and [for this] they should be provided with labourers.[47]

By the grace of God, innumerable muskets and cannon-pieces are manufactured in the country of this Government. Thus persons accompanying us carry those very muskets: [The Ottoman Ruler] should give us better craftsmen to manufacture muskets, cannon-pieces, clocks (*gharial*), glass, chinaware and mirrors, to accompany us [to our country]. This would be a source of pleasure to our master, and also of the strengthening of (f. 17a) the community's faith (*Din-i-milli*). The Christians who have obtained dominance in [our] country, have become dominant over and occupied [our] country owing to these very things. You, who are a great King of Muslims, should strive by all means to strengthen the True Religion. Whatever is required from the Government of our master will be furnished. By His grace, our master is in possession of all things needed. But the faithless Christians need to receive chastisement from the King of Muslims [the ruler of Turkey]. Whatever forces the Ruler of Turkey would send aboard ships, whatever expenditure is incurred on them will be paid by us during the time that they are with our master: whatever expenses have been fixed to be paid [by the Ottoman government], will be provided [by our Government]. Whenever [the Ottoman Ruler] asks for the return for his army, it will be sent back on the ships of our Government. Written on Eleventh Haidari, Jalu Year, Thursday, 14th Muharram, 12[00] Hijri [17 November 1785], camp Zafarabad.

[No text, ff. 17b–22a]

(f. 22b)

Statement of Instructions (*Hukmnama*) for Negotiations with the King of France

[The ambassadors are to make the following representations to the King of France:]

During the last thirty years, the English have taken possession of land worth rupees twenty-six crores [in annual revenue] in the country of Carnatic, Bengal, Surat and Gujarat, including Machhili Bandar (Masulipatam), etc., through collusion with the officials of the King of Hindustan, by means of deceit and treachery, and have committed much oppression and tyranny on Muslims and others. They have converted and inducted into their own faith (lit. race) thousands of men and women. They have seized Pondicherry two or three times, and made most of the French there their captives and prisoners, and inflicted extreme tyranny and oppression on the French people. All this must have been brought to your knowledge through letters and oral reports by your servants. Our mentioning the matter again is superfluous. In fact, the English over six or seven years ago marched against Pondicherry and (f. 23a), having forcibly brought it under their control, destroyed it.[48] They sent ships to seize the port of Mahe, which is within the territory of this Government. At that time our master [Haidar Ali] was engaged in an expedition into another country. He, therefore, wrote to the English: 'It is not proper for you to trespass into our country and use force against the French and seize the port of Mahe. Between us and the King of France, a cordial relationship has existed for a long time. Because of this we would be obliged to go to war against you. It would be better if you give up your design on the port of Mahe.' Despite repeated writing from our master, the English did not withdraw and occupied the said port. The moment he heard of this, our master was enraged. He withdrew from a country worth rupees five crores which he had brought under his possession from another ruler,—both from it and from the enemy's fort (f. 23b) that he had laid siege to and which was close to being captured. Without returning to the capital, but by-passing it, he marched into the country of the Carnatic. At that time the English army under the command of Munro ['Manroli'][49] with 3,000 Europeans and 15,000 men of this country, confronted the army of our Government. Another [English] commander, Baillie[50] by name, with 1,000 Europeans and men of this country, arrived from a different direction to a distance of five or six *kurohs*. Our master also divided his army into two armies, and leaving one army to face Munro, he made a forced march in the night and delivered an attack [on Baillie]. From dawn till four *gharis* [one hour, thirty-six minutes] of the day, Baillie's forces were subjected to capture and slaughter. Thereafter he turned back upon Munro. Not being able to resist, the said commander took to flight in all confusion, abandoning all military stores, such as weapons, tents, etc. The army of our Government captured or killed nearly three-fourths [lit. three parts] of the army of the enemy's forces. Munro fled with a small force (f. 24a), and entered Chennapattan (Madras). Our master addressed himself to the conquest of the country and territories of the Carnatic. By the favour of God, within a period of one year the entire territory and forts of the Carnatic came into the possession of the officers of our royal Government.

After this a general, Coote by name,[51] arrived from Bengal by sea, with a strong army. Our master also wrote a letter to Monsieur Souillac, who was the Governor of the port of Mauritius.[52] The letter said: 'For six or seven years the English had occupied Pondicherry and expelled the French. For meeting the old obligations of the bonds of unity that exist with the King of France, we had waged war with the English for one year. We captured and killed many of them. If your army also arrives, we will capture Pondicherry and hand it over to you, and inflict on your enemies a severe punishment.' Upon receipt of the letter, Monsieur Souillac sent Monsieur [de] Suffren,[53] the admiral (lit. 'commander of ships') (f. 24b), with ten war-ships, and Monsieur Duchemin with 2,000 Europeans.[54] On learning of their arrival, our master captured the fort of Cuddalore, Mahmud Bandar and other places. He had the French army, which arrived aboard ships, disembarked at the above-mentioned places, and furnished the ships of Monsieur Suffren and the army accompanying Monsieur Duchemin with grain, money, horses, camels, bullocks for drawing guns, tents, etc., in unlimited quantities for two years, and also gave them the rear part (*mawara'i*) of that country. During these two years the English came to fight time and again with the object of destroying the French army. Our master put the French army at a separate safe place and chastised the English army with his own army. The English becoming helpless, and sending their trustworthy men, solicited peace (f. 25a). They asked the precise question: 'The French should not be given aid and should be abandoned, for what can be obtained from the French in return for all this assistance? We will attend on you and be active in all manners of ways and will withdraw from the country of the Carnatic, which was in olden times under the King of Hindustan, and we will just keep ourselves at Chennapattan (Madras), and carry on our profession of trade.' Our master replied, 'We have had friendship with the French of old, and, having summoned them, have helped them in all kinds of ways. Without the French agreeing to peace, there can be no peace between us and you. And you must relinquish the country of the Carnatic, which was in the possession of Muslims, as well as Trichinopoly, etc., which was under this [Mysore] Government, which you have seized.' Our master revealed to all Frenchmen the contents of the negotiations with the English so that all Frenchmen are aware that for three years, thousands of commanders and lakhs of men of the army of this Government (f. 25b) tasted the cup of martyrdom in the war. Our master wrote many times to Monsieur Souillac that the entire country of the Carnatic has come under the control of this Government, and just one fort, that of Chennapattan, remains. Our Government has abundant forces for conducting wars on the land, but to prevent reinforcements reaching Chennapattan, ships are needed. Some ships needed to be sent immediately so that the fort of Chennapattan could be captured soon and handed over to the French. Monsieur Souillac did not send more ships owing to which cause the capture of the said fort was put in abeyance. Thereafter our master [Haidar Ali] fell ill. All the commanders and others requested him to move to the capital and, giving himself rest for some time, resume the war again later, while a strong army may be posted to reinforce the French till the [time of] return. Our master replied (f. 26a) that it did not behove rulers and commanders possessed of determination to [first] assist the French and then to leave the work incomplete, and return to the capital leaving just an army to reinforce the French: the treatment of his own illness and recovery must take place at this very place. However, a severe illness overwhelmed him. In those times also, those attending upon him began to insist on his return to the capital, but this was not agreed to.

In the end, in accordance with the will of God, he [Haidar Ali] died in the vicinity of Arcot. At that time His Highness, our master's son, let God make his authority eternal, was engaged in chastising the English in the territory of Calicut. After chastising them, the moment he heard this news, he proceeded by forced marches and entered the victorious camp [of Haidar Ali's army].

Monsieur Duchemin had already passed away one year earlier, and in his place Monsieur KANDBALIS (?) was the Commander of the French army (f. 26b).[55] Our master's son [Tipu] turned upon the English army with the intention to fight against them. The English, being unable to withstand him, took refuge in the fort of Wandiwash. When our [new] master (*Murshid*) also prepared for a battle at Wandiwash, the English did not find themselves strong enough to face him there. They destroyed the fort of Wandiwash, and, within the night, escaped and entered Chennapattan. In the meantime, the English army

arrived from Mumbai (Bombay) and, conspiring with the commandant of the city of Haidarnagar [Bednur or Nagar] belonging to the
Government, captured the said place through deceit and treachery.
Immediately upon learning of this event, our master left behind one
lakh horse and foot with the French army in the country of the Carnatic, and himself marched to Nagar. He took with him 300 French
horsemen under Monsieur [de] Cossigny ['Kusni'], with the object of
taking the port of Mahe after the conquest of Nagar and delivering it to
the French[56] (f. 27a). Immediately upon his camp reaching near the
town of Nagar, he fought a fierce battle for one day and entered the
city of Nagar. The English troops, comprising 2,500 Europeans and
12,000 men of this country, came out in front of the fort of Nagar to
oppose him. By the strength of God, he fought with them, and forced
them to retire into the fort and establish entrenchments. For one
month the English came out of the fort on some occasions, fighting
fiercely. At last a large number of them were killed, and the rest taken
prisoner; and the fort was captured. After the conquest of the city of
Nagar, news arrived that Monsieur Bussy ['Bhunsi'] has arrived at the
head of a strong French army.[57] Our master, believing that since now a
large French army has arrived, he himself should march against Koryal
[Mangalore] and other ports under Nagar, which the English had
brought under their possession, and after occupying them, should
return to the Carnatic. He accordingly marched to Koryal, besieging it,
and reduced the large English army, which was there, to straits, so that
its reduction was near.[58] In the meanwhile, the English appeared
against the French army, which was at Cuddalore, to force it to fight.
Monsieur Bussy, the Commander of the French army, told the Commander of the army of this Government (f. 27b): 'There is a large army
with us and another is aboard Monsieur Suffren's ships. We with our
own army would fight with the English, while you should go to the
rear of the English with your army and enter battle there.' The Commander of this Government's army,[59] acting according to the sugges-
tion of Monsieur Bussy, immediately left some troopers and foot under
a commander with Bussy, and taking the remaining army, went to the
rear of the English army. The English also divided their army into two
parts. One army was left to confront the army of this Government, and
the other marched to confront the army of the French, which was
encamped below the fort of Cuddalore. The English ships, which had
anchored at sea near Monsieur [de] Suffren's ships, moved and began

a battle. The French ships were defeated: some ships dispersed in the sea, and some took refuge near the fort of Cuddalore. The French army [on land] could not stand up to the English, and abandoning forty-five guns, a large number of muskets, tents, etc., in total confusion, took refuge in the fort of Cuddalore. The Commander of the government of Mysore also returned with his force and joined Monsieur Bussy. The cause of this entire setback was that (f. 28a) Monsieur Bussy, owing to his old age, had no control over his reason and senses, and the other commanders accompanying him were very inexperienced and simply carried out his orders.[60] The English now sent from their country a letter which had been received, about the terms of peace, to Monsieur Bussy, and declared peace. Monsieur Bussy, after seeing the written agreement of his country with the English government (lit. chiefs), suspended hostilities and sent to our master the letter of Mr Sadleir ('Setlar'), the second Governor ('Gonar') of Chennapattan, who had arrived in Monsieur Bussy's camp, along with his own letter favouring the conclusion of peace.[61] He (Bussy) also wrote to Monsieur Cossigny, asking him to break camp and return to the Mahe port. Accordingly, Monsieur Cossigny, without taking leave of this Government, broke camp and left.[62] This letter was received at a time when the fort of Koryal was on the point of being taken in a day or two. Our master felt that it was on behalf of the French that all this war had been undertaken. Now they had come to peace with one another, without informing this Government. There had been no need for us and the English to have fought. During (f. 28b) the four years of the war the English had repeatedly requested our Government that it should not help the French: 'We [the English] will ourselves conclude peace [with you] and will be obedient to you and will withdraw from Trichinopoly and other territories of this Government as well as the country of Carnatic.' We (Tipu's Government) did not accept this, in consideration of the feelings of the King of France, and so had to bear the burden of expenditure of crores [of rupees]. Now the French, without informing our Government, had concluded peace and set right their own affairs while spoiling ours. Now, except for war, no peace was acceptable. A letter of this substance was sent to Monsieur Bussy. Monsieur Bussy sent Mr Sadleir, the second Governor of Chenna-pattan, with his own letters, by the land route, to solicit peace. Mr Sadleir made a journey of two months to reach our master at the port of Koryal. He expressed much helplessness and importunity. Before his arrival, the fort of Koryal had been captured. After his arrival, for one month he [Tipu] did not agree to (conclude) peace, and had already made two or three marches with the intention of [invading] the Carnatic (f. 29a). At last, in view of Monsieur Bussy's pleadings, the expressions of helplessness and importunity by Mr Sadleir, and the exigencies of time, he (Tipu) agreed to conclude peace.[63]

Now we have travelled such a long distance, which none of the men of our country from the beginning of time till date has traversed, in order to come to this land. [We have done so] only to disclose the breach of promise and acts of disloyalty committed by your servants, since these unreasonable acts have perhaps been committed without your knowledge. Otherwise, this is not [according to] the ways of statesmen and persons of nobility. We hope to take a written statement of pledge and promise from you personally, and obtain knowledge of your inclinations, so that we may gird our loins to punish and destroy your enemies, who have always been [hostile] to you, since olden days. In this regard, if we receive the necessary satisfaction from you, we will by all means give assistance and make endeavour (f. 29b). You should first give us a written agreement and we will give you a similar written agreement thereafter to the effect that, first, a war of ten years should be undertaken against the enemy. During this period whatever happens by accident of fate, no peace would still be concluded [with the enemy].

You should send 10,000 European soldiers (lit. 'hat-wearers') with high-ranking commanders who may disembark at Pondicherry or the port of Mahe or Calicut, which is within the territories of this Government, wherever they wish. Wherever they disembark, they would be supplied with foodgrains and other items. Also you should direct the commanders of your army that they should follow the commands of our master in every respect. If in this they commit any fault, they would be punished after enquiry.

In circumstances of sincere friendship, the servants of our master are in the position of being your servants, and your servants are in that of our master's servants. This means that the servants of both parties are to be deemed to be under a single authority.

After the arrival of the [French] army, God willing, the entire country of the Carnatic including the fort of (f. 30a) Chennapattan would be conquered. Whatever had been assigned as *jagir* to the fort of Pondicherry, that together with the fort of Chennapattan and the territories attached to it, and besides it, the other sea-ports of that coast, would be handed over to the French. For conquering the country of Mumbai, Bengal, Gujarat, etc., an army would be assigned to accompany the French, and those territories too will be handed over to the French. After the pledged period of war [viz. ten years], from our two sides, when the time arrives for concluding peace with the English on behalf of our master and yourself, it is necessary also that the terms of peace should be settled in consultation between our master and yourself, and the peace treaty records the names of both governments. Copies of the peace treaty should be sent from both sides, that is, from your country to our master, while our master would send the said copies to you.

[Note:]

You should obtain a text of agreement from the King of France in accordance with what is written above, and thereafter you yourself should give an agreement, with appropriate contents.

Written on Eleventh Haidari, Jalu Year, corresponding to 14th Muharram, Thursday, 12[00] Hijri [17 November 1785].

[No text, ff. 30b–33a]

(f. 33b)

Statement of Instructions (*Hukmnama*) for Negotiations with the King of the English

[The ambassadors are to represent to the King of England as follows:]

For the last three years the men of the English Company have gained absolute authority in the country of the Carnatic, etc., and have committed unlimited atrocities and oppression on the inhabitants. This must have become known to you from detailed reports (?). It has come to our knowledge as well. Enormous revenue is imposed, and it is all divided [among the Company's servants] outside [your control], and only a small amount reaches your treasury (lit. stores). Now our master from such a long distance has sent us to you in order to describe to you the entire situation of the [late] war and the condition of these territories. The fact is that the men of your nation have inflicted such cruelty and oppression on the people of the Carnatic as is beyond human endurance. Besides, they have ruined many Muslims and (f. 34a) converted them to their faith. Therefore, a large number of

Muslims brought their complaints to our master, and our master has given them a place in his own country, letting them settle there. Thereafter the English extended their hand of oppression to the country of [our] Government which is in the neighbourhood of the Carnatic. Many times our master wrote to the English [governments] in the past, but they did not pay any heed. They also extended their hand of oppression to the country of Calicut ('Kalikot'). Having no alternative, our master [Haidar Ali] marched against the country of Carnatic and demanded of the [English] people at Chennapattan: 'Before the English secured authority in the country of Carnatic, we had led an expedition against the ruler of Trichinopoly, which ruler was separate [from that of Carnatic], for extraction of tribute [lit. give-and-take], and rendered him helpless.' The English, who were in Chennapattan for trade, had [then] only a small army. They too had come and joined the army of our master (f. 34b). Muhammad Ali, by name, the *'Amil* (Revenue Collector) of the country of Carnatic,[64] colluding with the English, made a secret pact with them. When the entrenchments of [the troops of] this Government reached up to the moat of the fort, the men of the fort, with expressions of helplessness and humility, begged for terms. A promise [of safety] was given to them on behalf of our Government and the place was brought under the possession of the officials of this Government. Our master, leaving one captain (*sardar*) with a small army, with the agreement of the said Muhammad Ali, marched away in another direction. At that time Muhammad Ali, conspiring with the English, called in the English and handed over the fort treacherously [to them]. The captain of our Government, along with his men, was kept prisoner for two years. Our master was then engaged in a campaign. On account of this he could not give due attention to this matter. Now, four years ago, our master, marching into the Carnatic, asked of the English: 'The said Muhammad Ali had seized nearly a crore of rupees and the fort of Trichinopoly through treachery: you should make him pay the amount or hand over our debtor (f. 35a) to us. We have arrived in the Carnatic to recover the debt owed to us. Besides this we have no other object.'[65] The English did not give a reply to this, but arrived prepared for battle. All these circumstances must have been brought to your knowledge from detailed reports.

Now, we have arrived, undertaking such a long journey that none from our people has undertaken to these countries since the beginning of time till today [and] none has appeared in this land [before us]. Our object is that you should order your representatives there to have our fort, along with the territory under it and the debt money, returned [to us] so that no disturbance or conflict may arise. In return for this order [issued by you], should you wish to seize any country and need the assistance of our Government's army to reinforce your men, a strong army shall be given to accompany [your troops]. Written on Eleventh Haidari, Jalu Year, corresponding to 14th Muharram, Thursday, 12[00] Hijri, from camp Zafarabad [17 November 1785].

[No text, ff. 35b–50a]

(f. 50b)

Statement of Instructions (*Hukmnama*) to Muhammad Hanif, Murad Khan, Ziyau'ddin and Muhammad Shafi'uddin

You should load the four vessels, namely, (1) *Fakhru'l Marakib*, (2) *Fathshahi Sughra*, (3) *Nabi Bakhsh*, and (4) the *ghurab* (galliot), with quantities of merchandise, textiles, black pepper, sandal, distilled sandal oil (*'itr-i sandal*), etc., and all of you four should get aboard them and put on board the *risala* of the *jaish* of Faqir Muhammad. The four of you yourselves who are going with [your] people, should get the people accompanying you aboard [the ships] according to the separate memorandum (*yad-dasht*), and take them to Jedda, Alighting there, you should sell there the merchandise with you and hand over a sum of 50,000 great *huns* to Ghulam 'Ali Khan, Nuru'llah Khan, Lutf 'Ali Khan and Ja'far Khan, taking receipt thereof. From Jedda [may be bought], cereal (*kashkak*, barley or wheat), a *man* of forty *seers* pucca at the price of Rupees 16 and *sari* (?), a *man* (f. 51a) aforesaid at Rupees $2^1/_2$—If there is a half to one rupee more or less, you should not consider it a hitch, and make the purchase. You should take the black pepper and sandal which Narsaiya,[66] the *Diwan* of Nagar, having weighed them, gives, including bags of *khadi* (coarse cloth), and, weighing these, give receipt thereof. At this place, the price of sandal per *man* of full forty *seers* is Rupees 11, and black pepper, Rupees 14. It is necessary that, keeping profits to the Government in view, these should be sold at proper prices at that place [Jedda]. Opening four bags of pepper, the cloth thereof should be weighed to establish [the weight]. At the time of giving receipt this weight should be deducted from the weight of [full bags of] pepper, and receipt should be given for the remaining weight. The established price of cloth is Rupees 2 for 100 *ankahs* (?). Details of it are recorded below. This should be sold at a little above or below these [rates], whatever seems proper for the time. You should buy the stone and lead, as mentioned above. Further, for the diet of men aboard ships, grain, etc., should be obtained, if the necessity arises, and be purchased according to the people's needs. Whatever grain they load from this place (f. 51b), you should record the account of the expenditure on it in detail, according to the regulations. Whatever is spent for those going in company [of the mission] to Turkey (*Rum*), and, accompanying you, which is to be spent, you should get recorded by the clerks (*navisindaha*), and bring it with you. After reaching Jedda you should, engaging in service one or two persons acquainted with commerce, pay them salary till the goods are sold. Whatever reward, etc., has to be given to the brokers, should be given to them. After the sale of the goods, if it is the season for return, you should immediately return. If it is not the season, the ships should be anchored in a protected place, so that at the time of season these should sail off and come to Koryal Bandar (Mangalore). If you have to stay there for four months, you should, all the four persons, disembark daily for buying and selling at the said port (Jedda), and come back aboard your ships four *gharis* before sunset, and reside there. If anyone remains on land during the night, he shall be an offender against this Government. After having anchored the ships for four or five days, the anchors should be lifted and the ships should be taken to a distance, and then made to stand re-anchored so that the ships are protected from the marine worm. The merchandise to be purchased and sold should be brought to the houses (*kothi*) of the merchants of the said place, giving them something in hire charges. For a watch over it, soldiers (*jawanan*) of the four *bargs*[67] and four or five men should be disembarked and placed there. You people should remain at night aboard your own ships, and in the day should go to the port to be with your goods. The Government ships, which are armed (*jangi*) (f. 52a), should each [including] the *Fakhru'l Marakib*, at the time of sunset [every] day, fire one gun. After the firing of the gun, the captains of all four ships of the *barg* (fleet?) should stand upon the [decks of] ships, and keep themselves alert at their own posts. For as long as the stay continues, they should follow this practice. At the time of the ships' departure, it is not necessary to fire guns. The insides (*darmiyan*) of the guns should be filled with gun-powder and cannon-ball (*gola*). Day and night the cannoniers should be kept posted near the guns. After a week the powder and ball should be taken out, the gun cleaned and the powder and ball put in again. At night, whether in voyage or at anchor, half the night one half of the soldiers should keep awake, and in the other half of the night, the other half of the men.

For the writing of the accounts of sales and purchases and issue of rations, etc., the following have been appointed: Muhammad Shafi', one person; *Karali* (?), three persons; *Gangpalla* (?), three persons; and *Asadullahis*, three persons. Every one [of these] who boards the ships, should write the account of the grain rations issued to persons aboard the ships. Whenever the ships anchor, he [Muhammad Hanif ?] should summon all the officials (*mutasaddis*), and should have the account of the expenditure of foodgrains and purchases and sales written down in front of all of them, and affixing thereon his seal and signature, bring it back (f. 52b), making all of them responsible for it. From Jedda or Musqat, seeds and saplings of almond, pistachio-nut, walnut (*akrot*), filbert-nut (*funduq*), bahi (?), common pear (*nashpati*) and yam (*alu*)[68] should be obtained; and the seeds of dates as also the gardeners who prepare the date plants should also be brought over. In that country there is much stone-coal (*sang-i angisht*). They should obtain stone-coal, either free or at some price in exchange of the *nilam*, whose stone and sand is put as ballast aboard ships, and bring it, loading it on all the four ships. Silkworms and those who culture them should also be brought (lit. should come) along with you.[69]

As per orders of this court (*hasbu'l hukm-i huzur*), Ghulam 'Ali Khan, Nurullah Khan, etc., should recruit *Rumi* (Turkish) and Mughal (Iranian ?) soldiers (*jawanan*); and, giving them advances (*musa'ada*), you people should send them [to Mysore]. For each [such] soldier you people should give Rupees 4 or Rupees 5 for purchase of foodgrains [and] diet for them. You should tell them to buy the grain for their diet, and loading it on the ships, start on the voyage to the port of Koryal. Twelve eunuchs (*khoja*) of the age of nine or ten years, of the Abyssinian (*habshi*) race or other race, should also be obtained and brought over.

(f. 53a)

[A] Persons posted on Ships

Men
41

	Persons of the *Jaish*, etc.		
Captains on ships: 2 on each	Porters	*Risala* of Faqir Muhammad from the Court	*Khallasi* (Sailors)
6 persons	35 [comprising]	250 persons *Sarang* (Mate) 9 persons	258 persons *Tandil* (Head of *Khallasis*)[70]
	Murad Khan, etc: 3 persons	*Solgani* (?)	10 persons
	On account of ...... [undeciphered] Koryal: 14 persons	16 persons *Mu'allim* (Navigator)	Carpenters 9
	On account of ..... [undeciphered] Khwushhalpur: 7 persons	9 persons *Kalyani* 8 persons	*Mashar* (?) 7 persons *Sarkari* 6 persons
	Ja'far Khan: 11 persons	*Talbhandari* 3 persons *Koldar* (?)	*Kochar* (?) 4 persons
(f. 53b)		45 persons From Court 20 persons	From Koryal 25 persons

[B] Cargo
269 *kanna* (?) [*basta?*]
Total *thans*: 13,622
Total *bandi*: 84,46,107.6
At Rupees 2 per hundred
Total: Rs 1,68,321, annas 2.

[Note:] In each *basta* and each *than* a statement (*chitthi*) has been put

(f. 54a to f. 56b)
[Details of items of cargo omitted][71]

(f. 56b)
At the time of the voyage [lit. arrival and departure] of ships the following persons as detailed below have been appointed to be put aboard:

Ships and galliot (*ghurab*):	4 vessels
	684 [persons]

[A] On the ship *Fakhrul Marakib:*   354 [persons]
Commanders: 2
   Muhammad Hanif
   Murad Khan
Officials (*mutasaddis*):   3 persons
   Muhammad Shafi Karani
   Gang Pada
   Ya'qub Khan *Asadullahi*
(f. 57a)
Persons of the *Jaish, Khallasis,*
   Koldars, etc. (comprising):   334 persons
Persons of the *Jaish,* including one
   Commander (*Joqdar*) and three
   Captains (*Sarkhails*), etc.:   150 persons
Khallasis and *Koldars,* etc.:   184 persons
Porters: 15 persons

[B] On the ship *Nabi Bakhsh:*   140 persons
Commanders: 2 persons
   Ziya'uddin, *Darogha*
   Faqir Muhammad, *Risaladar* of
   the *Jaish*
Officials (*Mutasaddis*):   3 persons
   Karani
   Gang Pada
   'Inayat Khan *Asadullahi*
(f. 57b)
Persons of the *Jaish,* including
   one Captain (*Sarkhail*):   49 persons
Porters: 8 persons
Khallasis and *Koldars:*   78 persons

[C] On the ship *Fat'h Shahi Mu'izzi:* 139 persons
Commander (*Sardar*):   Shamsu'ddin, *darogha azbad* (?)
Officials (*Mutasaddis*):   3 persons
   Karani
   Gang pada
   Asadullahi

Porters:	8
Persons of the *Jaish* including two Commanders (*Joqdars*):	49
(f. 58a)	
Khallasis, Koldars, etc.:	78

[D] On the galliot (*ghurab*):	51 persons
Captain: one man	1
Porters	3
Mutasaddi: Karani	1
Captain of the *Jaish*	1
Khallasis, Koldars, etc.	45

Besides these [goods], Ghulam 'Ali Khan, etc., should, for departure to Turkey (*Rum*), be put aboard the *Fakhru'l Marakib*; and if they are more [in number], on another ship, as is appropriate. At the time of return (f. 58b), such *hajis* as are coming from there should be put on board, and brought to Koryal, where they may alight. You should enquire from the Sharif of Mecca, and others, what things would be deemed approved and long-lasting as a gift (*nazar*) in the honoured Mecca, Medina, in the Shrine of the *Prophet (Hazarat Piran Pir)*, in Najaf, in Karbala, and in the shrine of Hazarat Imam Riza. Also, if silver doorways are sent [from here], would these be installed in the said places or not, and also, if in front of the said shrines, large caravan *serais* are established, and on top of them a second storey (*balakhana*) is built and a drum-house (*naqqarkhana*) added, would this be better or not. You should bring some persons expert in identifying gold and silver ore, at the time of your return. You should also bring 200 candies (*khandi*) of *hairakash* (?).

Further: the following goods have been supplied for sale: turmeric, seven candies; sandal scent, twelve *atl*; cardamoms, twenty-three candies; ginger, thirty-two candies; fans (*punkahs*), thirty-six; sandalwood drums, 70 (f. 59a). If *Bir* (?) and *Panjrasi* guns, of twelve-*ratl*-weight to forty-two-*ratl*-weight, can be had at price in the ports, and the distance to traverse is four or five stages [day-and-night voyages], you should take the ships there and bring the said guns, and also purchase European muskets and bring them. The sale and purchase of goods and merchants should be made [before] the beginning of the [sailing] season, and they should be sent here at the beginning of the season. It has been written above that a sum of 50,000 great *huns* should be given to Ghulam 'Ali Khan, etc., and a receipt taken. If the rates there for the black pepper and sandalwood are less than the rates written above, there is no harm: they should put them to sale. Written on Fifteenth Haidari, Jalu Year, corresponding to 14th Muharram, 12[00] A.H. [17 November 1785].

(f. 60b)

Statement of Instructions (*Hukmnama*) addressed to Muhammad Darvesh Khan, Akbar 'Ali Khan and Muhammad 'Usman[72]

You, together with the persons particularized below, [with] robes of honour, jewels, letters (*kharitas*), should go to Phulchari (Pondicherry), meet Monsieur Cossigny ('Kusni')[73] there, and give him the letter-bag. You should also give the letter to Monsieur Monneron ('Mandrun').[74] You should obtain all the articles you require at a price through the mediation of Monsieur Cossigny and load it on board the French ship. In consultation with Monsieur Monneron, you should go aboard the ship to travel to the kingdom of France. The money with which you have purchased grain, etc., for all the people accompanying you, should be recovered through deductions from everyone's pay. Out of all the robes with you, one embroidered robe and one *qahali* (?) robe are to be given to the queen of the King of France. If after you reach the kingdom [of France], [the money for] your expenses, etc., is exhausted, you may take it from the King of France or from bankers (*sahus*) (f. 61a) by writing a draft/bill (*tamassuk*), so that here the said amount would be conveyed by the Government to Phulchari (Pondicherry) [for payment]. You should pay court expenses [in France] as necessary and proper, small or large. You should bring one printer (*chhapasaz*) of books with you by giving him an advance of a proper amount. You should tell the King of France: 'Owing to God's benevolence and the Prophet's help, there are ten musket-factories under the Asadullahi Government, and innumerable muskets are manufactured here, and similarly, cannon-pieces. The requirement of friendship is that Your Majesty may send to our master other craftsmen capable of making new kinds of muskets and *bejars* and *bir*, i.e. iron cannon-pieces, and, besides these, clock-makers, makers of chinaware, glass and mirror-makers and other artisans of your country, ten each of every sort, so that the friendship may increase, and we may take them with us after giving them proper amounts of money in advance. Before our departure, our master has appointed the officers (*sardars*) Saiyid Ghulam 'Ali Khan, Lutf'Ali Khan, Nurullah Khan, etc., to negotiate on all these matters.'[75]

[Text of f. 61b missing]

(f. 62a)

He [Muhammad Darvesh Khan ?] should install the required provisions from his own resources. Taking them from him, you should distribute them among the people accompanying you, according to the rule recorded below. If he does not give them [to you], he should buy the required amount of grain, etc., out of the money in the Government treasury, and distribute it in accordance with the rules. During the ship's voyage, when the allowance (*bhatta*) will be given, the cash allowance for diet, which is specified in the certificate (*tasdiq*), should not be given. From the day that the ship's voyage comes to an end, the [issue of] grain, etc., should be suspended and the cash allowance for diet should be given, according to the certificate. All of you three captains should take the cash allowance for diet according to the certificate, and the grain, etc., required by them should be purchased on ship and on land. Two *Asadullahi* men should be given grain, etc., according to the rule, on ship and on land, from the Government.

(f. 63a)

The bags of letters which have been given to Muhammad Darvesh Khan:

Sixteen items
The King of France: One
In trust, for unnamed persons: Ten
Monsieur Souillac: One
Governor of Port of Kabat (?): One
English King: One
Monsieur Cossigny: One
Monneron: One

Robes of Honour
Five boxes
54 robes of honour
—

261 items of clothing
[A] Loom-embroidery (*karchobi*), *Jhali* (netting?) and
    Mahmudi (muslin)
12 robes of honour
[containing]
58 items of clothing
One box
[B] Burhanpuri [muslin]
12 [robes of honour]
53 items of clothing
One box

(f. 63b)
[C] White [cloth]
30 robes of honour
150 items of clothing
3 boxes.
[1] For the King
[A] Jewellery
5 items
1 *Falaki*
1 *Sarpech* [turban ornament]
·1 *Hadak*
2 *Angushtar* [finger-ring]
[B] Robes of Honour
7
32 items of clothing
[a] Loom-embroidery
2 [robes]
10 items of clothing
comprising
Gold 1
Silver 1
Mahmudi 8
[b] Gold netting
Two [robes]
10 items of clothing
[c] White cloth
12 items of clothing

[2] For French Notables
[A] Loom-embroidery
Two [robes]
11 items of clothing
(a) Gold
1 [robe]
5 items of clothing
(b) Silver, including turban ornament
[B] Golden netting
3 items
15 items of clothing
[C] Burhanpuri [muslin]
12
53 items of clothing
(1) of 5-fold robe (? *Panch-parcha*)
5
25 items of clothing
(a) 1st class: 3
(b) 2nd class: 2
(2) of 4-fold robe (? *Chahar-parcha*)
7
28 items of clothing
(a) 1st class: 6
(b) 2nd class: 1
[D] White [cloth]
30
150 items of clothing
(1) Turbans
30
(2) Unsewn cloth
80
(a) *Saila* 30
(b) *Dariya* 30
(c) *Do-patta* 30
(d) *Gulbadan* (flowered) 25
(e) *Mashru'* (cotton and silk mixed) 5

Notes and References

1 Persian MS Nos 4683 and 4685.

2 Asiatic Society Bengal, Calcutta, Persian MS No. 1677.

3 William Kirkpatrick, *Select Letters of Tippoo Sultan to Various Public Functionaries*, London, 1811.

4 Ibid., p. 264. He also did not get a copy of the 'journal of the embassy' to Constantinople. The latter has been edited by Mohibbul Hasan, *Waqa'I' Manazil-i Rum*, Bombay, 1986 (Persian text, hereafter cited as *Waqa'i'*).

5 See notes on them in the translation that follows.

6 A small port on the western coast.

7 Kabir Kausar, *Secret Correspondence of Tipu Sultan*, New Delhi, p. 60 (hereafter cited as *Secret Correspondence*).

8 *Waqa'i'*, p. 1.

9 Ibid., p. 2.

10 The change of decision to have the embassy proceed via Basra and not Jedda is assumed in Tipu Sultan's letter to Ghulam Ali Khan, &c., dated 1 March 1786 (Kirkpatrick, *Select Letters*, pp. 264–66).

11 Ghulam Husain Kirmani, *History of the Reign of Tipu Sultan*, translated by W. Miles, London, 1864, p. 144.

12 Archives Nationale, Paris, C 155, ff. 216–216b, cited in Mohibbul Hasan, *History of Tipu Sultan*, Calcutta, 1971, pp. 24 and 42n. See also Chapter VIII of the same work.

13 Mark Wilks, *Historical Sketches of the South of India, etc.*, edited by Murray Hammick, II, Mysore, 1930, p. 363.

14 *Foreign (Sec.) Pol. Proc.*, 26 September–25 October 1789, No. 96, Council Proceedings of 26 August 1789, p. 1849, cited in C.K. Kareem, *Kerala under Haider Ali and Tipu Sultan*, Cochin, 1973, p. 165.

15 Ashin Das Gupta, *Malabar in Asian Trade*, 1740–1800, London, 1967, pp. 114, 122; Introduction, *Waqa'i'*, p. 15.

16 *Waqa'i'*, Introduction, p. 15.

17 Cf. Kareem, *Kerala under Haider Ali and Tipu Sultan*, p. 165.

18 *Waqa'i'*, Introduction, pp. 2–3.

19 Wilks, *Historical Sketches*, II, p. 366. Kirmani tells us that 'ten lakh of rupees newly coined, valuable cloth with gold, jewels of great value etc.' were sent (*History of the Reign of Tipu Sultan*, p. 144).

20 Mohibbul Hasan, *History of Tipu Sultan*, p. 131.

21 Cf. Kirkpatrick, *Select Letters*, pp. 185–89, 209, 231–35, 282–84, being letters to Mir Kazim, dated 17 November 1785 to 24 April 1786. Tipu Sultan also wrote (16 January 1786) to his *dallal* or broker at Musqat (pp. 239–41), and on the same date to the Imam of Musqat (pp. 241–42).

22 Cf. Irfan Habib (ed.), *Confronting Colonialism: Resistance and Modernization under Haidar Ali /and Tipu Sultan*, Delhi, 1999, pp. xxix, xliv *n*41.

23 That this request was made is confirmed by French documentation: see M.P. Sridharan in *Confronting Colonialism*, ibid., p. 145.

24 Wilks, *Historical Sketches*, II, p. 366.

[25] It is not clear if this is a draft order or was actually issued. Such is the case with all the other *Hukmnamas* in this MS translated here.

[26] Ghulam 'Ali Khan was one of the most trusted officers of Tipu Sultan. He was a resident of Arcot and joined the service of Haidar Ali in 1780. Tipu made him Mir Sadr. He was chosen by Tipu Sultan to lead the embassy to Constantinople. On return he fell into disgrace for some time. He was again deputed by Tipu to negotiate the treaty with the English in 1792. He was then selected to proceed to Mauritius to negotiate with the French. After the fall of Mysore, the English gave him a pension sufficient for his maintenance. See *Waqa'i'*, Introduction, p. 1.

[27] Nurullah Khan was a Sayyid of Persian origin. He had been sent to Shiraz by Haidar Ali in 1770, with a view to seeking military help from Karim Khan Zand, the ruler of Iran (Wilks, *Historical Sketches*, II, p. 361).

[28] Mirza Lutf 'Ali Beg served as a military officer in Haidar Ali's army. For a short time he also held the position of an admiral; ibid., pp. 205–08; 361*n*, 362 and 498.

[29] Ja'far Khan was one of the four persons sent to Constantinople. Details about him are not available.

[30] Nagar is now known as Bednur. This town also bore the honorific epithet *Dar al Saltanat*. See Rev. Geo. P. Taylor, *The Coins of Tipu Sultan*, rpt 1989, pp. 11, 12 (hereafter cited as *Coins*).

[31] Tadri, a small port at the mouth of river Tadri in Kannara district.

[32] A special corps of soldiers. Haidar Ali had his *chelas* recruited from prisoners of war; Tipu Sultan formed his corps of *Asadullahis* of similar material.

[33] The *Sazawal* was an official in Mughal administration who had the authority to compel other officials (even higher in rank) to perform a particular duty or meet a particular obligation.

[34] Regular infantry of Tipu Sultan.

[35] On the antecedants of Faqir Muhammad, no data are available.

[36] Captain of a *jauq*, or company of men.

[37] Islambol was the name given by the Ottomans to Constantinople, whose Turkish form was Istanbul, the present official name.

[38] *Khundkar* was a designation specific to the Ottoman ruler.

[39] *Kullars*, apparently a species of subordinates.

[40] Tipu refers to the proposal again in his letter of 1 March 1786 to Ghulam 'Ali Khan and his colleagues, translated in Kirkpatrick, *Select Letters*, p. 265.

[41] *Bans* were rockets made of bamboo-sticks propelled by gun-powder.

[42] *Sang-i angisht. Angisht* means charcoal, and *sang*, stone.

[43] Equivalent to thirteen *fanams*. See Nikhiles Guha, *Pre-British State System in South India, Mysore 1761–1799*, Calcutta, 1985, p. 202.

[44] I cannot trace what *kandla* means: it was apparently a kind of tent.

[45] This fragmentary piece appears on fol.1 of the Manuscript. It must have been thought of by Tipu after the dictation of the text of instructions to the members of his mission to Istanbul had been completed. It was then apparently tacked on to the beginning of the draft of the instructions.

[46] According to Kirkpatrick's calculations, the Eleventh of Haidari, Jalu Year,

corresponded to 18 November 1785, while 14th Muharram 1200, according to H.G. Cattenoz's concordance, corresponded to 17 November 1785. In dates determined by lunar sightings this variation would not matter, but the weekday would be decisive. The 17th of November being a Thursday, one may suppose this to be the actual date of the missive. The problem, however, is compounded by the fact that on f. 12a the Haidari date is given as fifteen (in figure as well as words). One can only suppose this is a clerical error, since *yazdaham* and *panzdaham* in Persian writing are often confused.

[47] This canal is, again, mentioned in Tipu's letter of 1 March 1786 to Ghulam 'Ali Khan and his colleagues (Kirkpatrick, *Select Letters*, p. 266).

[48] The reference is to the English capture of Pondicherry in 1778.

[49] Hector Munro (1726–1805), the victor at the Battle of Buxar (1764), returned to India to command the Madras army as major-general, in 1779. After his defeat at the hands of Haidar Ali, in 1780, he commanded the right division of Sir Eyre Coote's army at the Battle of Porto Novo (July 1781).

[50] William Baillie, a Lieutenant-Colonel in the East India Company's forces, had supervised the destruction of French works at Pondicherry (1779), to which Tipu refers above. Baillie was defeated and captured by Haidar Ali in 1780 while attempting to join Munro in the engagement that Tipu now describes. Baillie died in captivity in 1781.

[51] Sir Eyre Coote (1726–83), who defeated the French Commander Lally at Wandiwash (1760). He assumed the position of Commander-in-Chief in India (1779), took the field against Haidar Ali, and was repulsed at Chelambakam, but won at Porto-Novo (1781).

[52] For Souillac, who, as Governor of the Isle of France (Mauritius), received Haidar Ali's proposals for help and cooperation in 1781, see S.P. Sen, *The French in India (1763–1861)*, Calcutta, 1958, p. 201. Souillac remained involved in the Mysore–French relationship down to 1788, when Tipu's embassy undertook its voyage to France aboard a French ship (ibid., p. 520).

[53] Pierre Andre de Suffren (b. 1729) was sent to the east as commander of the French fleet to the east in 1781. Leaving the Isle of France (Mauritius) on 7 December, he carried troops under Duchemin's command. Suffren was an active naval commander and fairly successfully challenged English naval supremacy on south Indian coasts during 1782–83. See ibid., pp. 266–71, 359–74.

[54] Duchemin, brought by Suffren's fleet, landed with his troops at Cuddalore in March 1782.

[55] In actual fact, Duchemin was seriously ill when he resigned his command to Hoffelize, on Bussy's orders, sent from the Isle of France in the summer of 1782 (ibid., pp. 282–83). How Hoffelize has been rendered as 'Kandabalis' is difficult to understand, unless there is a confusion with de Canaple, a high-ranking French officer under Duchemin and them under Bussy.

[56] According to the French version, when Tipu left the Carnatic, Hoffelize sent 600 French troops under de Cossigny to accompany him (ibid., p. 294).

Mahe was the French settlement on the Malabar coast, which the English had captured.

[57] Marquis C. de Bussy, the famous French Commander, who for some years in the 1750s held a dominant position at the court of the Nizam, was now sent again with a new expeditionary force. After spending some time in the Isle of France, he landed at Trinkomali in March 1783. His military operations in south India thereafter are described in ibid., pp. 342–78.

[58] Tipu's account of what happened at Cuddalore may be compared with the French reports summarized in ibid., pp. 349–59. See also Mohibbul Hasan, 'The French in the Second Anglo–Mysore War', in *Confronting Colonialism*, edited by Irfan Habib, New Delhi, 1999, pp. 35–48.

[59] Tipu does not name the Commander; he was Sayyid Saheb (Mir Mu'inuddin), Tipu Sultan's cousin and father-in-law.

[60] The French, however, attributed their reverse on 13 June 1783 to the passivity of Sayyid Saheb, Tipu's Commander, during the course of the engagement (S.P. Sen, *The French in India*, pp. 356–59).

[61] Anthony Sadleir and George Staunton were the two English Commissioners sent by Macartney, Governor of Madras, to Bussy, to convey the news of peace. Sadleir was second member of the Madras Council, and so next in rank to the Governor.

[62] According to S.P. Sen, *The French in India*, pp. 392–93, Bussy had sent orders to Cossigny to separate himself from Tipu's forces, but not to come away. But in September, without informing Bussy, Cossigny broke camp and marched off to Telicherry, to Tipu's great indignation.

[63] Tipu's account is not substantively inaccurate. See Denys Forrest's account of the proceedings of the English commissioners, Sadleir and Staunton, in his *Tiger of Mysore: The Life and Death of Tipu Sultan*, Bombay, 1970, pp. 76–88.

[64] This is, of course, the well-known 'Nawab of Arcot', who was technically 'the *faujdar* of Karnatak-i Haidarabadi', in Mughal official parlance. Tipu wishes to reduce his status further to a mere '*amil*, or revenue collector.

[65] This dispute over Trichinopoly and the amount Muhammad 'Ali owed to Haidar Ali went back to the mid-1750s. The point was raised by Tipu with the English representative, Brigadier-General Macleod, in negotiations held in August 1783 for concluding the Second Mysore War. (See Irshad Husain Baqi, 'A Conference between Tipu Sultan and Brigadier-General Macleod', in *Confronting Colonialism*, pp. 58–60.)

[66] On a subsequent dispute over the matter of supplies of goods from 'Nursia, the *Dewan* of Nugr', see Tipu's letter of 3 February 1786, addressed to Ghulam 'Ali Khan, translated in Kirkpatrick, *Select Letters*, pp. 250–51. Kirkpatrick notes (p. 250*n*) that Narsaiya is 'in other places' called '*Taalukdar* of Nugr'.

[67] *Barg*, meaning part or wing, perhaps the various categories of troops accompanying the mission. But see further on where we have *har chahar jahaz-i barg*, 'all the four ships of the *barg*'—where *barg* may mean fleet.

[68] The meaning of potato became attached to *alu* only in the nineteenth century.

[69] This early interest in establishing sericulture in Mysore may be noted.

[70] The meanings of *sarang (sarhang)* and *tandil* appear from Abu'l Fazl, *A'in-i Akbari*, translated by H. Blochmann, Vol. I, Calcutta, 1977, p. 290.

[71] These items cannot entirely be properly deciphered, though enough can be read to see that these are all textile items (*chhit, rumal, parkala, khadi, dopatta, doriya, khes*, etc.).

[72] The decision to send an embassy direct to Paris meant a change from the previous decision to have Ghulam 'Ali Khan and his colleagues proceed from Turkey to France. As late as 15 August 1786, Tipu Sultan was writing to Cossigny, Governor of Pondicherry, that this was his plan (Kirkpatrick, *Select Letters*, p. 377). But on 19 November 1786, he not only informs Monneron of the intention to send Darvesh Khan, Akbar Ali Khan and Muhammad 'Usman to Paris through Pondicherry, but also of the fact that they had set out for Pondicherry (ibid., pp. 444–45). The present statement of instructions whose date is lost must therefore have been written some time before 19 November 1786, but definitely after 15 August.

The French documents relating to this embassy have now been translated by Suman Venkatesh: *The Correspondence of the French during the Reign of Haidar Ali and Tipu Sultan, 1788–1789*, III, Bangalore, 1998. All the three ambassadors duly arrived in France by the *Aurore* in June 1788, accompanied by de Monneron. In the French documents, however, the name of Ali Akbar Khan is given as Akbar Ali Khan. The ambassadors embarked for India aboard the *Thetyo* in November 1788. The only success the ambassadors were able to achieve was the recruitment for service under Tipu of Mouriset of the French Royal Foundries, with four other craftsmen qualified to manufacture fire-arms and some other craftsmen (ibid., pp. 280–81).

[73] Cossigny was now Governor of Pondicherry, a position he held till September 1787, when he left it to join the post of Governor of the Isle of France. The letter from Tipu to Cossigny that this embassy was to take to him is published in translation in ibid., p. 48.

[74] Pierre Monneron was one of the three French Commissioners who negotiated with the English Commissioners at Pondicherry in 1784. The letter that the envoys were to deliver to Monneron may well be the one dated 19 November 1786, translated in Kirkpatrick, *Select Letters*, p. 444. Monneron was not then at Pondicherry. Arriving on ship from Mangalore, he departed on the same ship from Pondicherry with Tipu's envoys on 19 July 1787. (S. Venkatesh, *The Correspondence of the French*, p. 84 and passim.)

[75] It is not clear, since the text of f. 61b is unavailable, whether Tipu Sultan was still planning to send Ghulam 'Ali Khan and his colleagues from Constantinople to France, or had withdrawn their brief in view of this embassy sent directly to France. But from other indications it would seem he decided to rescind the project of Ghulam 'Ali Khan's embassy to France much later.

State Intervention in the Economy

Tipu's Orders to Revenue Collectors, 1792–97:

A Calendar

Translation by I.G. Khan

The eighteenth century is unique for a number of reasons. Whereas the second half of the century is remarkable for the manner in which the English East India Company was able to take over an entire subcontinent, its first half is marked by a rapid decline in the centralized, bureaucratized power of the Mughal emperor. The latter half of the century saw number of attempts to replicate the Mughal systems of military efficiency and revenue collection across a vast variety of regional environments—until they were subsumed by the needs of modern imperialism represented by the British East India Company.[1] The 'successors', such as the Nawabis of Awadh, Bengal and Farrukhabad, the Nizamat of Hyderabad, the Rajput kingdoms across Rajasthan, had their own *jagirdars,* their *diwans,* their *bakhshis,* their *faujdars* and their *qiladars*[2]—yet none of these potentates dared award *mansab* ranks to their elite. This was due to the fact that the Mughal emperor was still the sovereign and the rest, including the Marathas, acknowledged his suzerainty on paper. The canons of Turko–Mongol sovereignty that had been developed over a long era of almost 500 years[3] could not be assumed by its minions or opponents; nor could the people transfer their loyalties to just anyone who had the wealth and military resources to put together an army and assume charge over a set of districts whose very boundaries had been demarcated by the Mughal emperors. The Mughal concept of kingship drew its strength from the assumed compact between the Mughal emperor and the indigenous as well as immigrant elites to establish the Mughal emperor in a position of supreme authority and then to provide him with a loyal and centralized bureaucracy. It was also successful because of the willingness of the people to be ruled by those who were able to demonstrate their abilities to provide them security of life and property

66

as well as the freedom to adhere to their religious beliefs. In attempting a centralization in government similar to that of the Mughals, one would have expected Tipu to seek legitimacy from the oldest and most established political authority of his times, namely, the Mughal emperor in Delhi, Shah Alam II.

The Marathas had done so when they escorted him from Allahabad to Delhi in 1772 and installed him as their emperor so as to extract legitimacy for their return to the north.[4] The first Nizam who established an independent state in the Deccan, despite his disillusionment, always tried to have his man at the Mughal court. He advised his son to maintain the old association with the emperor, and his son was a keen aspirant to the post of Vazir in the turmoil preceding and after the death of Muhammad Shah.[5] Even the British admitted the nominal sovereignty of the Mughal emperor who gave them the right to collect the revenues of a part of his empire, and the British King and Parliament were initially hesitant about encroaching upon the sovereignty of the Great Mughal.[6]

Tipu, however, was not impressed with the mythology of Mughal supremacy. He knew of the humiliation of Shah Alam at Allahabad when he sought the protection of the British forces after the Battle of Buxar in 1764. Later, on his return to Delhi in 1772, he was simply a puppet of the Marathas.[7] Thus, when Tipu had his coins struck, they carried only his name and not the name of Shah Alam— something even the toughest contender for regional autonomy had not dared to do. To make matters worse, he even sent these handsome gold coins to the Mughal emperor as an offering. The impotent rage of Shah Alam was met with polite apologies.[8]

Under these circumstances Tipu felt that it was high time he broke free from the old paradigm by positing an entirely different concept of kingship, namely, the idea of the *Saltanat-i Khudadad,* in which he was merely an instrument in the hands of God, doing his bidding vis-à-vis the poor and the needy.

However, the rationalization of his authority could only be through the exercise of legal and military roles, based not just upon the tenets of Islam but also on the codes he had evolved suited to the need to guarantee the material welfare of his people. The orders that he constantly issued were aimed at providing them with gainful employment and at satisfying their needs for food, clothing, housing, education and natural justice. For this Tipu did not need a *lashkar-i du'a* or army of scholars on religion, like the one patronized by the Mughals. He needed to be his own scholar; and to judge from the books in his library, listed in a Catalogue by Charles Stewart (compiled soon after his death), his interests ranged far beyond the theology of Islam. He had acquired a large number of the texts and treatises that had once formed the staple of the Mughal elite, and was also in touch with the political developments in West Asia as well as in France, where a revolution was carried out in 1789. Thus, in the arts and sciences his library had the well-known copy of the *Jami' ul Ulum* of Ghaus Gwaliari. It was set in the format of the old Persian 'Book of Knowledge'-type of encyclopaedia, with 53 chapters on astronomy, geography, agriculture, horticulture, physics, music, magnetism, theology and sufism. The other famous encyclopaedia of the crafts, the *Majmuat us Sana'i'*, was also to be found in the library of the Sultan. He apparently laid great emphasis on the prediction of a person's character from his appearance, and one finds several references to books on geomancy. He also possessed a Persian translation of a French treatise on encampment and tactics for warfare. The library had several *Jawaharnamehs* or Books of Gems, with descriptions, and ways of recognizing a wide variety of precious stones. There were *Farsnamehs*, or Books on Horses, with instructions on how to assess breeds, their prices, and even a section on the management of stud-farms. Other books on animals included the *Shahbaznameh* and the *Khawas ul Haiwan*. Tipu himself ordered the preparation of a book of diagrams showing the lay-out of military camps, as well as a treatise on dyes and perfumes. In fact, Stewart says that Tipu had ordered close to forty-five new books to be compiled or translated from European sources by his English prisoners. He collected books on mathematics, geometry and Arab astronomy. He aimed at preparing a calendar which could mesh with the Hindu agricultural cycle as well as the Muslim lunar calendar. On medicine he possessed many treatises, especially the *Zakhireh Khwarizm Shahi*, *Jami al Fawaid* and *Riaz-i Alamgiri*. The first attempt at presenting Ayurvedic pharmacology in Persian, the *Ma'din ush Shifa-i Sikandar Shahi* by Bhuva bin Khwas Khan, was also found preserved in his library.[9]

With such a formidable array of information on virtually all aspects of revenue collection, agriculture, warfare and the crafts, it was quite natural for Tipu to intervene in the functions of almost all his top officials in the form of personal inspections as well as orders and regulations, which he issued quite frequently.[10] Most of Tipu's earlier orders have either been translated or published in calendars or books by Company officers eager to cash in on the interest this 'native' had generated.[11] However, even William Kirkpatrick's exhaustive calendar goes only as far as November 1793; as he admits in the Introduction to his book, 'the period between 1794 and 1799 is an absolute blank'.[12]

The documents at hand had apparently fallen into the hands of the Hyderabad forces, or were bought by Salar Jang. No matter how they got there, they are at present well preserved in the Persian Manuscript section of the Salar Jang Museum (Acquisition No. 3195, Farsi Nasr 100), and relate to the period following Tipu's humiliation at the hands of Cornwallis in 1792, when he lost half his kingdom. These orders seem all the more vehement as Tipu was clearly trying to reassert his personal authority—undeterred in his resolve to fashion his *Saltanat-i Khudadad* as a bulwark against the British occupation of his country. To the best of my knowledge they have not so far been studied or contextualized.

It is evident that the documents are a part of an album of about 50 orders from Tipu Sultan to a *Mir Asaf* or revenue commissioner, who was in charge of forty-five *taluqas* and four forts, and can be dated to the period 1795–98. As was to be expected of a man who had survived several conspiracies and had only recently suffered defeat at the hands of the English, the Introduction relates to the severity of Islamic injunctions against conspiracy and sedition. The *munshi*, writing on behalf of the Sultan, begins by reminding the officers of the four kinds of greed which weaken men: namely, women, wealth, life and land. Also, the three unclean things which ought to be avoided: namely, swine, dogs and heretics. He then goes on to define loyalty in terms of 'four kinds of *namak halali*'. For example, loyalty of the eyes implies that you stop all destruction of the property of the *Saltanat-I Khudadad* that you may witness. Second, if you hear sedition against the *sarkar* and punish forthwith anyone talking ill of the Sultan—that is loyalty of the ears. Speak in praise of the *sarkar*—that is loyalty of the tongue. And finally, to express loyalty of the hands, write, and wield the sword or the gun against the enemies of the *sarkar*. Opposition to these rules is the worst crime you can commit. God and His Prophet are everpresent witnesses, and then a passage from the *Quran* follows: 'I know that man is subject to temptations; but I am closer to you than your jugular vein.'

The specific orders then begin:

Order No. 1. Relating to the restoration and removal of *amils, qiladars, sar-rishtadars,* and *muqaddams.* They are in direct contact with the Sultan, therefore they must never be disloyal and must be of good moral character. Those that disobey will always be punished, but those who are loyal and possess *taluqas* are under the supervision of the *Mir Asaf's* court. Every year in the month of Haidari (sixth month, according to Tipu's *abtath* numerals), accounts of every *ijara* in every village under every *muqaddam* and every *amil* must be collected for the entire six months, according to the rates fixed by the Sultan, and submitted under the seal of the *Asaf* with the name of the *muqaddam* and his village. *Nine lines and a half line.* (This length is always noted as the end of every order.)

Order No. 2. The *Asaf* must take accounts from the *amils* and *sar-rishtadars* of income and expenditure, along the following lines: that in such and such *taluqa*, such and such *muqaddam* was given the *ijara* of such and such village for 200 *rahti*. The balance of the previous year was 50 *rahti* for which a separate *patta ijara* was obtained. (Details of current accounts follow.) All these details, with the number of cultivators and ploughs, and the increase in their numbers, must be prepared by the *Sadr* and then taken to the *Mir Asaf.*

Order No. 3. For the four forts that are in your charge, make four copies of this order (and forward them to the respective *qiladars*). According to this order, all the stores in the fort must remain fully stocked. After six months all the items, except salt, must be changed. The lead-shot and gunpowder need not be changed. And you must ensure that all the personnel are at the posts assigned to them. The salaries of the *qiladars, amaldars* and *piyadas* must be estimated. Make their payments from your collections after deducting tax due from those holding lands and *jagirs*, and obtain the receipts from them. Send the remainder to the central treasury after entering all details in the register.[13]

Order No. 4. Regarding the disbursal of monthly salaries to soldiers, make sure that men of the regular army are paid by the thirty-seventh day. The *piyadas* must be paid by the fortieth day and the men with landholdings ought to be paid by the thirty-fourth day. And in all these payments, ensure that the taxes due on their lands are 'deducted at source'.

Order No. 5. This order relates to those forts in which repairs are in progress. Let the *qiladars* and *amils* supervise the work in progress, and let the *Asaf* move about and inspect all such works and send a detailed report to the Sultan.

Order No. 6. In all the territories under you, once every year, go to all the *taluqas* and listen to the complaints of injustice and violence. Make it very clear to the perpetrators of violence that there are laws and there are punishments. And to every *muqaddam* do not give *ijara* for more than one village—whether large or small; and never two villages to the same *muqaddam*.

Order No. 7. Since *amils* collect cash from the peasants, ensure that they give separate receipts to each cultivator. The cultivator can pay his dues in three instalments to the *muqaddam*, who must pass it on to the *amil* as and when it is paid to him. No land can be given in gift, *jagir*, or daily allowance, to any soldier, without the permission of the Sultan. And those who bring marshlands and riverine floodlands under cultivation must be encouraged. In these lands, try and extend cultivation of sugarcane and/or paddy.

Order No. 8. In all our lands traders must be permitted to trade in items produced within our territories only. If any trader brings in goods from outside our territories, his goods must be confiscated and placed in your custody. All imports are banned except horses, elephants, mules, camels and guns (*tufang*). And do not charge anything above the *rahdari huzoor* (royal octroi). Let not foreigners (*mardum i mulk i ghair*) move about our territories. Wherever you see them, imprison them and inform the Sultan. These instructions are to be conveyed in the strictest terms to all *amils* and *qiladars*.

Order No. 9. In cases of those (*amaldars'*) courts, wherein the potential to pay more than 5000 *rahti* does not exist, let them collect just 5000 *rahti* and send them to the royal presence with the *qiladar*.

Order No. 10. In the territories in your charge and in all the villages, there are men who have been forced to work as servants to rich cultivators. Take these men, give them a plough or/and five *rahti* cash as well as two *ihya* of grain (1 *ihya* = 320 *sers*, which were to be called *deks*)[14] as *taqavi* loan, so that they may start cultivation on their own. Let the *muqaddam* be the guarantor for the return of this loan, which may be recovered over three years.

Order No. 11. There are canals and wells and dams; have them repaired and start cultivation in the lands around them. Those dams which are in disrepair must be repaired and land adjoining them (or reclaimed by them) taken into cultivation. Furthermore, there are points where a new dam will provide land for cultivation; have them constructed and start cultivation.

Order No. 12. All newly-recruited youth and armymen are ordered to present themselves before you. Inspect them and verify their guarantors and have *pattas* written out regarding their services.

For the forts in need of repair, and for the supplies needed for the gun carriages (*araba e darakhsh*), get carpenters, ironsmiths and labourers as per requirements; collect also the iron, etc., necessary for these works.

Order No. 13. In the forts and *taluqas* in your charge there are a number of infantrymen. Deploy them at the *chowkis* and order them to ensure that no person of foreign lands or even *sarkar* lands enters our territories without seeing a pass with the stamp and signature of the Sultan. Let also the *muqaddams* and the people in general be asked to watch out for strangers. This is not meant to restrict the movement of our common people and traders.

Order No. 14. In relation to the collection of cash by the *amaldar*, for every 1,000 *rahti* of assessed value of an area, he may recruit one soldier at the rate of six *fanam* per month for a period of twelve months. And let the *amaldars* ('*ummalan*) be empowered to decide on the recruitment and dismissal of such revenue *piyadas*.

Order No. 15. 400 bullocks and cows have been assigned to the territories under your jurisdiction; and even the *taluqa* for their rearing has been decided. The salary of their caretakers will be paid by the *amil* directly to each attendant. The information-gatherers must report the details to the *Sadr Maweshi* (or superintendent of livestock).

[Note: The importance of this officer and his department must not be underestimated, as bullocks formed the backbone of the entire system of transportation, both civil and military.]

Order No. 16. Being sent to you is a headman of the axe-wielders. The Sultan desires that Muslim axe-men be given employment and axes be procured for them.

Order No. 17. The Saiyids and the Quraishis are men of the highest religious affiliation. Let them be provided with villages for their maintenance.

Order No. 18. This order is for the *muqaddams* under your jurisdiction to maintain mares of good breed and to take their offspring and to bring them before you; these are to be taken into your own

72

charge. Train them yourself. Furthermore, let the *muqaddams* and the *amils* be warned that they must not let the population of tigers and bears in their areas survive at all. They must be killed and the skins sent to the Sultan.

Order No. 19. The following soldiers have been assigned to the different *amils* for employment and sustenance, as per the schedule given below:

Taluqa Tapsamundar—Numbers given

Taluqa Hulikal—Numbers given

Taluqa Awwal, Mai Samundar—Numbers given

Taluqa Dudballa—Numbers given

Taluqa Hotridurg—Numbers given

Taluqa Doyam, Mai Samundar—Numbers given

Taluqa Banglur—Numbers given

Taluqa Gondana—Numbers given

[And so on for another twenty-four entries, each with the number of soldiers assigned shown against them. It ends with the remark that in case any assignee does not have the cash to start cultivation, give them five *rahti* cash and two *ihya* of foodgrains as *taqavi* loan. This loan may be recovered over three years. Anyone making dams, or digging a well for cultivation, is to be given irrigated land as *inam* land.]

Order No. 20. According to the *Ayat e Karima*, anyone who steals property worth more than two-and-a-half rupees shall be punished with the cutting off of his or her hands.

Order No. 21. In the territories under your jurisdiction, the following are the forty-five *taluqas*:

Taluqa Alinagar—one unit

Taluqa Awwal, Nilungal—one unit

Taluqa Doyam, Nilungal—one unit

Taluqa Sondikul—one unit

And so on, to list all forty-five *taluqas*

Order No. 22. Orders regarding the deployment of cattle in the different *taluqas* and the provisions for them in a detailed tabular form. Even their breeds are specified.

Order No. 23. Information being sent that 4,771 *piyadas* have been sent to the areas of different *amils* under your jurisdiction to undertake cultivation as per details given below:

From the royal headquarters—800 men

From Yusufabad—650 men

From Banglur—2,301 men

From Hotridurg—300 men

From Hoskote—560 men

From Najkal—120 men

From Bihrandurg—40 men

Total—4,771 men

Let them be deployed in extending cultivation.

Order No. 24. The following men in the following numbers are being sent to you for manning the *chowkis.*

From Hoskote, fifty men; and from Najkal, thirty men. According to the orders of the *Sadr*, they must keep alert and guard the outposts to be manned by them.

Order No. 25. All the newly-recruited men of the army recruited by the *qiladars* must be presented before you for inspection and approval. And let the date of their enrolment be recorded for the calculation of their salary. And those having land, let the *Asaf* and the *qiladar* keep them in their own contingent. And there is no need to send them to the Sultan. And send the muster-rolls of all men and their salaries as are in your charge to the Sultan so that they may be entered into the registers.

Order No. 26. To all the *taluqadars*, all headmen, all *sarrishtadars* of the villages, it is ordered that the accounts of the past arrears be sent forthwith. Also, that the cesses have been abolished and so collect only that which is legal and they should send their collections to you (the *Mir Asaf*). The *Asaf* and his *mutasaddis* (officials) must go to every village and *taluqa* and collect only that which is ordained by the Sultan.

Remove all the hardships of the peasantry and deduct your expenses before handing over the rest to the *amils*, and make sure you take a receipt.

Order No. 27. About the strengthening and repairing of the earthen dams in your territories. Appoint one labourer who has his own bullock for carrying the earth per every 50 *dhira* of dam work (one *dhira* = forty-eight *nirangusht* or thumb-breadths of about $9/10$ inch each). The men will be paid in terms of three *rahti* dry and three *rahti* irrigated land for his upkeep. The earth must be taken from the inner side of the dam and placed on top. Trees of *babool* (cassia) and toddy must be planted on the outer slope to make it stronger, and also to provide wood for construction.

Order No. 28. This is regarding the steps to be taken for increasing the number of ploughs and cultivation in each *taluqa*. The Sultan has assessed the agricultural potential of every *taluqa* and in accordance with his orders, get a list of all the cultivators and the numbers of ploughs compiled for each village. Go about and persuade them to work harder. To those who are not working due to lack of capital, give them *taqavi* of five *rahti* and two *ihya* of grains and land for cultivation. And move about the kingdom and ensure that violence is not being inflicted upon the *raiyats* as the *muqaddams* used to do earlier. Take a bond from the *muqaddams* as safeguard against violence and let it be deposited with the *Mir Asaf* of *Kachehri Huzoor*. By the force of this agreement and the *patti* given earlier, as well as the force of the seal of the Sultan, the peasant will feel secure and work harder. Send all details of accounts to the Sultan and inform the *Mir Asaf* of *Kachehri Huzoor*.

Order No. 29. To those employed in the army and other offices, assign them *jagirs* for their sustenance. And let the spies watch over them for any instance of violence, following which their *jagirs* must be confiscated and resumed to the crown lands. And no other *jagir* is to be assigned to them even under pretext of increasing cultivation.

Order No. 30. Take from the traders in grain and fodder only those duties as are approved by the Sultan. Let not the *amils* harass them in any way.

Dated 5th Haidari 1222 Mauludi or sixth month of the year 1795–96.

Seals of the *Diwan* of Tipu Sultan and receipt by Saiyid Mohammad Sadiq also occur on this page.

Order No. 31. Ordered that they issue orders from their courts to the *taluqa* that the items listed below be sent to the royal presence every year without delay or excuse after making the necessary payments:

Turban, white, 25 *dhira*; *do-patti* @12 *fanam*, 3,000 pieces; khadi, 300 pieces; velvet, *yak-patti*, 500 pieces; velvet, *do-patti*, 500 pieces; *thaan babri reshmin*, 300 pieces; . . . ropes, iron balances and *sailah yaktari* @ 2 and 2.5 *rahti*, get 100 pieces . . . be sent to the royal presence.

Order No. 32. Items such as grains, oils, ghee, are not to be exported out of our territories. So also, let not any item come in from outside excepting horses and camels, nothing else.

Order No. 33. Do not wait for orders to collect the revenue every year. Go ahead and collect the dues without fear and send them to the royal treasury. Furthermore, you are to instruct every *amaldar* and *qiladar* to provide a good horse worth 300 to 400 rupees to their brothers or any relative and send them to the Sultan, so that they may be accommodated among the *sawars* attached to his court. Those refusing to send their sons and relatives with good horses will not have their contracts renewed.

Order No. 34. It is ordered that *pucca* brick *masjids* are built in all the forts. They shall be utilized to provide education to the children of the soldiers and the officers. Exhort them to come for prayers. And they must be taught the books *Zad al Mujahidin* and *Murid al Muja-hidin* which can be taken from the royal chancery (*nawishtkhana*). There is a *qazi* in all your courts, see that he is paid three *rahti* and he will ensure the lighting of the lamps. Proper names must also be given to the children of the Muslim subjects and the *qazi* must perform the *Bismillah* ceremonies for the sons of the nobles.

Order No. 35. Details of handing over charge by *amil* who has been removed, to the *amil* newly appointed. Take all the accounts and have a public gathering held and let it be documented and send all accounts to the Sultan.

Order No. 36. To the animal traders let it be made clear that all offspring of horses mating with mules will be first offered to the *amil*, who will purchase them for Rs 200–300 each, as they are excellent for carrying loads. All information about the numbers of such mules in your area must be compiled and sent to the Sultan.

Order No. 37. If from an unbeliever (*mushrik*) you take one *imami*, then from the Muslim trader take one quarter less.

Order No. 38. To the news-reporters in your territories: let all ordinary as well as extraordinary events be reported to the Sultan. Also report the causes behind these events.

Order No. 39. It has been decided that in your territories 50 workshops of iron will be established. Of these ten will produce steel and forty, iron. They can be more but not less than 50. The steel and iron ingots will be of one *dek* (one *ser* weighing twenty-four rupees) or $1^1/_4$ *dek* or $1^1/_2$ *dek* or $1^3/_4$ *dek* and send them to the Sultan. All excess may be sold in the market. Iron that is soft is good, and that which is hard is not useful. These 50 shops must produce any iron or steel item required by the Sultan.

Order No. 40. To the *Mir Asaf Kachehri*: Inform your subordinates to keep an eye out for flintstone (*sang e tufang*) deposits. Collect them and send them to the royal presence. Also collect samples of different kinds of stones and send them to the Sultan for selection. Those that are selected must be quarried and collected and sent to the royal court on carts. There is no need to have them chiselled or cut.

Order No. 41. To the *Mir Asaf*: There is always an excess of farmers opting to cultivate wheat, maize, barley, etc. Provide them with seeds for the next crop. And try and extend the land under rice. And send these grains to the Sultan every year as per his requirements. But before you go for the annual *Eid ul Zuha* prayers and presentation before the Sultan, take with you the accounts of all the *amils*, all the population, all that is left to be collected, all the *nazrana*, all the Sultan's levy of grains, all the details of violence against the peasants, and take with you the gunmen provided by the Sultan and come to his presence.

Dated 6th of Jafari 1223 (*c.* 1796–97). Signed *Munshi Sadr.*

Order No. 42. This is regarding the despatch of honey, wax, gum arabica, and the four types of nuts, as well as redwood or *patang* on hired carts by the *amils* of the areas where they occur. If these areas are already given out on *ijara*, deduct the cost of this forest produce from the amount payable by the revenue farmer (*mustajir*). Let this practice be pursued zealously every year. A minimum amount of wax and honey to be sent is also indicated.

The order is dated 8th of the month Jafari of the year Saz or 1223 (or third month of 1796–97).

Order No. 43. As a gesture of patronage the Sultan has ordered that all trade carried on by his *Asafs* and his *amils* shall be exempt from all state levies. Furthermore, if they use their own men and money to bring more barren land under cultivation, they shall pay only 50 per cent of the rates levied from the rest.

[Note: This seems to be aimed at winning the loyalty of the intermediaries. However, even more significant is this attempt to encourage capitalistic tendencies in his officials by encouraging them to trade and to invest in capital-intensive agriculture.]

Order No. 44. This order relates to the appointing of *Naib Malik ut Tujjar* to assist the *Mir Asaf* and one *mutasaddi* to assist each *Asaf*. These *naibs* shall send their *gumashtas* to the *taluqas* and collect information on the trade in gold, silver and sandalwood. These items must not be traded in by anyone except by the *Naib Malik ut Tujjar*.

Order No. 45. This order relates to the collection of sandalwood saplings that grow in the *taluqas* in the territories under you. The sandal tree sends forth small saplings in the ground around the tree. The *Naib Malik ut Tujjar* must have them dug out and dried and sent to the royal court.

Order No. 46. Every year the *Asafs* and the *Amils* come to the royal court for the *Eid al Zuha* celebrations, and they are accompanied by many of the *muqaddams* and the *mutasaddis* of the villages under their control. These men are given rice and grains and presented before the Sultan, who gives them a *pan* each. After this they must be sent back to their posts forthwith so that agricultural work does not suffer.

Order No. 47. In areas under your jurisdiction, there are lands allocated for the grazing of state draught cattle. It has been seen that cows belonging to the local peasants are being allowed to enter into these pastures and this is resulting in the despoiling of the breeds of the state bulls that are strong and tall, while the local breeds are small and weak. Let the *amils* ensure that the local cows are kept away from state bulls. Let the weak offspring be sold to the local peasantry. And let the *darogha* and the *amil* of the grazing lands keep count of the cattle population and tour the entire area. They must see whether the climate and the water is suited to cattle-rearing. If an area is found unhealthy, let the cattle be shifted to cleaner climes. Let this *darogha* accompany you when you come for the *Eid* celebrations.

Order No. 48. Regarding the despatch of *sailah* cloth *yaktara* from your *kachehri*, as per details given below. It is imperative that this cloth be sent without delay or excuses to the royal court. The rate to be paid for the *sailah* should be between eighteen and twenty-five *fanam* per piece.

Order No. 55a [Obviously the photocopies of the entire set could not be procured]: Let not the soldiers or anyone else distil alcohol in your territory. If any case is reported go out and verify the facts and then cut off the hands of the offender. Similar punishment is to be meted out to those who cultivate *bhang.*

Order No. 56a. Muqaddams are solely for the collection of cash dues. Those peasants not having the cash dues to pay their tax can do so in four instalments. [Details of payments, responsibilities and documentation follow in the original order.]

Order No. 57. You must send iron ingots as per details given below; and on each ingot you must stamp the words '*Falak Shukoh*'. [There are details of about forty workshops which will produce the *dhuri* (clamps?) for the gunpowder boxes, and ten workshops which will supply the royal court with ingots of steel. The details of the *dhuri* and the ingots are given in tabular form and can be the subject of an entire range of studies on the technology under Tipu.]

Order No. 58a. Renewed order dated Jafari or fifth month of the Mauludi year 1225, or 1798–99, according to which the order already current about the items required to be sent to the royal stores has been modified. The old list has been renewed and a number of new items have been introduced which are as follows: [a list of seeds, spices, grains, oils, textiles, etc., follow]. The *munshi* adds: 'Also prepare a sample as per the design sent by the Sultan and send it back for approval. Apart from these send *dhuri* (?) for the gunpowder boxes @ thirty per annum; bullets for handguns, 60 per month; brushes for currying horses, 3,000 per annum.'

Order No. 56b. In the *taluqas* which fall under your region and which produce tobacco, let the tobacco trade be given on *ijara* to any party which can pay @ twenty-five *rahti* per 1,000 of assessed value of that *taluqa*. He may pay in four instalments and may take a loan after necessary sureties are put up. Furthermore, if the markets show that a higher amount may be taken, then let it be fixed at more than twenty-five per 1,000.

Order No. 57b. Let all the trade in silver, gold and copper, both struck and unstruck, be given out on farm to anyone willing to pay the state a sum @ fifty *rahti* per 1,000 of the net assessed value of the *taluqa*. Let the men be attentive and serious and the monopoly will be theirs. The amount is to be paid in four instalments, and if he requires a loan, the *Asaf* must take responsibility for repayments. If it is found that the rate can be higher, then let it be enhanced.

What we have just examined is evidence showing the depth of intervention exercised by an innovative monarch; one who was clearly less worried about form and more about the substance of governance. His strict control over the fiscal resources of the *Saltanat-i Khudadad* enabled him to sustain a centralized military apparatus under his personal command. Wherever responsibility is delegated, there too detailed and specific orders come from the Sultan. The *Mir Asaf*, who was to collect revenues and mobilize resources for the army, is reduced to providing sustenance for out-of-place soldiers and carrying out orders, that is all. The large army and Tipu's control over agriculture and even livestock enabled him to enforce his monopoly over vital items of trade. He was showing the other indigenous rulers that the tools of trade monopoly and strict revenue control used by the British Company could be used as effectively against them—to keep them out of India's markets.[15] According to Tipu, once the barriers became costly and unprofitable for the British, they would leave our country in peace. This, for the British, was the main reason why Tipu and his 'experiment' had to be destroyed.

Notes and References

[1] For a general view of the impact of the colonial intervention on our economy in the eighteenth century, see Irfan Habib, 'The Eighteenth Century in India's Economic History', *Proceedings of the Indian History Congress*, Mysore, 1995. For a wider contextualization of this century, see Athar Ali, 'The Eighteenth Century: An Interpretation', *Indian Historical Review*, Vol. V, pp. 175–86.

[2] For a perceptive interpretation of the eighteenth century and the emergence of Awadh, see Richard Barnett, *North India between Empires*, Berkeley, 1982.

[3] For an early attempt at configuring the essentials of this vital institution, see Iqtidar Alam Khan, 'The Turko–Mongol Theory of Kingship', *Medieval India: A Miscellany*, Vol. II, Aligarh, 1972, pp. 8–18.

[4] See also references to the Mughal as the *Padishah,* and the Maratha resorting to his authority to over-ride mutual disputes, in J.N. Sarkar, *Decline and Fall of the Mughal Empire*, Vols. II–IV, passim.

[5] Cf. Yusuf Husain, *The First Nizam: The Life and Times of Nizamul-Mulk Asaf Jah I*, Bombay, 1963, p. 200. Interestingly, another upstart group that decided to stay aloof from the Mughal 'black hole' were the Ruhelas. When faced with the choice of siding with the emperor in the 1750s or maintaining their distance from the other power-brokers, they chose to keep away. Only one of them (Najib Khan) went over to the crown and he was able to use the institutions of Mughal sovereignty so well that he rose to become the dictator of Delhi. As Vazir and Amir ul Umara, Najib kept the Marathas and the Jats at arms-length, yet within the ambit of Mughal sovereignty. For details, see Nuruddin's *Tarikh e Najib ud Daulah,* as well as Shiv Prashad's *Tarikh-i Faiz Bakhsh*, MS copy, Salar Jang Museum. It would be useful to compare the Ruhela state and its ideology with that of Tipu's Mysore, and the recent researches in Iqbal Husain, *Rise and Decline of the Ruhela Chieftaincies,* New Delhi, 1990, and I.G. Khan, 'Ruhela Military Technology and Ideology', in C.J. Dewey (ed.), *The New Military History of South Asia*, New Delhi (forthcoming), would be of help.

[6] See letters to Clive, Hastings and the constraints on Wellesley, in Dodwell, *Cambridge History of India*, Vol. 5, passim.

[7] Later, in 1792, Shah Alam II was even to send letters of congratulations to the acting Governor General in Calcutta, Col. Stuart. See translation in Kausar Kabir, *Secret Correspondence of Tipu Sultan*, New Delhi, 1980.

[8] Cf. details in L.B. Bowring, *Haidar Ali and Tipu Sultan*, p. 212, vide Geo P. Taylor, *The Coins of Tipu Sultan*, Delhi, 1914, 1989 rpt, p. 29.

[9] The military charts have been reproduced in Mahmud Hussain, 'Encampment Charts of Tipu Sultan's Army', in Irfan Habib (ed.), *Confronting Colonialism: Resistance and Modernization under Haidar Ali and Tipu Sultan*, New Delhi, 1999, pp. 185–87. For an idea of the breadth of his knowledge, see Charles Stewart, *Memoirs of Hyder Ally Khan and his Son Tippoo Sultan (in a Descriptive Catalogue of the Oriental Library of the late Tippoo Sultan)*, Cambridge, 1809, pp. 96–118. Compare these treatises with the texts current among the Mughal nobles, discussed in I.G. Khan, 'Technical Literature and the Mughal Elite', paper read at the Conference on Indo–Persian Literature, MSH, Paris, 1993. See also I.G. Khan, *Agriculture, Warfare and Knowledge: Technology and Training in 18th Century North India* (forthcoming).

[10] His orders were being collected and translated even as he ruled. Thus, in 1792 Burrish Crisp, an English officer, translated Tipu's revenue regulations which he had sent to the present and future *amils* and *sar-rishtadars* of the second district of Waumloor, dependency of the *kuchehri* of Awulpatam. See details in Nikhiles Guha, *Pre-British State System in South India*, Calcutta, 1985.

[11] Burrish Crisp, *The Mysore Revenue Regulations*, London, 1792. The other highly useful translation is William Kirkpatrick's *Select Letters of Tippoo Sultan to Various Public Functionaries including his Principal Military Commanders; Governors of Forts, and Provinces; Diplomatic and Commercial Agents etc. etc. Together with some addressed to the Tributary Chieftains of Shanoor, Kurnool and Cannanore and Sundry Other Persons*, London, 1811. These were the more balanced accounts; the rest of the literature was aimed at demonizing Tipu in order to justify their role as liberators of the people of India from this fanatic and debauch. For an excellent critique of this literature, see Kate Teltscher, *India Inscribed: European and British Writing on India 1600–1800*, New Delhi, 1995.

[12] Kirkpatrick, *Select Letters*, Introduction.

[13] This order reinforces the thesis of Burton Stein and Mohibbul Hasan that Tipu was continuing with his policy of fiscal centralization in order to sustain a larger military organization controlled directly by him. See Burton Stein, 'Fiscal Centralization in Mysore' *South Asia Researches*, Vol. 2; M. Hasan, *The History of Tipu Sultan*, Calcutta, 1971.

[14] See Regulations 74–80 for an explanation of the new weights and measures, in Crisp, *Mysore Revenue Regulations*, quoted verbatim in Nikhiles Guha, *Pre-British State System*, pp. 194–97.

[15] Cf. C.A. Bayly, *The Imperial Meridian: The British Empire and the World, 1780–1830*, London, 1989, pp. 59–60.

The 'Mémoires' of Lieutenant-Colonel Russel concerning Mysore

In the Service Historique de l'Armée de Terre, Château de Vincennes, Paris

Translation by Jean-Marie Lafont

Most of the Frenchmen who served Hyder Ali and Tipu Sultan did not publish any memoirs or any account of the events they witnessed. In the review of F. D'Souza's *Quand la France decouvrit l'Inde*,[1] Aniruddha Ray noticed 'Tipu's [...] absence',[2] which was also the case with Guy Deleury's compilation, *Les Indes florissantes* in 1991;[3] the few exceptions include Le Goux de Flaix[4] and Maistre de la Tour.[5] Maistre de la Tour's *Histoire* was translated and published in English in 1855,[6] and it was deemed so interesting at that time that the English translation was 'revised and corrected by His Highness Prince Gholam Mohammed, the only surviving son of Tippoo Sultaun'.[7] Maistre de la Tour, however, has not been taken very seriously by contemporary Indian historians, especially since Jadunath Sarkar cast some doubts on his reliability.[8] This is a rare case of Sir Jadunath Sarkar's quick reading of a French text: Maistre de la Tour, in his book, traced the history of Hyder Ali and Tipu Sultan from what he personally learnt and witnessed during his stay at Mysore right from 1771, and subsequently from French officers and soldiers who served them in the field till the late 1770s. The 'naive confession' alluded to by Sarkar[9] is about the new war in the Carnatic (1780–83), and Maistre de la Tour,[10] as well as Russel, were at that time in France. They had no other information on India except that coming through London, because of the superiority of the British navy which had cut off communications between India and France.

One should not be surprised to find that no published contemporary account has survived of a militarily covert operation which was deemed to be secret and classified. The officers who took part in it have left only manuscript documents, and the fact is that Maistre de la

82

Tour, though the information he published in 1783 tallies pretty well with these unpublished documents, was *not* a member of the military team secretly dispatched by the French government to Mysore in 1769. He does not figure on the list of these officers, and he is specifically mentioned in Hugau's papers[11] as being a French 'merchant' from Provence with some medical skill, who tried to play the military man in Mysore with not much success.[12] We therefore understand Jadunath Sarkar's satisfaction when he found in Goa an anonymous account by a French officer who participated in the Carnatic campaign of Hyder Ali in 1780. He immediately translated it into English and published it in 1941.[13] He also referred in a footnote to one of Lallée's letters written to his brother on the same topic, published in Franch in 1934.[14] However, French archives have some more documentation on this still little-known aspect of the Franco–Mysorean military co-operation, and I have recently analysed some of the documents found in France concerning the contingent of Hussars who served Hyder Ali and Tipu Sultan from 1769 to 1785.[15] In fact, the information contained in the private and official papers of Hugau, Bouthenot, Russel and Piveron de Morlat covers the whole range of the Franco–Mysorean military cooperation during that period, and they also include a brief account of the first contingent of Hügel's cavalry in the service of Mysore from 1761 to 1764. In this article I will concentrate on the Russel papers in the Service Historique de l'Armée de Terre (SHAT), Château de Vincennes, under the reference M-249.

Five documents written by Russel, two letters and three (or two) memoirs (the *Mémoires* covering 106 pages), are kept in the Service Historique de l'Armée de Terre. They are:

1. Letter dated 26 May 1781, covering the dispatch of the first *Mémoire(s)*.
2. Note giving Russel's biodata and listing his military services till 1780.
3. 'Mémoire sur le Nabab Hyder-Ali-Kan dit Bahader ou le grand (Mai 1781)', pp. 1–58.
4. 'Observations sur la guerre que fait Hyder contre les Anglais à la côte de Coromandel', no date [May 1781], pp. 59–69.
5. 'Project d'une expédition dans l'Inde (Novembre 1781)', pp. 70–106.

Document 1

This letter is a brief document covering the dispatch of the first *Mémoire*[16] (nos 3 and 4), but it has the interesting information that 'this memoir only contains a very succinct result[17] of my papers on Hyder and India'.[18] Russel says that he was sent on a political and military assignment to Hyder Ali Khan with Hügel, and in June 1772 he succeeded him as commanding officer of the French detachment.[19] He remained with the Nawab till 1778, always campaigning, and he gives a list of the sieges and campaigns (with dates) in which he participated with the French troops.

Document 2

The second document contains Russel's biodata. He joined the army in 1753 as a 'cadet' in the Régiment du Royal Ecossais, then volunteered to join the Regiment of Lenoncourt Cavalry in 1756. He was promoted sous-lieutenant in the Royal Duex-Pont in 1758, sous-lieutenant of Grenadiers in 1760,[20] and first lieutenant in 1762. He participated with this regiment in the campaigns of 1758 to 1762, and he gives the list of battles and 'affaires' in which he was engaged.[21] Russel does not mention in this official letter his demotion and lack of promotion in the following years, but Michel Turiotte rightly ascribed it to the fact that, being a commoner, this experienced officer had no chance against the young officers of noble stock who got out-of-turn promotions at that time of 'reaction nobiliaire'. A promotion to the rank of captain came only in 1769, when he was offered the job of serving with Lieutenant-Colonel Hügel.[22] Hügel died in 1772 from wounds received at the Battle of Melkota,[23] but before dying he advised Hyder Ali to select Russel as the next commander of the French troops.[24] Russel was promoted Lieutenant-Colonel of Cavalry in 1773 on Hyder's recommendation, and was awarded the prestigious Saint Louis Cross. He commanded the detachment for full six years, till Puymorin[25] replaced him on 9 June 1778. While travelling back to Pondicherry, he came to know that the city was besieged by the British. Disguising himself as a Muslim, he crossed the British lines to join Bellecombe, the Governor General, who appointed him his *aide de camp*.[26] He became a prisoner of war after the capitulation of Pondicherry, and was back in France in October 1780. These documents, dated 1781, are signed 'Lieutenant-Colonel Russel, former Commander of the French troops'.[27]

Document 3: 'Mémoire sur le Nabab Hyder-Ali-Kan dit Bahader ou le grand'

'Mémoire sur le Nabab Hyder-Ali-Kan dit Bahader ou le grand'[28] is 58 pages long. The first fifteen pages tell the story of Hyder Ali Khan from his birth in 1720 and his first contacts with the French at Trichinopoly in 1752, till 1771, when he was informed of the arrival of Hügel at Srirangapatnam with eight officers and two subaltern officers.[29] There is an interesting mention of the brilliant action of Hyder Naik at Trichinopoly,[30] when he captured 400 muskets and an unspecified number of horses. On Dupleix's recommendation to Nandi Raja, the Maratha general, Hyder was allowed to raise a troop of 400 sepoys equipped with these muskets, and as many horsemen for mounting the horses he had taken from the British.[31] The elevation of Hyder provoked the growing suspicion and jealousy of the *darbar* of Mysore, and Russel gives a detailed account of Hyder's unfolding *coup d'état* in 1761,[32] with the help of Hügel and 300 Hussars who joined him in Bangalore after the fall of Pondicherry. We find details of the help Hügel gave to Hyder in the capture of Srirangapatnam.[33] Having secured his hold on the country, Hyder embarked upon a policy of conquests, seeking to seize Kolar, Hoskote, Matagueri and Sira.[34] He received the title of Nawab from Basalat Jang in 1762, following which he changed his name from Hyder Naik to Hyder Ali Khan. He then extended his domination over 'Gran' [big] and 'Chauta' [small] Balapour [probably Dodballapur] and Chiteldrouk. Russel devotes only one page to the conquest of 'Bisnagar',[35] but describes the battle of Sanour [Savanur], in which Hügel and the French troops distinguished themselves.[36] The conquest of Sonde [Sode, Sunda], whose Raja escaped to Goa, brought Hyder Ali close to a conflict with the Portuguese. Russel simply states that Hyder would have besieged Goa, had not Hügel decided to leave him at that time: a decision which obliged the Nawab to change his plans.[37] The three following pages[38] cover the period 1765–71 with the conquest of the Malabar coast, the war against the English and their puppet Nawab Muhammad Ali Khan,[39] the Maratha invasion of Mysore, and the preparations made by Hyder to fight the Marathas at Melkota.

Hügel and his officers had arrived in Srirangapatnam a few days before the battle, and they joined Hyder just before the fateful day when 'Mr Fortin was killed, all the other officers wounded, and Mr

Hügel died from his wounds in the first days of May 1772'.[40] From Pondicherry Russel hastened to Srirangapatnam and assumed command of the French troops.[41] He vividly describes Hyder's efforts to rebuild his army, whose regular troops were upto 15,000 infantry and 10,000 cavalry in February 1773. The French Hussars joined them for the conquest of Coorg,[42] and then for the reconquest of the places lost to the Marathas (1774–75). Hyder then moved against Basalat Jang, who was besieging Bellary. After a quick march,[43] while approaching the army of Basalat Jang at Bellary, 'Hyder ordered his infantry to form into columns. The artillery was in the intervals, the cavalry on the wings, my troop behind the infantry. He kept that order while moving, and as soon as we were at gun-range he ordered us to open fire "à boulets perdus".' The confusion was complete in the enemy's camp, a general rout followed and Basalat Jang's army was almost completely destroyed or captured.[44] Hyder had carefully omitted to tell Russel that Basalat Jang had his own French troops (Lallée's corps), and Russel discovered a number of wounded French soldiers after the fight, whom he took care of.[45]

He then gives details of petty military operations in 1775, mostly against the Marathas and their allies. In December Hyder started the seige of Gooty where, on 10 January 1776, Russel, at the specific request of the Nawab, led the storming party, climbing an ascent at the head of his Hussars.[46] The citadel surrendered only after its ramparts were blown up with mines and stormed by the troops. The siege of Chiteldroog, started during the first days of July 1777, was also a difficult affair: it took 75 days of 'tranchées ouvertes', and it was only after the capture of the sixth fortification wall ('sixiéme enceinte') that the besieged commander decided to surrender.[47] By the end of 1777 Hyder Ali, after a month of 'marches et contre-marches', managed to close in on the Maratha army and fought the Battle of Daguerie on 1 January 1778:[48] 'We marched upon them [the Marathas] with the elite of our forces, leaving the main baggage with the main body of troops [. . .]. Hyder formed his vanguard with 4,000 cipayes, my troop and eighteen guns: one seventeen-pounder, one twelve-pounder, two English nine-pounder "coulevrines" and [fourteen] other six- and four-pounders. We marched in column, the artillery in front, my troop in the centre. The army followed us at one gun-shot range, the infantry formed into a square with the baggage in the square, and the cavalry on the wings and at the back. We marched slowly, in that compact order, against the Marathas, who occupied the best ground. When we came to half-gun-range, our field pieces opened fire on their vanguard, which retreated on the left after our second volley. We continued marching in the same order for one league [four kms] when we saw at the top of a hill the "Eléphants de Pavillion".[49] We climbed up the hill in front of them and we attacked them the same way as before. They again retreated on the left. They reappeared one league afar, still drawn in a battle-line, and at sunset, just as we came at gun-range, they forded the Tombandra river under darkness. We resumed the pursuit at 4 pm.'[50] Then, in March 1778, when the army was on the Tombandra [Tungabhadra] river, it was suddenly threatened by two powerful Maratha armies, and the army of Basalat Jang. The enemy forces, mustering more than 1,00,000 men, were overwhelmingly superior to that of Mysore, and Hyder decided to fall back to Srirangapatnam, retreating 'in reversed columns, and I was in the rearguard'.[51] Russel then explains, over six pages,[52] how the unfolding events at the Maratha court—the Raghuba affair—and the extraordinary acumen of Hyder saved Mysore from a devastating invasion. As soon as the three armies separated, Hyder crossed the river again and started reoccupying some strategic positions at the top of the hills. When Puymorin arrived, in June 1778, Russel 'gave him in good condition the French troop which [he] had formed and disciplined'.[53]

Russel then sums up his relations with Hyder Ali: 'During the six years I commanded [the Hussars], I did not leave Hyder for one single day. I followed him in all his expeditions, being twice a day with him or his son in the trenches during the sieges. I was always in the most perilous places in the battles or in the storming parties, and I was often consulted for erecting the batteries, conducting the siege works and dealing with the military service.'[54] Russel acknowledges the fact that Hyder was an outstanding general, and that he was at his best while besieging a city: 'When he is besieging a place, he himself directs the works, draws the lines, erects the batteries. As soon as the first entrenchment is ready, he builds a "canonnière" for his son,[55] who does not leave the trenches until the surrender of the place. Twice a day Hyder visits the works. It is there that I saw him becoming more human,[56] enjoying himself and becoming amiable. There he trusted me the most, and he asked for my advice with utmost interest.'[57] Most interesting is the care Hyder Ali took to train Tipu Sahib in the art of storming cities. Russel, who befriended Tipu Sahib and has painted a wonderful portrait of him,[58] underlines the following details: 'When I was with him [Tipu], which happened at least twice a day when we were besieging a place, while waiting for his father in the trenches, he questioned me on our manners and customs, our military forces, our way of conducting military operations. He asked me what he should do when he will be the master [of Mysore]. He told me his reign would be advantageous for France, for my troop [of Hussars] and for me. He enquired whether the French had any territorial ambitions in India. I reassured him, telling him that all we wanted was to maintain our position and protect our trade.'[59]

Russel gives two statements of the forces of the army of Mysore, which I reproduce (translated into English) hereafter. The first describes the army as it stood in June 1778 when he left Mysore, and it is as accurate as it can be, coming from a commanding officer who had just completed six years of active service in the force.

Statement on the Forces of Hyder-Ali-Kan
On June 1778

Troops

Cavalry	30,000
Cipayes [*Sipahis*]	20,000
Piedars [*Piyadas*]	1,50,000
Auxilliaries	12,000
[*Kam*]*altis* or Pioneers	10,000
[Total] Indians	2,22,000 men
French under the orders of M. de Puymorin	300
Europeans in the other corps of the army	600
[Total] Europeans	900 men
Total	2,22,900 men

Artillery

Iron guns, thirty-two-pounder	4
Iron guns, fourteen- and eighteen-pounder	60
Field guns '*en fonte*' [brass]	100
Howitzers	2
Pierriers [stone-throwers]	12
Total	178 guns

'This total does not include the mortars and the bombs taken by Hyder from the British when he reoccupied Mangalore in 1767.'[60]

The second statement is about the forces which Hyder Ali could have had with him in the Coromandel when he moved against Madras: the estimation is based on what Russel could conjecture in Paris when he wrote this *Mémoire* in May 1781:

Army of Hyder on the Coromandel Coast

Cavalry	30,000
Cipayes and Topaz	20,000
Cipayes and Topaz commanded by	4,000
M. de Lallé [sic]	
Piedars	90,000
Auxilliaries	12,000
[Total] Indians	1,66,000 men

French under the orders of M. de Puymorin	300
French under the orders of M. de Lallép [sic]	500
Europeans in the other corps of the army	600
[Total] Europeans	1,400 men

'From the statement I give above of Hyder Ali's artillery, we can be certain that he has with him whatever is necessary in field-guns and siege-guns'.[61]

Russel then describes the sophisticated provisioning system of Hyder Ali for providing to the needs of the troops from his magazines: 'He always has at Patann [Srirangapatnam], his capital, enough provisions to feed for ten years 10,000 cavalry and 20,000 sepoys. The store-houses at Hydernagar [Bednur] and Bangalore have more or less the same capacity.'[62] He gives a statement of the British army—43,000 men[63]—and affirms that 'the English army cannot resist Hyder Ali's'.[64]

Having thus written a short but comprehensive description of the action of the French troops since their inception in the army of Mysore out of the numerous 'Recueils' he brought back to France in 1778, Russel concludes this *Mémoire* with a lively description of Hyder Ali Khan's character,[65] followed by a shorter, but most interesting description of Prince Tipu Sahib's character,[66] which we publish in English translation as an Appendix.

Document 4: 'Observations sur la guerre que fait Hyder contre les Anglais, à la côte de Coromandel'

This second *Mémoire*, undated, has only eleven pages.[67] Although it has a separate title, it is clearly part of the preceding one, as can be seen from a reference to Raghuba and the Marathas.[68] It does not add much to the information we have, except for two successive affirmations by Russel that the French government's intention in sending this military mission to Mysore was to strengthen Hyder Ali and use him against the English East India Company.[69] Russel then plays a military game, of what would happen during the war when Hyder besieged Madras.[70] His assumption, which proved to be false, is that d'Orves, the French admiral, would neutralize the British navy in the Indian Ocean, and that the French government would deal with it in the Channel,[71] preventing England from sending reinforcements to India.[72] According to him, Madras, then, would not be able to resist Hyder Ali.[73] Russel insists on the fact that Hyder Ali has been able to convince Nizam Ali as well as the Marathas that it is in their own interest to expel the English from India, and he is certain that Hyder will succeed in keeping them on his side.[74] Hyder has already taken Mahé[75] and Tellichery,[76] and he will successfully capture all the other possessions of the East India Company in the Coromandel.[77] Hyder, according to Russel, started the present campaign because he was certain to receive French assistance against the British. Russel repetitively promised such help while he was serving in Mysore, and the purpose of the *Mémoire* is to provide the French government with 'useful observations at a time when it is considering the importance of dispatching such help in order to accelerate Hyder's success'.[78] Then, Russel criticizes the anti-Hyder lobby in Paris and Versailles, which was casting doubts on Hyder Ali's strong opposition to the English.[79] He further criticizes the proponents of a purely military operation, insisting also upon the political and diplomatic aspects of the expedition.[80] Recalling Hyder's own elevation to power in the context of the English East India Company's policy[81] and Dupleix's own position in India in 1754, Russel affirms that Hyder Ali is following a long-prepared plan[82] to take over India and reduce the English East India Company to its original size. He was only waiting for the next Anglo–French war to join the fray, and in 1778 he would have certainly come to the help of Pondicherry—Russel is quite emphatic on this point—'had he not been fighting 200 leagues away [800 km] inland to reduce Princes who were still capable of opposing him and helping the Marathas to invade Mysore'.[83] It is only after the completion of that campaign that he invaded the Carnatic with all his forces.[84] On the last page of the *Mémoire*, Russel reminds his readers of Hyder's success in inciting the Marathas and the Nizam to join him against the English: Hyder Ali will certainly reduce the East India Company, and perhaps the French Compagnie des Indes, to a mere couple of trading posts, since he is an ambitious man who can be contained only by superior power.[85]

Document 5: 'Mémoire secret. Project d'une Expédition dans l'Inde'

The 'Mémoire secret' sent by Russel to de Castries, Ministre de la Marine, is thirty-seven pages long.[86] It is dated November 1781, the time when Bussy secretly left Paris for Spain, where he was to board a man-of-war to sail to India. The expeditionary force was already at Brest, ready to embark on Soulange's squadron, which actually made its first unsuccessful attempt to break the English blockade, with tremendous losses, in December 1781.[87]

Russel refers to his previous *Mémoire* in which he explained the military assistance Hyder Ali could give the French in their fight against the English. The present *Mémoire* informs the minister of the dangers of trusting Hyder Ali too much, although he is the only native power who could help the French to retrieve their position in India, for he is also the only one who could prevent them from doing so. The three purposes of the French military intervention should be: (1) the destruction of the British power in India, (2) the preponderance of French trade, and (3) subsequently laying the foundations of formidable power, more through a peaceful and wise policy than the use of arms.[88] The expedition must be conducted on a large scale, so that the French are in a strong military position at the end of the war. The French navy in India[89] and in France[90] should get the upper hand over the British navy, so that Hyder Ali and the French corps were left to deal with only the land forces of the East India Company.

Hyder's policy, according to Russel, is to become the master of India and to reduce the English as well as the French to their small original trading posts in order to get from them 'at the best price the products of Europe, especially guns (artillery) and ammunition'.[91] In a footnote, he strongly advocates banning the sale of artillery to Hyder by French merchants;[92] and, if the French felt compelled to sell them, let them take their time and sell only defective guns.[93] Back to the main text, the Colonel emphasizes the necessity of a quick and strong operation, so that Hyder Ali would acknowledge the French as one of the main factors of his success,[94] and give them in exchange a most favoured position in the settlement of India after the victory. For this reason, Russel advocates the sending of 12,000 men to India,[95] to be divided into three legions of 4,000 men, each commanded by a Colonel.[96] A corps of sepoys commanded by European officers should be attached to each legion. The field artillery should be sufficient for an army of 30,000 men. Siege and position artillery should also be imported on a large scale, along with as much ammunition as possible according to the space available on the ships. Since Hyder Ali could grow suspicious about such a strong force landing in India, only 6,000 men would land first. The others would come as soon as necessary.

A long section, Section IV, entitled 'Politique à observer',[97] starts with the advice that the French Commander-in-Chief and his senior officers must be well aware of Indian politics,[98] with the General alone being informed of the details of the government's policy.[99] There is no need to list here the seventeen articles of Russel's advice to the Commander-in-Chief, although some of them, and some of the footnotes he attached to these articles, are worth noticing. In case Hyder Ali was reluctant to give back Pondicherry to the French with permission to erect new fortifications in the city (article 1),[100] Russel writes in a lengthy note (No. 5) of two-and-a-half pages,[101] interesting for its pseudo-Machiavellianism and colonialist content, that the French should carefully conceal the fact that they came back to India with any interests or ambitions, and they must [secretly] consider Hyder Ali as the greatest [Indian] enemy of their own hegemonistic designs. That is why the French General should not accept any native units, neither cavalry nor infantry, from the Nawab, because they could turn treacherous (article 12, note 8).[102] The French General must be the only one in charge of night operations, for which he will use only troops under his command (article 7, note 6).[103] Article 15 reads as follows: 'Ask the Nawab that all the French in his service be incorporated into the French army';[104] while article 16 concerns the 'European deserters' whom Hyder should not be allowed to enrol any more in his native units and his artillery. Note 11 to article 16 suggests that this drastic restriction should even be extended to Indian officers and soldiers in the service of the French, who should be forbidden to join the army of Mysore under the Franco–Mysorean agreement. After these seventeen articles, Russel calls the attention of the French Commander-in-Chief to the situation of the Dutch on the Malabar coast. He refers in note 13[105] to the treaty signed in 1774 between Hyder and the Dutch authorities at Cochin, according to which the Dutch were to send 1,500 European soldiers to Hyder in lieu of his permission to them to open factories at Mangalore and other places. But they did not send any troops, and a Dutch settlement called Chetoit was captured in retaliation by Hyder. Russel, in this note, expatiates upon Hyder's ambitions in respect of Travancore: because it was a very rich state, and also because he could then attack the English from the south. Another interesting piece of information in the same note concerns 'the troops that we allow them [the Dutch] to raise in France': if sent to India and used by the Dutch against Mysore, Hyder could imagine that the French and the Dutch have decided to act together against him in India.

When the French General meets Hyder Ali,[106] he is to give him state presents and negotiate the Franco–Mysorean treaty with him. He should also request permission to meet Tipu Sahib[107] and offer him state gifts, along with the personal gifts Tipu had requested Russel to send him from France in 1778: taffetas 'ciré' of different shades to make coats, 'gold and silver water' from Danzig, looking-glasses, and a toiletry set with good soaps.[108] Other notables should also receive gifts: Prince Karim Sahib, one of Hyder's sons 'du sérail'[109] and his most preferred child, Mir Sahib[110] and Muktum Sahib[111], the most important brahmins, the first two *chobdars* who would be in charge of the negotiations, other *chobdars* and servants in Tipu Sultan's and the princes' houses.

Section VI is about 'Alternative à prévoir pour les négocia-[tions]'.[112] If Madras was captured by Hyder before the French army arrives in India, the Nawab might not be inclined to give the French any advantageous concessions, unless he can use them for his own aggrandizement or defence. Note 19[113] cites Travancore as the country Hyder wanted to annex first, and Russel mentions the roads which Hyder built in the forests towards Cochin as a preliminary step for the invasion of Travancore.[114] The French could help Hyder Ali to conquer Travancore if proper diplomatic measures are taken in France concerning the Netherlands. Concerning defence, note 20[115] says that after the destruction of the British in India, the Marathas and Nizam Ali might grow suspicious of Hyder Ali's power, and unite against him once again. In that case, if Hyder was reluctant to accommodate the French, they could play the Maratha card against him. The French General, in any case, should keep the French squadron with him for clearing the Indian Ocean of the British navy, bringing in the second division[116] and provisions for the troops, for being used to sail out of India in case of difficulty.[117]

'In case Hyder Ali Khan refused [to secure] Pondicherry' for the French,[118] one should induce him join in an attack on Bombay, and after that on Surat. If he did not agree, the French could do it themselves, provided they had an alliance with the Marathas and Nizam Ali.

Section VIII[119] considers the possibility that no agreement is reached with Hyder Ali for fighting the English. The first step, in that case, would be to negotiate a treaty with the kings of Travancore and Tanjore, and then move on with an attack on Bengal. Russel is emphatic about 'the immense resources that the English are getting from that place even during the present war'.[120] He says that the local princes are ready to join the French against the English, provided the French came with a considerable army. After that, the French General should call in the second division[121] and discuss again with Hyder Ali the question of Pondicherry. If Hyder still rejected the demand of the French, they could ask Tanjore, or preferably Travancore, for permission to wait there, and then storm Bombay. Once in Bombay, the French should enter into an alliance with the Marathas and the petty princes of the eastern coast, write to the Great Mughal at Delhi, and then try to capture Surat, before returning with the army to Travancore. From there, the French General should start negotiating again with Hyder Ali. In the meantime, he should take appropriate action so that the French officers in Hyder's service desert with their troops and join the French army. The same could be done for the other European officers serving Mysore. Many soldiers, sepoys and topazes, could be enticed to join the French against Hyder, and even the native commanders hired by Hyder, with their cavalry units, could be won over. Russel even dreams of Tipu Sultan joining the French against Hyder, since he too was reeling under his yoke! If Tipu acted this way, most of the Mysore army, especially the cavalry, would follow him.[122] Then, the French General should attack Hyder Ali in such a way that he cannot make a retreat to

Hydernagar [Bednur], because of the strength of the place and the resources of the countryside. The main issue then would be to prevent an alliance between Hyder Ali and some other country-power, like the Marathas.

Section X, the last section,[123] deals with the 'Politique avec les Princes du Pays'. Russel has no doubt that if the French can reduce Hyder Ali, they will become the 'arbitres des intérêts de tous les indiens'.[124] It will then suffice to explain to the Indians that 'the intention of the French is to protect them, provide them with a secure existence, give back to the princes whatever territories had been taken from them'. They would only be requested to pay a small tribute proportionate to their income and accommodate *Vakils* at their court, who would keep the French informed of what was going on in their *darbars*. Everything would be taken care of kindly, especially the peasants,[125] who would not run away any more on the approach of 'our armies'. Russel waxes eloquent on the peaceful conquests which will follow. This wise policy 'will make France the master of the most beautiful and richest country in the world',[126] and that will be a boost for French commercial enterprises. Ultimately, 'the ability of France to have an impressive navy always in a state of preparedness will unavoidably[127] give her preponderance over her rivals'.[128]

A short 'Recapitulation'[129] starts with the clear affirmation that the purpose of French military intervention in India must be the conquest of all of India, not only of the present English possessions there. If we can fight the East India Company with Hyder Ali as an ally, the British will be soon expelled from India. But we shall soon after be obliged to fight the Nawab as well: 'He is in possession of immense treasures, and is the master of one of the most beautiful parts of India.' According to Russel, there will be no injustice done to Hyder Ali if the French deprive him of his possessions, since they helped him so much in acquiring them! And the French will solely give back to their original owners part of the very extensive kingdom of Mysore. Last, but not least, there is of course the possibility of Hyder's demise, which was why Russel had befriended 'Pytin-poun-Saïl' [Tipu Sahib] when he was in Mysore.[130]

Such is the content of this interesting file kept in the Service Historique de l'Armée de Terre, Château de Vincennes, Paris. A political analysis of these documents has been offered by the author in a previous publication.[131] I would like here to emphasize some other aspects of Russel's *Mémoires*, which might give a better understanding of the thinking in France concerning the French who served the Indian states from the 1750s onwards.

As mentioned in the beginning of that study, not much of the documentation on Hyder Ali and Tipu Sultan kept in French archives has been used, not to speak of publication. S.P. Sen wrote his magisterial *The French in India*, because he was able to work in the Pondicherry archives, which were transferred to France after 1954 and are now kept in the Centre des Archives d'Outre-Mer at Aix-en-Provence. Because of the intricate connections and almost permanent conflicts between the Marathas and Mysore, V.G. Hatalkar collected in Paris, mostly from the Archives Nationales and the Bibliothèque Nationale, an impressive number of microfilms and photocopies of documents concerning Hyder and Tipu Sultan, for his monumental work on the relations of the French with the Marathas.[132] Suman Venkatesh has recently published an English translation of these photocopies kept in the Karnataka State Archives.[133] However, many more documents remain to be explored in France concerning the Franco–Mysorean connection from about 1750 to 1799. As stated before, the papers, official or private, written by Hugau, Hügel, Russel, Lallée, Bouthenot and several other anonymous French officers who served in Mysore— including the one published by Sir Jadunath Sarkar in 1941—cover the whole story of the Hussars' corps in the service of Mysore from 1770 to 1785, with several feedbacks for the period 1761–64, when Hügel and his cavalry first served in Hyder Ali's army. The most significant parts of these manuscripts, translated into English, could be published in one volume of a collection dealing with the French sources of Indian history, if some governmental or private sponsorship could be found for their publication.

The English translation of Piveron de Morlat's *Mémoire sur l'Inde*, a manuscript of 450 pages in 4°, is under preparation.[134] It covers extensively the 1778–85 military and political involvements of Hyder Ali and Tipu Sultan, as perceived by the French Agent (Ambassador) attached to the *darbar* of Mysore. Other manuscripts of Piveron, e.g., the documents pertaining to the capitulation of the British garrison at Mangalore in January 1784, are still awaiting detailed study, not to speak of publication. And there are other documents still to be traced. As we have seen, Jadunath Sarkar alludes to a letter of Lallée published in French in 1934.[135] In 1878, the correspondence of Lallée with his family, covering forty years of service (*c.* 1750–90) with Basalat Jang, Nizam Ali, Hyder Ali and Tipu Sultan, was preserved in the Château de Romilly [Savoy]. The Château does not exist any more, and I have not yet been able to trace Lallée's private papers among the descendants of the de Motz de la Sale family. But it is evident that documents exist in France on the Franco–Mysorean connection, which could shed fresh light on the Sultanate of Mysore, similar to the documents we have already used for the French in the service of the Sindhia and Maharaja Ranjit Singh.

The second aspect I would like to emphasize is the diversity of these testimonies. Some historians today are as puzzled as Bussy was in the late 1770s, when they read the reports advising the French government to follow so many different, often contradictory, policies towards India. No document, of course, can be taken at its face-value, but the difficulty is to assess, for each and every document, its relative importance. The first *Mémoire* is a testimony to what was done by the French, and especially by the French commander of the Hussar corps between 1772 and 1778, to modernize the army of Mysore and fight along with the Mysorean forces according to the instructions of the French government. Being a king's officer, Russel did his duty in transferring, without reluctance, military technologies to Mysore, and in training the Mysorean forces according to the most modern European systems of warfare. This policy was continued after Russel's departure from Mysore, first by Colonel Puymorin, who died from a wound received in action in 1782, and then by Colonel Bouthenot, who died just after his return to France in January 1787.[136] This first *Mémoire* is, according to me, the most important document of the Russel papers.

People not familiar with the practice of military officers, especially commanding officers, of that time may be surprised—and probably amused—at the way Russel, in the two following *Mémoires* (Documents 4 and 5), developed his plans for military operations in India which were to lead, on paper at least, 'infailliblement' to victory.[137] These *Mémoires* are in fact, a different type of document—war games, which are still practised today, 'with very different tools', by any officer in any army of the world: how, from a given situation, to fight a battle and win a victory against all odds.

The interest of these two documents does not lie therefore in their military value. They are interesting because of the clearly advocated colonial policy proposed by Lieutenant-Colonel Russel while advising the French government on the aims and prospects of a costly military expedition to India, and the bias they suddenly reveal in the author's mind against Hyder Ali. If we go by the royal and ministerial instructions sent by the French government to its officials in India, it is clear that, with the brief (though 'brilliant') exception of Dupleix in 1741–54,[138] there was no intention on the part of the French to colonize India the way they did North America (Canada, Louisiana, etc.) or the Caribbean (Haïti, etc.), and as the British did in India after 1757. Lally's instructions (1757), just like Bussy's instructions (1780–83), were simply to destroy the British power in India and to give back to the Indian rulers part of their territories which had been conquered by the English East India Company. That was (and remained even in 1802–03, during Decaen's aborted expedition) the official policy of France. That does not mean, of course, that all the French lobbies in India (Pondicherry), the Mascareignas (Ile de France [Mauritius], Ile Bourbon) and France shared the espousal of such a disinterested or far-sighted policy.[139] Lieutenant-Colonel Russel thought the only purpose of such an expensive expedition to be the conquest of India by the French.[140] Some people in France did not share the same analysis. At exactly the same time, on 11 November 1781, King Louis XVI signed his *Mémoire of the King*, which was to serve as 'Instructions' to Marquis de Bussy, Commander-in-Chief. These instructions clearly stated that the object of the French expedition to India was to liberate the Indian princes from the yoke of the English, and not to make any territorial conquest.[141] Is it necessary to add that Lieutenant-Colonel Russel's personal feelings, whether right or wrong, did not modify the policy of the King of France and his government on matters related to India?

Appendix

Character of Petin Pousall,[142] *Son of Hyder-Aly-Kan*
(Translated from the French, pages 55–58)

[p. 55] Tipu Sahib, also called Sahibzada,[143] was educated as a prince who was to succeed a conqueror. He is not as tall and strong as his father. He has a distinguished appearance, is very smart and quick in physical exercises. He is the best horseman of the whole army.

The prince is thirty-two years old. He has shown from his early childhood that he can follow the path of his father because of his quick understanding, his eagerness to learn, his interest in politics and war, his love for glory. He has the same passions as his father, but not the vices. He is particular about following exactly the commands of his religion. He has moral principles, is careful not to depart from them, and is critical of his father's behaviour.

Tipu Sahib is an upright [p. 56], sensible and grateful gentleman. He seems to like friendship. He was married by his father six years ago, but had only one daughter when I left. He is nice when his father is not around and if he is not afraid of being reported.[144] He then speaks openly, trustfully, to the people he loves, especially about war, politics and governance. When I was with him, which happened at least twice a day when we were besieging a place, while waiting for his father in the trenches, he questioned me on our manners and customs, our military forces, our way of conducting military operations. He asked me what he should do when he would be the master [of Mysore]. He told me his reign would be advantageous for France, for my troop [of Hussars] and for me. He enquired whether the French had any territorial ambitions in India. I reassured him, telling him that all we wanted was to maintain our position and protect our trade. He was then making plans to fight the English (whom he hates) and their Nawab Mahamat-Aly-Khan [p. 57]. He often told me: 'I want to expel them from India. I want to be the friend of the French all my life.'

Tipu Sahib fears his father more than he loves him. He is ambitious like him, and impatient to reign. Whatever precautions he can use to dissimulate his feelings, they could hardly escape the penetration and vigilance of Hyder. That is probably what entreats him [Hyder Ali] to be so cautious, and not to give any parcel of authority to his son. That is why also he only gives him the [resources] strictly necessary for life, so that he does not collect any partisans.

Tipu Sahib has an elevated character. He is only looking for opportunities to distinguish himself. He is sometimes rash, but he also showed that he can be clever and cautious in war. He has an enlightened ambition. He is perfectly aware of the importance for an Indian ruler that no European nation near him grows too powerful.

He knows how to appreciate merit. He promises a lot, but his father does not give him the means to fulfil his commitments. [Hyder Ali] gives him money with such parsimony that he is obliged to borrow from the *socards* [*sahukars*], or [p. 58] money-lenders for his necessary expenses. He however spends sparingly, loves order, is very strict in military discipline. He gives great hopes, but the limitations imposed on his actions do not permit one to say whether his coming into authority would result in good or bad things.[145]

Notes and References

[1] Paris, L'Harmattan, 19XX.

[2] *Journal of Historical Research*, X, 2000, p. 111.

[3] *Les Indes florissantes. Anthologie des voyageurs francais (1750–1820)*, Paris, 1991.

[4] *Essai historique, geographique et politique sur l'Indoustan, avec le tableau de son commerce par Mr Legoux de Flaix, ancien officier du Genie, de la Societe Asiatique de Colcota [sic]*, 2 volumes, Paris, 1807. This is not acknowledged as a publication on Mysore, since Legoux de Flaix wrote mostly on economic affairs and covered the whole of India. But in his preface he informs his readers that he spent many years in Hyder Ali's service as a civil and military engineer. There is however no information concerning what he did in Mysore in the 448+460 pages of his essay.

[5] *Histoire d'Ayder-Aly-Cawn, ou Nouveaux Memoires sur l'Inde*, 2 volumes, Paris, 1783.

[6] *The History of Hyder Shah, alias Hyder Ali Khan Bahadur: and of his son, Tippoo Sultaun*, by M.M.D.L.T., General in the army of the Mughal Empire, rpt, Delhi, 1976.

[7] Ibid.

[8] 'A French military adventurer in India, named Maistre de la Tour [. . .] claimed to be "an eye-witness of his [Hyder Ali's] conquests]", yet he naively confesses: "We can give no details of the operations of Haider in the present war, having no other materials than the relations of the English",' in J. Sarkar, 'Haidar Ali's Invasion of the Eastern Carnatic, 1780', *Islamic Culture*, XV, 1941, pp. 214–28; reprinted in Irfan Habib (ed.), *Confronting Colonialism: Resistance and Modernization under Haidar Ali and Tipu Sultan*, Delhi, 1999, pp. 21–34.

[9] *The History of Hyder Shah*, p. 225.

[10] He was back in France at that time.

[11] Hugau met him in Mascate and called him Maistre only, adding that the man then came to Srirangapatnam. 'De la Tour' was perhaps added by Maistre to his name when he returned to France.

[12] Hugau lost his way (as he says) or deserted (as his brother officers said without mincing words about it) after the Battle of Melkota. What he writes concerning his French colleagues who stayed in Mysore must therefore be read with some caution.

[13] Irfan Habib (ed.), *Confronting Colonialism*, p. 21n. Let us say here that J. Sarkar was puzzled by the following sentence: 'I met son tinate dans cette pagode', which he translated as: 'He placed his tent in that Pagoda' (p. 32), with a footnote (p. 34, note 3) trying to make sense of the word 'tinate'.

Piveron de Morlat probably used the same word (written 'tenate') with the following explanation: '[troupes] a ses ordres positifs'. See my own comments on this word in Piveron's *Memoire sur l'Inde*, forthcoming.

[14] Ibid.

[15] 'Military Cooperation between Mysore and France according to Some French Sources, 1750–1785', paper presented at International Seminar on Tipu Sultan, Bangalore, 4–6 May 1999 (forthcoming).

[16] Dated May 1781, like the covering letter.

[17] The meaning here is 'resume'.

[18] 'qu'un resultat tres succinct de mes Recueils sur Hyder et sur'. I do not know whether these 'Recueils' (manuscript books and notes) have survived.

[19] 'La troupe francaise'.

[20] Each regiment, in Europe as well as in the 'French' regiments of the Indian states (e.g., the Corps de Francais de Raymond, in the Nizam's service) had one elite company of Grenadiers.

[21] These took place in the course of the Seven Years' War.

[22] Hügel, an excellent Cavalry officer, was captain of Hussars at twenty-three. He had been in the service of Hyder Ali from 1761 to 1764, and was now sent on a secret mission to Mysore in order to modernize the Nawab's forces.

[23] This is Russel's version of the demise of Hügel. We know that there was a severe outbreak of dysentery in Mysore in 1772, and that Hügel died from the epidemic.

[24] Two observations here: the first is that Hyder Ali, who had a high regard for Hügel, ordered his mortal remains to be buried in front of his palace at Srirangapatnam. The second observation, collected from the *Mémoire* (no. 3), is that Russel had been sent by Hügel direct from Ile de France (Mauritius) to Pondicherry on a political mission. On being informed of Hügel's demise and his own appointment, he hurried to Srirangapatnam and assumed the command of the French troops on 9 June 1772.

[25] Spelt Pimorin.

[26] According to the *Mémoire* (no. 3, p. 38), he first crossed the British lines to reach Tranquebar. From there he sailed to Pondicherry, where he arrived on 19 August 1778.

[27] E.g., p. 106: 'L. Russel, Lieutenant-Colonel de Cavalerie, ci-devant Commandant les Troupes francaises aupres d'Hyder Ali'.

[28] 'Memoir on Hyder Ali Khan, called Bahadur or the Great'.

[29] pp. 1–6.

[30] An attack of a British convoy by a party of French and Mysorean troops.

[31] pp. 1–2.

[32] pp. 2–8.

[33] p. 4: 'Hyder fit attaquer les retranchements par les Francais qui les emporterent, et mirent l'armee en deroute.'

[34] pp. 8–9.

[35] pp. 10–11. This is in fact the country of Canara, with its capital at Bednore.

Maistre de la Tour is more prolix on this conquest and the prodigious riches Hyder found in the capital, Hydernagar: *History of Hyder Ali Khan*, pp. 53–59.

[36] C. Hayavadana Rao, *History of Mysore*, II, Bangalore, 1946, pp. 482–85. No mention of the French.

[37] '[Hyder Ali] eut assiege cette place [Goa] si le depart de M. Hugel ne lui eut fait changer de dessein.' Hugau, more explicitly, wrote that Hügel and his French troops refused to help Hyder in the invasion and attack of Goa since Portugal was at peace with France.

[38] pp. 12–16.

[39] With the lightning advance of Hyder Ali on Madras.

[40] Supra, note 23.

[41] pp. 17–20.

[42] p. 20.

[43] Forty leagues 120 kms in three days.

[44] p. 21.

[45] p. 21. 'Most of them would have died miserably if I had not spent 4,000 Francs to give them all the medical assistance they required.'

[46] p. 23. 'I was the first in the place.'

[47] pp. 26–27.

[48] pp. 28–31. Daguerie for Dodderie? The date given by Russel does not tally with those of other records.

[49] Elephants bearing the Maratha standards.

[50] pp. 28–29. This way of moving, so different from what we know of the Mughal armies in the 1740s, is comparable to the French (and indeed European) armies in the field after the various military reorganizations of the mid-eighteenth century. See my study on this topic 'Observations on the French Military Presence in the Indian States 1750–1849', in T.S. Mathew and S.J. Stephen (eds), *Indo–French Relations*, Delhi, 1999, pp. 199–234. See also my 'Benoit de Boigne in Hindustan', in *INDIKA Essays in Indo–French Relations 1630–1976*, Delhi, 2000, pp. 177–204.

[51] pp. 31–32. 'En colonnes reversees dont je formais l'arriere-garde'. The rear-guard is the most exposed position in a retreating army. Hyder had 4,000 elite infantry and 3,000 cavalry to protect his rear.

[52] pp. 32–36.

[53] p. 37.

[54] p. 37.

[55] Tipu Sahib.

[56] 's'humaniser'.

[57] pp. 52–53.

[58] pp. 54–58. See the English translation in the Appendix to this essay.

[59] p. 56.

[60] pp. 39–40.

[61] p. 41. For an analysis of the differences between the two statements, I refer the reader to my study, 'Military Cooperation between Mysore and France'.

[62] pp. 41–42.

[63] Cavalry 4,000, sepoys 30,000, piedars 6,000: total, 40,000 Indians. Plus 3,000 Europeans.

[64] p. 44.

[65] pp. 44–45.

[66] pp. 55–58.

[67] pp. 59–69.

[68] p. 69, '*J'ai deja fait observer dans le cours de ce memoire* [emphasis mine], en parlant de l'entreprise de Ragouba contre le jeune roi de Ponin [Pune]'. This refers to pp. 32–36 of the manuscript.

[69] pp. 59, 65.

[70] pp. 60–61.

[71] p. 61.

[72] p. 62.

[73] pp. 61–63.

[74] pp. 63–64.

[75] The French enclave on the Malabar coast, captured by the English on 19 March 1779.

[76] An English trading post north of Mahe.

[77] p. 65.

[78] p. 66: 'Mes observations peuvent etre utiles dans un moment ou doit juger de l'importance des secours capables d'accelerer le succes d'Hyder'. The date is May 1781. Rochambeau's army had been in North America since July 1780, but had not been able to engage the English because Washington could provide no transport for their heavy artillery. De Grasse and Suffren had left Brest with their squadrons in March 1781, and Bussy was to leave France for India with his army, an army as strong as Rochambeau's, in November 1781. Cornwallis's capitulation at Yorktown on 19 October 1781, with 8,000 soldiers, 162 guns, twenty-two flags and forty ships, was not yet known in France. For the chronology of these military operations, see J.M. Lafont, 'French Military Intervention in India compared to the French Intervention in North America 1776–1785', in *Proceedings of the Seminar on Tipu Sultan*, Asiatic Society of Calcutta, October 1999 (forthcoming).

[79] pp. 66–67. Bussy had decided to act along with the Marathas and the Nizam. He was ultimately obliged to land on the Coromandel coast and ally himself with Tipu Sultan because of accidental circumstances.

[80] p. 67: 'Je ne serais pas plus etonne que l'on eut assure qu'il n'y a point de politique dans l'Inde, et qu'il suffit d'y avoir de l'argent et des troupes. Il en faut sans doute. Mais sans une connaissance parfaite des moeurs, des usages et des interets differents, comment prevenir les perfidies, manier les esprits, diviser ses forces, preparer les evenements et s'en servir avec avantage?'

[81] p. 67: 'le systeme des Anglais'.

[82] Ibid: 'un plan forme depuis longtemps'.

[83] p. 68: '[Hyder Ali] serait bien certainement venu secourir Pondichery s'il n'eut ete a 200 lieues dans les terres occupe a reduire les Princes qui pouvaient encore contrarier ses dessins et favoriser les incursions des

Marathes dans see Etats.' The French in Paris were accusing Hyder Ali of having kept aloof from the war when the British besieged and captured Pondicherry. Let us remember here that when Russel left Hyder Ali's camp to return home, the news of the siege of Pondicherry had not yet reached the *darbar* of Mysore. Russel heard of it 'en route'.

[84] p. 68: 'Aussi n'a-t-il pas manque apres cette expedition [. . .] de [descendre] avec toutes ses forces a la Cote de Coromandel'.

[85] p. 69, the last three lines of the *Mémoire*: 'C'est en un mot un ambitieux avec lequel il faut etre le plus fort si l'on ne veut pas devenir sa victime.'

[86] pp. 70–106.

[87] See, for details, J.M. Lafont, 'French Military Intervention in India compared to the French Intervention in North America'.

[88] p. 71. Russel, as I explain in the paper quoted in note 87, belonged to the imperialistic and colonialist lobby of the French army. He perfectly knew what most of the French political circles ignored, viz. that the British empire was being built with Indian money.

[89] p. 72: again a reference to the squadron under the command of d'Orves in the Indian Ocean.

[90] Ibid: with reference to a request to the French government to prevent England from sending reinforcements to India.

[91] p. 73.

[92] p. 73 note 1, continued on p.74 at the top of the page.

[93] p. 74. This must be read as a strong criticism of what had been done previously and was still going on in 1781 to provide Hyder Ali with excellent war material and highly trained specialists, like Russel himself!

[94] Russel is apparently unaware that this statement contradicts the contents of his footnote no. 1.

[95] The maximum number considered by Bussy for a successful operation in India. Russel, in his foonote no. 2, advises the minister to send along with the army the full equipment for 30,000 men and a number of 'saddles à la hussarde', best suited for riding in India.

[96] p. 75: 3,000 infantry, 400 artillery, 600 dragoons (light cavalry).

[97] pp. 77–88.

[98] As opposed to General Comte de Lally and his Etat-Major during the Seven Years' War.

[99] That was the case with Bussy, and the reason why Bussy's arrival at Ile de France (Mauritius) being delayed by unexpected circumstances, the first troops under Duchemin landed on the Coromandel coast, not knowing that Bussy wanted a combined operation with the Marathas and the Nizam's forces starting from the Malabar coast.

[100] p. 78.

[101] pp. 78–80.

[102] p. 81. The French will raise their own units of native cavalry, 4,000 men, and infantry (5,000 to 6,000 sepoys and topazes).

[103] Combined operations at night with Indian units were the nightmare of French officers.

[104] p. 83: i.e. the French Hussars under Puymorin, the French party of Lallee and other officers and soldiers in the service of Mysore. Russel however anticipated a strong resistance from Hyder on this point, and his note 10 advises the French General not to insist too much on the topic if Hyder refuses at once to comply, but 'profiter de toutes les occasions pour renouveler cette demande'.

[105] A long note extending from p. 84 to p. 86.

[106] Section V: 'Arrivee du General chez Hyder Ali', pp. 88–90.

[107] The manuscript systematically and clearly reads Pytin-poun Sail or Sael, not Saib or Saeb. It is however undoubtedly Prince Tipou Sahib.

[108] p. 89: 'du taffetas cire de differentes couleurs pour faire des mateaux, de l'eau d'or et d'argent de Dantzick, des lunettes d'approche, et un necessaire avec de bonnes savonnettes.'

[109] 'From the seraglio'. To be distinguished from other children Hyder had 'outside' his harem.

[110] Brother of Tipu's mother, his 'Mammu'. p. 98, note 18.

[111] Another brother-in-law of the Nawab. He was Governor of Srirangapatnam in 1778: ibid., note 18.

[112] pp. 90–94.

[113] pp. 90–91.

[114] Legoux de Flaix (supra, note 4) mentions as a spectacular achievement the road built by Hyder Ali in the mountains for the conquest of Coorg. My feeling is that he was involved in this engineering *chef d'oeuvre*, but I have no evidence of this. We know however that the French troops were involved in the conquest of Coorg by Hyder.

[115] pp. 92–93.

[116] The 6,000 troops which had not yet landed in India. Russel does not say where they could wait. Ile de France did not have the resources to feed 6,000 soldiers for too long.

[117] Usually the land commander did not have any authority over the admiral, a fact which proved to be militarily disastrous for the French at the time of Dupleix, Lally and in 1778. In 1781, Admiral d'Orves was put under the command of Bussy, Commander-in-Chief of the land forces. Suffren, who succeded d'Orves, worked particularly well with and under Bussy, whatever has been written about their collaboration since 1783.

[118] Short section VII, pp. 94–95.

[119] pp. 95–101.

[120] p. 96: '[les] resources immenses que les Anglais en [= from Bengal] ont tire meme pendeant cette guerre'.

[121] Here, p. 97, Russel says that these 6,000 troops have been waiting in Cape Town or at Ile de France (Mauritius). A long note 22, pp. 97–98, explains again why it is essential not to raise the suspicion of Hyder by landing 12,000 troops in India.

[122] p. 101. The reason, according to Russel, is that most of the army leaders are deeply attached to Tipu.

[123] pp. 102–104.

[124] p. 102.

[125] Called 'les aldiens', people living in the Aldees (Aldeas).

[126] p. 103.

[127] 'Infailliblement' is the most usual locution at the end of a French military *mémoire* in which a war has be won . . . on paper!

[128] p. 104.

[129] pp. 104–06.

[130] p. 105.

[131] J.M. Lafont, 'Military Cooperation between Mysore and France according to Some French Sources'.

[132] See his *Relations between the French and the Marathas [1688–1815]*, Bombay, 1958, p. 281, Bibliography. See also his monumental *French Records Relating to the History of the Marathas*, 6 volumes, Bombay, 1978 to 1985.

[133] *Correspondence of the French during the Reign of Hyder Ali and Tipu Sultan*, 3 volumes, volume I, Bangalore, 1999.

[134] The only existing manuscript is also preserved in the Service Historique de l'Armée de Terre, Château de Vincennes.

[135] Supra, note 8.

[136] He was thirty-nine. He died from amoebiasis contracted during his service in India.

[137] They remind the French reader 'infailliablement' of the Pichrocoline War in Rabelais's *Gargantua*.

[138] As can be seen from the passing references to Dupleix in the *Mémoires*, Russel is an admirer of the Governor-General.

[139] When the French started building their 'Second Empire Colonial' in 1830 (Algeria) and expanded it in the east (Indo–China) and Central Africa, it became fashionable to criticize and ridicule Louis XVI's government for his failure to do the same in the 1780s. The cult of Dupleix spread in France in the 1850s, and flourished under Napoleon III's Second Empire. It is ironical to observe that the statue of Dupleix in Pondicherry was installed in 1870, the year the French Second Empire collapsed at Sedan.

[140] As emphasized in one of my studies quoted above ('Military Cooperation between Mysore and France according to Some French Sources'), Russel, as a king's officer and, later on, as the commanding officer of the French corps in Mysore, faithfully implemented his government's policy to transfer military technology and knowledge to Mysore. However, as a French subject convinced that such a policy was counter-productive for French interests in India, he tried to call the attention of his government to the dangers of reinforcing the army of Mysore. There is no contradiction between these two positions. All over the world, how many military officers since then, including today, have obeyed their government's orders and often died in doing their duty, even while they did not agree with the policy followed and the orders issued by the government? In 1835, Alfred de Vigny called it *Servitude et grandeur militaire*.

[141] Correctly analysed by S.P. Sen, *The French in India*, pp. 305–06, with reference to the French official documents then kept in the Pondicherry

Archives, now in the Centre des Archives d'Outre-Mer, Archives Nationales, Aix-en-Provence.

[142] Underlined in the text. Sic, for Tipu Sahib. I replace everywhere else in the text, *Petin Pousail* by Tipu Sahib.

[143] *Sabdaja* in the text.

[144] i.e. to his father, by the spies around him.

[145] The remaining part of page 58 is blank.

Essays

Tipu Sultan's Quest for Legitimacy and his Commercial Measures

Nikhiles Guha

The last fifteen years have seen important additions to the historical literature on the career and achievements of Tipu Sultan, who ruled Mysore from 1782 to 1799. Asok Sen's article on the material conditions of the time was followed by my book-length survey of the Mysore kingdom in the eighteenth century as an important instance of pre-British state formation in south India. Within Karnataka itself, the need has been felt for a closer look at the life and times of the Sultan. The continuing interest outside India is evidenced by the writings of Anne Buddle on the historic relics, and Kate Brittlebank's discussion of the interaction between the forces of tradition and change within the Mysore kingdom during this period.[1] The Indian History Congress, by bringing together articles on the Sultan presented at its various sessions within the covers of a single book (*Confronting Colonialism*) under the editorship of Irfan Habib, has enabled us to view the recent growth of scholarship on the subject in a proper perspective. Not only have the new writings extended our knowledge of the diplomatic and military events of the time on the basis of fresh evidence, they have helped us to look beyond individual personalities to the general forces at work. The bicentennial of the death of Tipu Sultan provides a fresh opportunity to examine the general conditions in which he lived and worked. More particularly, we will be discussing in brief the circumstances that inhibited his progress and contributed to his downfall.

Question of Legitimacy

Let us start with the question of legitimacy. Kate Brittlebank regards this as the key to understanding the Sultan's motivations.

111

Earlier we might have seen in this an attempt by the British to justify their appropriation of power as outsiders, by contending that the Muslim rulers had done the same before them. But there is no denying the fact that Tipu Sultan himself was concerned with the problem. Thus, immediately after the Treaty of Mangalore (1782), which ended the second Anglo–Mysore War, he sent an envoy to Constantinople to secure confirmation of his title to rule from the Ottoman Caliph. One can find precedence for this kind of action in the history of the Delhi Sultanate. Iltutmish had obtained the Caliph's investiture in AD 1229 to crown his life's work. Muhammad bin Tughlaq, when faced by enemies all round, had tried to strengthen his position by obtaining support from the Caliph in 1342. Firoz Shah Tughlaq, more orthodox in his religious views, had twice received the patent of rulership from the same source during the first six years of his reign (1351–88). In the following century, Sultan Mahmud of Malwa (1436–69) similarly received confirmation of his position from the Caliph.

In approaching the Caliph Tipu was returning to past instances, which had been set at abeyance during the 200 years of Mughal rule in India. The Mughal emperors had no need for support from abroad. In fact, Emperor Bahadur Shah (1707–12) almost provoked a Shia–Sunni riot in Lahore by ordering that the name of Ali be preceded by the title '*wasi*' (i.e. executor, of the Prophet's will) during the Friday prayers. This was a Shia innovation and implied that the first three Caliphs were usurpers. Ultimately, however, the order had to be withdrawn in view of massive protest from the Sunnis.

For the succession states, i.e. those that grew up on the ruins of the Mughal empire, the emperor's writ was still legally binding, no matter how weak and ineffective the occupant of the imperial power might actually be. Before approaching the Caliph for confirmation of his position, Tipu had, in 1783, offered to pay a large sum of money to the emperor besides *peshkash*, if granted a *sanad* for Arcot and a rank of 7,000. But the English foiled his attempt, and so he was left with no choice but to approach the Caliph for confirmation of his right to rule. So far as the legality of his position was concerned, Tipu compared less favourably with other Indian rulers of the time. The first Nizam had come to the Deccan as a representative of the Mughal emperor. The Maratha conquests in the Deccan and their collection of *chauth* and *sardeshmukhi* had received sanction from the emperor at the time when Balaji Vishwanath signed the treaty with Hussain Ali in 1718.

Even Haidar was on firmer ground. He had been the *dalvai* of the Raja of Mysore and had obtained charge of the *sarkar* of Sira from the Mughal emperor. Moreover, he had retained the old ruling family of Mysore as the figurehead of administration. Tipu dispensed with this fig-leaf of legality. In 1787 he had already adopted the title of *Badshah*. His desire to have this new title acknowledged by other rulers was clear from his insistence that the Peshwa should address him in this style, during the treaty with the Marathas in April 1787.

Tipu secured from the Ottoman Sultan recognition of his title of an independent king, along with the right to strike coins and have the *Khutba* read in his name. Tipu's desire to draw the Ottoman Sultan into a military alliance did not succeed because Turkey at the time was involved in a war against Russia and Austria, and depended on the support of England. In the words of Kate Brittlebank, Tipu regarded the Caliph's sanction more 'as the icing on the cake so to speak, than an essential ingredient of his place at home'. For Tipu was not prepared to be circumscribed by the theories of Islamic kingship, in spite of the fact that he called his kingdom *Saltanat-i Khudadad* (God-given government) and appealed to the Caliph for favour. His ambassadors to Cutch in 1796 were instructed to request the ruler to join him in 'prosecuting holy wars'. Tipu's call to all Muslim rulers to unite was also heard at Karachi and Kabul.[2] That much of this was prompted by political motivation was realized by Edward Moor, a shrewd English officer who took part in the Third Anglo–Mysore War. He observed:

> His subjects, he may possibly think, will with more reverence listen to his mandates when sanctioned by the authority of religion, and his armies will, with more awe, contemplate the power and dignity of the sovereign and general, when the abilities they admire are annexed to the spiritual sanctity of his character.[3]

We may point out here that in the shifting circumstances of eighteenth-century politics in India, alliances were not made or broken on grounds of religion alone. Thus, the Nizam might ally himself with the Marathas who, in the time of Baji Rao I, had raised the cry of 'Hindu Pad Padashahi'. The English, on their part, were ready to join hands with any Indian power that was ready to oppose Tipu. Wilks informs us that one reason why the Nizam did not enter into an alliance with Tipu in 1795 was the latter's refusal to swear by the *Koran*. But this is not accepted by Mohibbul Hasan, who points to other practical reasons as to why the alliance could not take place.[4]

Tipu's search for legitimacy does not support the impression, which Wilks tried to create, of the Sultan trying to dismantle the existing system in a hurry out of a spirit of restlessness. I have shown in my research how the specific instances cited by Wilks to prove his point—reform of the calendar and of weights and measures—were undertaken more as measures of convenience than anything else. Tipu's attempt to project himself in line with the existing tradition was inspired by motives of expediency. The Hindu ruling dynasty, which he had deposed, was continually plotting to get back power, and was not averse to joining hands with the English for this purpose. However, Tipu did not allow his eyes to be clouded over by communal considerations, as may be seen by his employment of Hindus in high offices of state. We have the examples of Purnaiya, who held the post of *Mir Asaf*, Krishna Rao the Treasurer, and Suva Rao, the Chief *Peshkar*. Tipu's large donations to the Hindu temples of his kingdom may also be remembered in this connection.[5]

The Commercial Conflict

Commercial considerations played a large part in bringing about the Third Anglo–Mysore War between Tipu Sultan and the English in 1790. The reasons may best be understood in the light of the trade between Asia and the west during this time. One of the principal articles of merchandise that brought sea-farers from the west to the orient was pepper. The English, in the late eighteenth century, had two main sources for obtaining the commodity: Malabar on the west coast of India and West Sumatra. After the Second Anglo–Mysore War, Tipu resolved on a blockade of his kingdom. In a letter to the *faujdar* of Calicut on 2 February 1788, he explained his motive thus: 'How long (in this case) will the above-named (enemy, the English) remain? He will, in the end despair of making either sales or purchases, and depart from thence.' Lest the English detain his goods while passing through the Carnatic, he did not send his agents as before to Pondicherry to buy vermilion. *Vakeels* passing through the Nawab of Arcot's territories in February 1787 were asked to hide their goods and travel by night to avoid detection by the English. There are letters to show also that it was Tipu's policy to stop the sale of rice to the English, Portuguese, etc., and intercept anyone who came from their side even in disguise.[6]

The impact of this bitterly affected the English. The Court of Directors urgently pressed Fort Marlborough, their headquarters in West Sumatra, for 'extending as much as possible your pepper investment, which although at all times desirous, is more essentially so at the present as the price of the article on the Malabar coast is so high as to leave no profit thereon, either at the English or China markets.'[7] Tipu's example was being followed all along the western coast of India. Thus, the Prince of Cherikal issued orders to the effect that all the pepper produced at Randaterra was to be gathered in his name, for he too was determined to monopolize the sale of the article.[8] The local merchants could thereafter purchase pepper only at the rate of Rs 160 a candy, and even this with difficulty.[9] The Raja of Travancore, another important supplier of pepper, could not make up for this shortfall, though the English were eager to buy 550 candies of pepper from him in 1787 at not less than Rs 105 a candy.[10] James Thomas, a local Bombay merchant, was in 1789 willing to supply 160 lbs of pepper to the English at Rs 155 per candy. He had purchased the same at Cochin for Rs 145, and charged the additional ten rupees as cost of transport.[11] The supply of cardamom, an article that sold at a rate between 3s. 2d, to 12s. 8d per lb. in the London market, also stopped reaching the English from Calicut. An inferior quality of cardamom grown near Cotiote was all that the contractors could now provide. They could assure supply of 560 lbs at Rs 140 a candy (twelve lbs were taken in these deals to be a measure of 140 candies).[12] To add to the difficulties of the English Factory at Tellicherry, Tipu Sultan's vessels hovered in the neighbouring waters, as all through 1789 the Sultan tried to starve them to submission by depriving them of their supply of rice. The French at Mahe were strongly discouraged from shipping rice to that quarter.[13]

Pamela Nightingale, in her *Trade and Empire in Western India 1784–1806*, has shown how pressure from the English private traders who had been affected by Tipu's imposition of a blockade on the products of his kingdom, was an important factor in influencing Henry Dundas, the President of the Board of Control, to go to war against Mysore. The authorities of the Company could not decide for a long time as to whether the profits to be derived from the export of products of the west coast of India to the Chinese market, like pepper, cardamom and teak-wood, justified the cost of maintaining Bombay Presidency and places like Tellichery and Anjengo. The private traders plying their business in the area, however, had no doubts about this; they held out the prospects of a very profitable trade. Therefore, they repeatedly requested Dundas to pursue a strong policy.[14] Both Holden Furber in *John Company at Work* and Van Lohuizen in *Dutch East India Company and Mysore* have shown that the money to be obtained from the sale of Cranganore and Ayicottah by the Dutch Company to the king of Travancore in 1790 was guaranteed by the Jewish merchants of Cochin with similar objectives in mind.[15]

John Holland, the Governor of Madras, was on the other hand reluctant to enter the fray in support of the ruler of Travancore when the latter was attacked by Tipu Sultan shortly afterwards. Both he and his brother were removed from the Madras Council for not complying with the Governor-General's orders to go to war immediately. Actually, as the principal creditor of the Nawab of Arcot, he feared that the Nawab's debts might be annulled the moment a war was declared. This also shows how the personal interests of the Company's representatives played an important role in determining the nature of the Company's policy in general.

We need also to look in greater detail into the local reaction to Tipu Sultan's blockade. The Bibi of Cannanore was among those who strongly supported the Sultan. This was despite the fact that, at the time under discussion she annually exported a considerable quantity of pepper in her vessels and sold it at different ports of India on her own account.[17] On the other hand, there were a few native merchants from whom the English Company purchased pepper through annual contracts. Between December and January each year, when the crops were so far advanced that some idea could be formed of the quantity of pepper likely to be obtainable, the Commercial Resident of the English Factory at Tellicherry assembled the contractors among whom the most important was a local merchant named Chokra Mousa. Associated with him were eleven others (mostly under his influence), who determined the price at which the pepper was to be sold. The quantity to be delivered by each supplier was determined by written contract. Generally half of the money was advanced at the time, although occasionally the total amount was paid to the contractors. The price varied from Rs 110 to Rs 120 per candy of 520 lbs. The merchants, in turn, gave a certain sum to some respectable *guada* or chief, who agreed to deliver a stipulated quantity of pepper at Honavar to the Company at two rupees a candy less than the Company's price. The investment was safe, as the pepper merchants were men of wealth.

All the pepper procured from the southern districts was obtained by means of small traders. A part of the produce was bought directly from the cultivators in the regions near Tellicherry. The traders dealing with the English Company enjoyed a special profit: while a candy of pepper was weighed at 600 lbs at the time of procurement, its weight was raised by 40 lbs at the time of delivery. It was naturally to the interest of these traders, therefore, that the British should stay. After the fall of Tipu Sultan, the leadership of the area passed into the hands of Chokra Mousa.[18] There is evidence that he was drawn into the conspiracy against Tipu before the outbreak of the fourth and final Anglo–Mysore War. We also read of another influential Moplah officer in Tipu's revenue service, Shaikh Shahabuddin, who also acted against the interests of his master.[19]

These local interests apart, the general inhabitants of the kingdom remained loyal to the Sultan even in the most adverse circumstances. Thomas Munro observed during the Third Anglo–Mysore War that 'even when forced to shut himself up in his capital, his authority continued so firm in the distant provinces, that the Marathas could not by any means convey information of their approach to Lord Cornwallis, or advise him that they had left Dharwar till they joined him at Seringapatam'.[20] Even after the fall of Srirangapatnam, a section of Tipu's followers were convinced that they had the strength to carry on the fight. But Fath Haidar, his eldest son, turned a deaf ear to their advice in the hope that he might be allowed to rule if he submitted.[21] Whether the Mysore kingdom would still have been able to continue the war of resistance against the English even after the death of Tipu, is open to doubt. But we cannot overlook the statement of Arthur Wellesley on hearing of the submission of another commander of the Mysore army, Qamaruddin, without resistance.

> If he had remained in arms, we never could have settled this country unless we incurred the enormous expense of keeping our army in the field and even then the operations to be carried on would be liable to all the hazards of protracted military operations. He has saved us this at least, and has thereby rendered us a service almost as great as any of those rendered by His Highness the Nizam.[22]

Notes and References

1 Kate Brittlebank, *Tipu Sultan's Search for Legitimacy*, Delhi, 1997, p. 71.

2 'Translation of Instructions from Tipoo Sultan to Meer Hubbab Collah and Meer Mohammad Rezza sent on an embassy from Zemaun Shah', in M. Wood, *A Review of the Origin, Progress and Result of the Late Decisive War in Mysore*, London, 1800, Appendix, Paper A, No. 21, p. 213.

3 Edward Moor, *A Narrative of the Operations of Captain Little's Detachment and of the Mahratta Army Commanded by Purseram Bhow during the Late Confederacy in India against the Nawab Tipu Sultan Bahadur*, London, 1794, p. 203.

4 Mohibbul Hasan, *History of Tipu Sultan*, Calcutta, 1951, pp. 181–82.

5 See, on this point, Surendranath Sen, 'The Shringeri Letters of Tipu Sultan', in *Studies in Indian History*, University of Calcutta, 1930, pp. 155–69; A. Sibbaraya Gupta, *New Light on Tipu Sultan*, Salem, 1967, pp. 88–93; G.K. Kareem, *Kerala under Haider Ali and Tipu Sultan*, Cochin, 1973, pp. 200–09.

6 William Kirkpatrick (trans. and ed.), *Select Letters of Tippoo Sultan to Various Public Functionaries*, London, 1811, letter no. CCCCXXXII, p. 471. See also letter nos XIX, pp. 32–33; XX, p. 35; CCVII, pp. 241–42; CCCXII, p. 457; and CCCCXXXIV, p. 473.

7 John Bastin, *The British in West Sumatra*, Kuala Lumpur, 1967, Document No. 67, pp. 85–86.

8 Tellicherry to Bombay, 11 November 1786, *Commercial Department Diary*, Vol. III, Maharashatra State Archives, Bombay, p. 333.

9 Tellicherry to Bombay, 6 October 1786, in ibid., pp. 19–20.

10 Anjengo to Bombay, 27 November 1787, in ibid., Vol. II, p. 270. See also Anjengo to Bombay, 30 April 1788, in ibid., p. 54.

11 James Thomas to Bombay Government, 17 December 1789, in ibid., Vol. IV, p. 249.

12 *Tellicherry Consultations*, 21–22 October 1788, in ibid., Vol. III, p. 54.

13 Bombay to Tellicherry, 6 May 1789, *Secret and Political Department Diary*, Maharashtra State Archives, Bombay, No. 39, pp. 216–17. Malet, Resident at Poona, 25 July 1789, in ibid., p. 368; and Malet, Resident at Poona, 17 August 1789, p. 378.

14 Pamela Nightingale, *Trade and Empire in Western India, 1784–1806*, Cambridge, 1970, pp. 38–59.

15 J. Van Lohuizen, *The Dutch East India Company and Mysore*, S. Gravenhage, Martinus Nijhoff, 1961, pp. 151–52 and Holden Furber, *John Company at Work*, Harvard, 1948, pp. 245–46.

16 Furber, *John Company*, p. 247.

17 Malet, Resident at Poona, to Cornwallis 5 February 1790, *Poona Residency Correspondence*, Vol. III edited by N.B. Ray, Bombay, 1937, pp. 54–67.

18 Francis Hanitton Buchanan, *Journey from Madras through Mysore, Canara and Malabar*, Vol. 2, London, 1807, pp. 407–08, 420, 531, 535.

19 Mohibbul Hasan, *Tipu Sultan*, p. 325.

[20] Munro to George Brown of Leith, 10 August 1791, in G.R. Gleig, *Life of Major General Sir Thomas Munro*, Vol. I, London, 1831, pp. 132–33.

[21] Kirmani, *History of Tipu Sultan*, translated by Col. W. Miles, Calcutta, 1958, pp. 129–30.

[22] Arthur Wellesley to Mornington, 13 May 1799, in *Supplementary Despatches of Field Marshall Arthur Duke of Wellington, 1797–1805*, edited by his son, Vol. I, London, 1859, p. 217.

France and Mysore

A History of Diverse French Strategies

Aniruddha Ray

I

The extensive French documentation on Tipu Sultan has thrown up different images of the Sultan, which are often contradictory, Oscillating between that of a tyrant and a modern revolutionary, the images do not fully reflect the varied French attitudes. This is mainly due to the lack of proper classification of the documents which are yet to be analysed.[1] While the contemporary classical French historians in the early twentieth century looked upon Tipu Sultan as a missed opportunity for the French to create an Indian empire,[2] recent Indian historians, with access to sources in English and the Indian languages, have looked at the overall relationship between Tipu Sultan and the French as well as the achievement of Tipu Sultan in an attempt to rectify the distortion of his image as seen through the tinted lens of the victors.[3] In such an image-building process, the French policy towards Tipu Sultan has taken the back seat. Only Mohibbul Hasan has made a partial attempt to present a structure of the relationship between the French and Tipu Sultan. Yet, even in his work, the different strands of French perceptions of him and the changes in them through the passage of time have not been given close enough scrutiny. Moreover, some of the crucial documents, like those relating to Tipu Sultan's embassy to Zaman Shah of Kabul, were not seen by Hasan.[4] On the other hand, the work of S.P. Sen[5] is far more exhaustive so far as French documentation is concerned. But he was writing on the French in India and not on Tipu Sultan, and thus, while generally accepting almost uncritically the French view on their dealings with Tipu Sultan, he was not really concerned with the overall picture of Tipu as seen by the French. In the present essay our concern is with the different strands of the French attitude towards Tipu in the context of the overall

120

French policy in India, and to see what changes occurred in the French perceptions of Tipu in the continuously changing situations in France and India.

The beginning of the eighteenth century did not find French commerce with India in a happy condition. The decline of the French Company, due to the blockade of their ships at Surat and in Bengal and the lack of funds,[6] necessitated a change of masters of the Company, with a take-over by the merchants of St Malo. From the 1720s the situation improved, but the rapid expansion of the English Company's commerce naturally worried the French; the problem of the administrative structure of the French also caused concern. A *Mémoire* of 1730[7] succinctly defines the problem as due to two factors: (a) lack of adequate commerce, and (b) lack of proper administrative control to enforce economies.

The problem was complicated by the expansion of consumption and consequently the increase of demand in France for Indian goods, mostly spices and textiles, which the Company was unable to supply in full. As a result, France had to buy second-hand from the English and the Dutch, which cost more. The *Mémoire* calls for commerce with India worth 20 million livres as optimum.

Yet, with expanding markets in France and Europe, the French Company made good profits between 1725 and 1759. An anonymous French *Mémoire*[8] places the sale of Indian goods between 1726 and 1756 at approximately 432,000,000 livres, while the expenses, including the capital cost of construction of ships, is put at approximately 370,000,000 livres, leaving a profit of 62,000,000 livres. It is also estimated that France annually consumed Indian goods worth 20 million livres, the optimum predicted earlier.

These data, however, conceal real losses in certain areas. The Company had extended its operation to places like Karikkal without permission from the Directors, and the commerce of such places was not self-supporting.[9] Between 1739 and 1741, the Company lost 12 million livres and was forced to get a subvention of 6 million livres from the government.[10] Yet, in the net, between 1726 and 1743, Indian commerce still brought in 126 million livres. With expenses deducted, the profit should have been in the region of 42 million livres, but the audited accounts showed a profit of only 30 million livres.[11] This brought forth the question of administrative reform, which included the policy of expansion and the formation of profitable political alliances proposed by Dupleix. The question that was never resolved at home among the French bureaucrats was whether to aim, through political alliances which involved active military participation, at getting lands whose revenues would then sustain the French commerce in India, or to have far-flung bases at different ports without interfering in the affairs of the inland powers. Owing to the lack of a decision on their part, the Indian powers would regard the French as vacillating and untrustworthy.

The French imports of Indian goods began to decrease from 1746 till 1751 when, owing to a diversion of their resources to military expenditure these suddenly began to rise to new heights.[12] They fell again in 1756 and with some minor ups and downs, continued to fall till 1762. From 1764 (after the Seven Years' War) the imports began to rise, almost touching the peak achieved in 1751–52, although there was another fall from 1766 onwards. The sale of Indian goods in France also began to fall from 1769 and reached its lowest level in 1771. The sales picked up again soon after and reached their highest peak in 1776, from when they began to fall again.[13]

Despite the profits coming from the trade in the Philippines.[14] the condition of the Company was gradually becoming desperate. After the reorganization in 1764 the Company paid off the accumulated debts, helped by the relaxation of government control. The situation had created so much alarm that in 1769, the king had to suppress some of the privileges.[15] A further reorganization came as a consequence of the Edict of 1770.[16] These difficulties brought home the truth propounded by Dupleix, that only the revenues of newly-acquired territories would usher in profitable commerce.[17] The Seven Years' War had ruined the French Company in India and they had to depend more on buying goods from the English Company, who had become the masters of Bengal after the grant of the Dewani in 1765.[18]

At the same time, from the middle of the eighteenth century, complaints from the French manufacturers of textiles against the use of Indian goods were becoming loud and clear.[19] This coincided with the knowledge of the enormous expenses incurred by France in the Seven Years' War, which gradually encouraged the view that the continuing rivalry with the English in India would not give any profit. It was also suggested that the China trade would be far more profitable.[20] However, the Company's view was that the import of Indian goods was enriching France and, by 1761, several *Mémoires* pointed out the advantages of Indian commerce.[21]

It is clear, therefore, that in these trying situations and with the losses suffered by the Company, there was no single strand of opinion on Indian commerce. In this debate, once again, Dupleix's dictum was lost sight of.[22] The French official view gradually came to the conclusion that the superiority of the French fleet in the Indian Ocean was *sine qua non* for profitable commerce. Obviously this was the policy laid out by the Ministry of Marine, which held the charge of the colonies and which attached far more importance to holding ports of call than territories inland in alliance with Indian powers.

II

After the restoration of the French territories in India in 1765, several projects reached Paris calling for opposition to the English in India, to recover the lost glories of France in the east. The Minister of Marine, Choiseul (1758–70), developed the French navy. Choiseul's real object was, however, to invade England with a diversionary attack in the Indian Ocean. In this, Ile de France would serve as the base. A large number of ships and troops were sent there. But the plan was not pursued and was allowed to lapse after the fall of the minister.[23]

It was on the eve of the American War of Independence that naval construction began again, coinciding with the successful diplomacy of Vergennes that isolated England in Europe. But there was no corresponding financial success, and this brought about the fall of the shortlived ministries of Necker and Calonne.[24]

In India, the French began to rely on military preparedness. Law de Laurestan, the Governor of Pondicherry, had fortified Pondicherry and appealed to all the French soldiers serving under different Indian princes to join the French forces at Pondicherry. The latter, however, did not wish to leave their secure positions for an uncertain future.[25] Paris was at that time beset by economic and social problems and was not in a position to send any effective forces. Unlike the English, the French did not have enough troops at Pondicherry to withstand another English attack. The indifferent attitude of Paris towards the colonies marked the tenure of Law's governorship till January 1777.[26]

The change at Paris began with the appointment of Sartine as

Minister of Marine and Colonies in 1776. Once again the plan of the restoration of the French glory in the east was avidly discussed, and particular attention was given to the rebuilding of the French navy. Despite such an understanding, no decision was taken at the outbreak of the hostilities in 1778.[27] The repeated pleas of Bellecombe, the Governor of Pondicherry, to Paris, to approve the plan of forming a league of Indian princes against the English, fell on deaf ears.[28] The inactivity and the indecision of Paris were largely due to the financial problems facing France at the time. But they were also due in no small measure to the conflicting projects sent from India.

Jean-Baptiste Chevalier, Governor of Chandernagore from 1767 to 1778, was on amicable terms with the English. Despite this, the English had begun to put pressure on French trade in Bengal and Bihar, restricting their purchases of saltpetre and opium. Chevalier's increasingly loud protests to Fort William did not improve matters.[29] Frustrated, Chevalier submitted to Paris a project of joining a league of Indian princes of northern India against the English, who would be simultaneously attacked by the French navy. This overlooked the fact that the Indian princes were jealous of each other and often in conflict among themselves, thus preventing any chance of united action. Chevalier also planned to forge an alliance with the Mughal emperor, Shah Alam, with a large French force and Indian sepoys trained by the French to back him for a confrontation with the English.[30] Paris did not want to offend England, having already abandoned Choiseul's plan, and refused to send troops.[31] Only some French adventurers veered towards the Mughal emperor and the Nawab of Oudh, more for their personal interests than for the glory of France. One of them, Rene Madec, submitted a plan to Chevalier to land French troops at Sind or Thatta, away from English control,[32] which was forwarded to Paris by him. Once again Paris lingered over the plan and finally sent Colonel Montigny to send a detailed report,[33] by which time Chandernagore had fallen to the English and Chevalier arrested by them; and Madec had left for France.[34] Chevalier, impatient at the delay, sent another plan to Paris for the landing of troops at Chittagong, which would then proceed to Dacca to liberate it. He assured Paris that the Marathas and the Mughals would join such a move, and Ile de France would be the base of operations. Chevalier even drew up a draft treaty with Mahadaji Sindhia and sent it to Paris.[35]

Chevalier's plan of a war with the English was opposed by

Law at Pondicherry, as well as by de Boigne, minister at Paris. Meanwhile, Rene Madec had consulted the Mughal emperor on the Thatta project and sent his approval to Paris.[36] A revival of the Mughal empire would obviously conflict with the interests of regional powers like the Jats, Marathas, Rohillas and Sikhs, as also the Nawab of Oudh. But Madec's plan would give the French a firm base to operate from, away from the English arms. However, no response came from Paris.

On the other hand, Law[37] had planned to install the French in southern India, from a well-fortified Pondicherry, Mahe and Karikkal. The port of Trincomale would be the French port of call. This would revive French superiority in the Indian Ocean, arousing support from Indian powers, among whom Haidar Ali and the Marathas would act as kingpins. Law suggested the formation of an anti-English coalition with Haidar Ali, the Marathas and the Nizam. He asked for the acceptance of an alliance with the Marathas, as proposed by them in 1772, as they were the strongest of the Indian powers and sufficiently spread out to attack the English at different places. Law categorically rejected Chevalier's plan of landing at Thatta. The divergence between the two was great as Law concentrated on southern India and the Deccan without any reference to the Mughal emperor. Law's idea of the success of the French over the English rested on the continual flow of wealth from India to France and the cyclic investment in the typical functioning of a colony that would serve as the motor of European enterprise in India. He suggested two stages of attack: first, in the Malabar coast, where Haidar Ali and the Marathas would help, and then an attack on Bengal, which was a modification of Chevalier's plan. Law however emphasized that Bombay needed to be captured.

Bellecombe, succeeding Law at Pondicherry in January 1777, believed that a large *sipahi* force should be raised in India under French training, as France would never be able to send a large enough force to India. But he was realistic enough to emphasize that unity among the Indian powers, particularly between Haidar Ali and the Marathas, would not be possible. He also planned to have Ile de France as the base for sending troops to India, thus keeping the centre of operations in south India and the Deccan. As for the Indian powers, he preferred alliance with one instead of trying to build a united alliance of all against the English, which was not feasible.[38]

By 1781, when Bellecombe's last *Mémoire* was written,[39] Haidar Ali had become far more powerful in French eyes, as seen in an anonymous *Mémoire* written in May 1781.[40] Interestingly enough, the *Mémoire* asked the French to justify their conquests against the possible attack of Haidar Ali, as he was trying to reduce the European powers in India. The contradiction between European imperialistic designs and Haidar's ambition was clear.

The distrust of the French living in close proximity to Haidar Ali can be seen in another *Mémoire*, written at the end of 1781.[41] Implying that Haidar was militarily far more powerful than the English, the *Mémoire* adds that in Arcot Haidar had destroyed everything and even demolished the rest-houses of travellers—a situation which would not be liked by the mercantile community. In the process, millions of Indians had also perished. Haidar Ali had usurped much of the Maratha dominion and driven the English out. The author calls upon the French to fortify the coastal areas, although he concedes that Haidar Ali had given the French whatever they had asked for.

At the local level of French thought, therefore, there was deep distrust of Haidar Ali's ambition and suspicion as to his ambitions. The author cites the secret hatred of the Nizam for Haidar Ali as well as the dissensions among the Marathas[42] that would adversely affect any attempt at unity among the Indian powers. The author proposes a Franco–Maratha combination to drive the English from Bengal,[43] thus confusing the issue or rather ignoring his own earlier assessment of the situation.

The author is also distrustful of Tipu Sultan, then still a prince, whom he accuses of not understanding the French contribution to Mysore.[44] He believes that even Pondicherry was not safe from Tipu (and he was not the only Frenchman to say that), and that the English too did not recognize Tipu as being very friendly towards the French.[45] Once again, the author calls for a greater role of Ile de France (with a reduced role for Pondicherry), so as not to attract the attention of Tipu.[46] This distrust is spelled out rather pompously: 'Tipu is more of our creation than our ally.'[47]

A third *Mémoire*[48] quite naively argues that the English would not help the Marathas if France would not do so and presented a defeatist attitude when it called for peaceful relations with the English in Asia. Obviously such an attitude suited the increased export of goods from India to France, after the setback in 1778–79.[49]

Basically, therefore, the *Mémoires* urged the French not to rely on any Indian power, acknowledging at the same time the impossibility of a united Indian alliance against the English. They therefore called for greater participation by French bases (especially Ile de France) outside India, and proposed only a limited role for Pondicherry, which was obviously more vulnerable to any hostile action by the English.[50] That the French in India did not want any confrontation with the English was clear and this must have been understood by Tipu, whose action in bypassing them, can only be understood in the light of this situation.

However, there were shades too in the local French opinion. While a *Resumé* of 1793[51] suggested that the main object should be the recovery of the French possessions in India, another letter[52] proposed that support should be given to Tipu Sultan and the Marathas. Yet another *Mémoire* suggested the sharing of possessions with the English and the Marathas after paying taxes to the latter.[53]

III

The appointment of Duchemine in 1782 to lead the expeditionary French force to India from Ile de France by itself did not mark any real change in the French policy. The change was in the instruction to him to establish a firm base in India in alliance with Haidar Ali and thereby to facilitate the subsequent operation of Bussy in the interior.[54] It was not clear whether Duchemine's would be a supportive one or whether he would strike with as much force as possible. He was asked to negotiate with Haidar Ali and conquer the Carnatic, with the expenses to be born by the Mysore ruler. Duchemine decided to strike but insisted on a formal treaty with Haidar Ali, obviously to safeguard the possessions in the Carnatic. The French were to give over to Haidar Ali the newly-conquered Carnatic, while their alliance with other Indian powers was not ruled out.[55] The emphasis of the French policy had shifted to an alliance with Mysore, although the earlier policy of uniting the other powers had not been given up. There were, however, elements of mutual irritation and distrust in the Franco–Mysore relationship from the very beginning. Haidar Ali was irritated at the French insistence on a formal treaty as he did not rate the French army very highly. On the other hand, the local French commander, De Launay, suspected him of secretly making a compromise with the English.[56] At the same time, Piveron de Morlat, the French representative, believed in Haidar Ali's sincerity.[57] The deaths of Haidar Ali and Duchemine did not change the situation. Both Morlat and Duchemine's successor, Hoeffelitz, believed that Tipu had no military talent like his father, and thus were now sceptical of the advantage to be derived from a continued reliance on Mysore. We have already seen the contradictions and vacillations reflected in the different *Mémoires*, most of which expressed local French sentiments and assessments.

Bussy's *Mémoire* of 1777[58] challenges such opinions and tries to formulate the basic policy in the following terms:

(a) Earlier reports were written from ignorance.

(b) Re-establishment of French power would be very expensive.

(c) An alliance or unity among the Indian powers was not possible due to their own jealousies, mistrust and ambitions, and the Marathas should be chosen as the major ally.

(d) The English had become very powerful in India.

Bussy recommends an alliance with the Maratha confederacy on political terms, and advocates an attack on Madras.

One can see that there was nothing new in Bussy's proposal except that he did not consider Haidar Ali as the best ally and wanted a direct confrontation with the English. The *Mémoire* did not find a receptive ear in Paris as the French were engaged in North America till 1779–80, after which they turned towards India.[59] By that time the French army in India was in a pitiable state and Haidar Ali was treating it with contempt. Bussy therefore changed his earlier stand and advocated sending a large force to India to convince the Indian powers of the superiority of the French forces. Once again he proposed cooperation with the Marathas while recommending that the main French action should be in south India, with a large expeditionary force sent from France.

Bussy's views did not find favour with the new Minister of Marine and Colonies, Castries, who, in 1782, renewed Chevalier's old theme, viz. an attack on Bengal by sea with a simultaneous attack by a land force operating with Najaf Khan and the Mughal emperor[60] to create a re-enactment of the drama of Shuja-ud Daulah before Buxar. One can see how distant Paris was from the realities of the Indian situation. As might be expected, Bussy criticized the plan as impractical since large ships would not be able to enter the Ganges river, while Najaf Khan was a doubtful starter.

Mohibbul Hassan[61] justifies Tipu's decision to leave the Coromandel to go to Malabar to defend it from the English; but this naturally annoyed Bussy, who had by now arrived in India. But his own plan of uniting with other Indian powers did not show much progress, as the latter regarded the French as committed to Tipu.[62] To dispel this idea, Bussy was opposed to any alliance with Tipu, having already categorized him as a tyrant. Strangely enough, relying on his own earlier experiences, he advocated alliance with the Nizam, one of the weakest of the Deccan powers. The failure of supply of provisions to the French by Tipu's general and Tipu's sudden departure convinced him of Tipu's duplicity. On the other hand, the peace between England and France and the sudden withdrawal of the French from the war, particularly when Mangalore was about to fall, increased the image of the undependability of the French in Tipu's mind.

As seen earlier, Bussy did not favour any alliance with the Mughal court, where the internal dissensions among the Mughal nobility prevented any action. Yet, he did not immediately reply to the Marathas who had proposed a formal treaty, and whose acceptance he had advocated earlier. One reason for the delay may have been that Bussy had no money, very little provision for his army and no transport facilities to make any operation feasible. Consequently, he was waiting for the larger force to arrive. The open rift between Tipu and Cossigny led to complaints and counter-complaints in which Bussy was submerged. He himself had a coloured view of Tipu Sultan.[63] This in turn led Tipu to distrust the French more. Even before his death in 1785 Bussy still clung to his impractical view that the only course left open to the French was to form a ring of alliances with the Indian powers.

The view that a treaty with Tipu would harm French interests was not Bussy's alone. Souillac, Governor of Ile de France, was of the same opinion, and tried to influence the French in India by writing to Cossigny to the same effect.[64] Souillac wanted Tipu to be beaten so that he would be dependent on the French for military support. By 1783, Minister Castries had changed his earlier views and now favoured an alliance with the Marathas. But by that time, Nana Phadnavis had got tired of waiting for a French reply and favoured a settlement with the English.[65] The shift in the policies of the Marathas, however, depended more on their internal contradictions than on the potential support of the French. The Nizam, since the loss of his territories to Haidar Ali, had always regarded Tipu as a usurper. Bussy's dilatory methods and the vacillation in Paris had created a chain reaction among the Indian powers not favourable to the French.

It would be a mistake to think, however, that Bussy wanted Tipu to be completely beaten and deserted. As a matter of fact, he did try to persuade the Marathas not to attack Tipu.[66] But the basic difference in policy between Bussy and Castries lay in the conflicting views on the location of the future centre of French power in India. Castries wanted Mahe to be the centre,[67] while Bussy did not want it to be close to either Tipu or the Marathas. Besides, Mahe, to Bussy, was not a good port.[68]

These contradictions in the formation of French policy naturally pulled it in different directions. There were differences of opinion between Paris, Ile de France and the French in India.[69] Along with these, there were often complete changes of policy depending on the changing conditions in India and France, which was soon to be overwhelmed by revolution. The situation was also coloured by the bitterness between the French and the English in India, who gradually began to put restrictions, particularly in Bengal, on the lucrative French trade of opium and saltpetre. The French ambition in India was finally crushed by the subsequent administrative reorganization and the Revolution. The centre of the French empire in the east was transferred from Pondicherry to Ile de France, along with stores, ammunition and French troops, which had to remain content as a commercial centre with only 300 troops.[70]

IV

The military victories of Tipu over the Maratha–Nizam combination changed the views of Souillac and Cossigny. They now wanted an alliance with Tipu[71] since the Marathas had remained divided and generally lukewarm to French overtures. But the French proposal of a commercial treaty in October 1788 was rejected by Tipu, who wanted military help as the basic minimum, and had directly sent an embassy to Versailles.

Although the French had been able to overcome their sense of frustration over the events of 1781–83, no definite policy emerged after 1785.[72] The French in India, as seen earlier in several *Mémoires*, had hoped that there could be a diplomatic alliance with the English to protect French interests in the east. But these hopes had little chance of coming to fruition since there was no corresponding gain in it for France. By early 1787, Castries too had abandoned his earlier strategy of a north Indian drive in alliance with the Mughal power, thus virtually shelving the projects of Chevalier and Madec. Since the Nizam was considered to be close to the English camp, Castries had no choice but to favour an alliance with Tipu, the only power left in the south to confront the English.[73]

The three centres at Paris, Ile de France and Pondicherry, distant from each other, often worked at cross-purposes, not being aware of the changes in policy on time. From 1785 onwards, Souillac, from Ile de France, attempted to settle the differences between Tipu and the Marathas with a view to forming an alliance with both, while Castries, as seen above, had located Tipu as the only secure ally. The Maratha leader Nana Phadnavis wanted a categorical reply to the Maratha proposal of 1782, while Souillac was assuring him that military help was not being given to Tipu and no treaty existed between the French and Tipu. By that time, the local French sentiments were growing hostile to Tipu: Montigny blamed Tipu for his oppressions and held that Tipu had inherited the wicked qualities of his father.[74]

By 1790, the situation was quite unfavourable to the French. The distrust of Tipu by the Marathas in the wake of the military victory had resulted in the signing of the Anglo–Maratha alliance in 1790. Only the Nizam, thwarted by the English, turned towards the French at Pondicherry, but there all the powers for such a decision had been abandoned to Ile de France.[75]

Till 1783 the French regarded Mysore as their traditional ally, a sentiment echoed in several *Mémoires*, although the means to recover the lost possessions of the French in India had varied. The Treaty of Versailles of 1783, in which the French made a separate peace with the English, left Tipu high and dry. He squarely blamed the local French authorities for not letting the French court know of the real state of affairs in India, and so sent an embassy directly to France, though the ambassadors had naturally to sail from Pondicherry.[76] This was reflected in Tipu Sultan's cavalier attitude to the French proposal in 1788, already cited—a sequel to Tipu's request for military support in his war with the Marathas, while Ile de France had ordered the withdrawal of all French troops from India. Once Mysore got involved in the Third Mysore War (1790–92), the fact that the French were at peace with the English left Tipu Sultan to face defeat alone. But the letter of de Fresne of 2 March 1792 clearly saw not only the humiliation of Tipu Sultan but also the destruction of French hopes in India.[77]

De Fresne argued that Tipu had more energy and less talent.[78] The entry allowed to the English through the *ghats* without resistance and the shoddy defence of Bangalore led to Tipu's humiliation. But he did not lose all hopes. He asked the minister to raise troops in India on the French model with the help of Duplessis, the French commander at Pondicherry. He also asked that troops be sent from France for Tipu.[79] This was a question that was tied up with a policy decision to be taken in Paris, where India was at the back-seat for the moment, owing to the internal upheavals caused by the French Revolution.

The Revolution did not usher in any consistent line of French thought. Even the delegates from Pondicherry differed in their general attitude and on the policies to be undertaken. Louis Monneron, the delegate from Pondicherry, suggested in 1790 that Tipu Sultan was the only strong Deccan power, while the Marathas, the Mughals, the Nizam and Tipu together, surrounding the English on all sides, could throw the English into the sea.[80] In the same year the inhabitants of Ile de France came to Paris and made a representation to the National Assembly not to abandon Pondicherry and Ile de France.[81] In 1791, Charles Mallet, Additional Deputy of Pondicherry, criticized Monneron for giving false information by attributing imaginary power to Tipu Sultan.[82]

With the arrival of the delegates of Pondicherry in France, the Ministry began to think of establishing quicker communication with India. It was suggested that instead of going directly to India, it should go via Ile de France while French agents should be posted at the consulate in Cairo.[83] Yet the conflicting expressions of opinion continued. In one *Mémoire* it is suggested that the Indians were only waiting for an opportunity to throw off the tyranny of the English and it calls upon France to recover her old possessions in India.[84] A letter to the Director from India called for support to Tipu Sultan and the Marathas, to destroy the English possessions in India.[85] This is contradicted by a *Mémoire* which, on the contrary, suggests the sharing of India with the English and the Marathas.

In October 1791, the National Assembly took a decision to send additional troops to Pondicherry, which reached Pondicherry in September 1992. While Malactric had replaced Cossigny as Governor General in Ile de France, Lescallier and Dumourier arrived at Pondicherry as civil commissioners.[87]

Lescallier met Tipu Sultan, who wanted 6,000 men, scaling

down his earlier demand of 10,000, with artillery, to be placed under his disposal. He suggested that the conquered coasts would belong to France, while the inland areas would belong to Tipu.[88] Lescallier's report gives in full the text of Tipu's letter.[89] Meanwhile, as war between England and France broke out in early 1793, Pondicherry fell and Lescallier escaped to Ile de France, from where he first wrote to the National Convention and later arrived in Paris with a letter from Tipu.

It is interesting that in his letter Tipu Sultan reverts to his grouse that the former French ministers had not communicated his requirements to the king, and that the French were withdrawn from the siege of Mangalore when a separate peace concluded with England, thus exposing him to the enemy.[90] Other proposals remained the same. Lescallier had written to him from Ile de France to keep him in good humour till the arrival of the French forces in India,[91] while on 17 April 1796, Louis Monneron had signed a treaty with Tipu Sultan.[92] Thus Tipu was assured of the landing of the French forces both by the French in India as well as by Ile de France. Yet the Ministry took the decision not to ratify the treaty as negotiation with England for peace had started.[93]

The administrative reorganization of the French Company made Ile de France the centre of French power in the east, practically forsaking Pondicherry. This was the result of pursuing two contradictory objectives since the foundation of the Company in 1664.[94] On the one hand, the islands, including Madagascar, were regarded as a necessary stop on the voyage to the Indies; on the other, these were treated as fully developed colonies, though Madagascar had gone out of the pale of the French empire by the end of the seventeenth century. After the reorganization, Ile de France was regarded as the base for launching large-scale military expedition to India. With the start of the revolutionary war on the European continent (1792), these French colonies naturally took a backseat in military strategy. The French thinking on India was rather defensive, seeing its potential as a diversion to keep the English fleet occupied in the Indian Ocean and to prevent them from attacking the French ports. Till 1796, Paris did not give much thought to Ile de France either: de Suffren, the French naval commander, preferred Pondicherry to Ile de France as his base.[95] In 1796 another crucial problem came to the fore. The Assembly at Paris wanted to free the slaves working in Ile de France. This would certainly hurt the interests of French slave-owners on the island, and the Directory wanted to keep the existing structure. It also wanted a naval expedition to be sent to the Ile, to keep the English engaged.[96] As a result, no help could be given to Tipu when he needed it most and the vacillations of the French finally became one of the key factors for the downfall of Tipu Sultan.

V

The commencement of the Anglo–French War in Europe in 1793 gave the French an opportunity to land troops in India. The English fleet was then not in a position to guard the whole of the Indian Ocean.[97] The French wanted Tipu Sultan to join the war, to tie up as many English soldiers as possible. But, as seen above, there was no real French effort to regain their lost possessions in India.

Two events, well-recorded, hastened the fall of Tipu Sultan. One was the misadventure of Ripaud and the Malactric proclamation from Ile de France which reached Calcutta in early 1798.[98] The other was the expedition of Napoleon to Egypt (1798–99) and the invasion of Zaman Shah of Kabul, who twice reached Lahore with his army practically unopposed. This coincided with the revolt of Vizir Ali,[99] the ousted Nawab of Oudh, at Benaras, who seems to have organized a string of revolts among the Bengal and Bihar zamindars. This was the image of the concerted threat that Wellesley presented to London, by which Tipu was supposed to act as the kingpin in the south and Vizir Ali in the north. Recent researches have shown that there was no such concerted design,[100] nor was there any plan by Napoleon to land troops in India or to march to India, a dream he later envisaged in isolation at St Helena.[101] Paris, perhaps, wanted him to be far from France, and forwarded to him a draft copy of the proposed treaty with Tipu Sultan.[102] What is important is that Wellesley forcefully utilized this pretext of a critical situation to force his way through to success, although this was achieved more by the blunders of Tipu Sultan and the treachery of his officials than the skill of the English army.

Interestingly, what had remained unnoticed so far was that in a report to Napolean as First Consul, after the fall of Tipu, Pierre Dubec, Captain of the French troops and Ambassador Extraordinary to the court of Tipu Sultan, stated that the Governor of Ile de France (Malactric) had promised to send a large force to Tipu, and that it was this news that led the English to attack Tipu.[103] Although there is no corroborative evidence in the English documents, the circumstances show that there was a broader understanding, if not a clear commitment, between Tipu and the French than has hitherto been believed. The reported advice of the French to Tipu Sultan on the eve of his fall to flee from Srirangapatnam,[104] may suggest their expectation of the possible landing of a French force, although by that time the French navy had been dispersed at the Battle of Trafalgar and all possibility of a French naval intervention in Indian waters had disappeared.

VI

One can discern, therefore, several strands in the French attitude towards Tipu Sultan. These changed through different periods of time due to the changing conditions in eighteenth-century France and India. As a result, no clear policy of forcing the issue in India was ever consistently pursued and no primacy was therefore given to an alliance with Mysore in the strategic framework of the French in the east. The contradictory streams of French thought, often stemming from the different perceptions of their authors, led to different assessments of the Indian reality; and these were generally coloured by an excessive concern with the immediate benefit to French trade and political interest.

The confusion was complicated by the emergence of three different French centres of power—Paris (and Versailles), Ile de France and Pondicherry—while there were only two (London and Calcutta) in the case of the English. As the eighteenth century progressed, the focus in London became far clearer—the territorial possessions inland were to be the major plank and the ports would be merely the funnels. This strategy was pursued by successive English administrators in India despite Pitt's Act of 1784 and the directives of the Court of Directors not to get involved in local disputes. The French, on the other hand, had reduced the influence of Pondicherry by reorganizing the apparatus and increasing the number of decision-making centres, which often worked at cross-purposes, given the state of communications prevailing at the time. The resulting confusion and delay naturally heightened the insecurity of the Indian power, who could not take the military support of Pondicherry for granted. The failure of the French to sustain Tipu Sultan in 1790–92, in the background of the lack of a consistent policy, in turn, spawned a number of explanations and rival strategic proposals. The vacillation of the French between a policy of alliance with Mysore, with the Marathas, or with an alliance (projected) of all Indian powers, made the French more and more untrustworthy in the eyes of the Indian powers. The French remained basically a European power and more concerned with their territorial interests in Europe then with their colonial interests. In a way, both parties, Mysore and the French, could not shake off their historical legacies. The limited modernization of Tipu, depending on a centralized bureaucracy, did not create a class in Mysore with which the French could find any rapport. The formation of the Jacobin Club at Srirangapatnam was not an insignificant event; but neither for the French nor for Tipu Sultan was it a bond sufficiently strong. The English acted as catalysts in hastening Tipu Sultan's fall by seizing the opportunities offered by French domestic troubles and vacillations, to isolate and destroy Tipu Sultan.

Notes and References

[1] A large number of French documents in transcripts concerning Haidar Ali and Tipu Sultan are preserved in the Karnataka State Archives, Bangalore, apart from documents in archives in Paris, Aix-en Provence, London, New Delhi and other places.

[2] For example, see J. Michaud, *Histoire de la Progress et de la chute de l'Empire de Mysore*, 2 vols, Paris, 1801; W. Weber, *La Compagnie Francaise des Indes (1604–1875)*, Paris, 1904.

[3] Mohibbul Hasan, *History of Tipu Sultan*, 2nd edn, Calcutta, 1971.

[4] For details, see Aniruddha Ray, 'Tipu Sultan and the Invasion of Zaman Shah: The English Reaction', in *Sultan*, Vol. IV, 1986, pp. 13–25. The original document is in the *Archives du Ministere des Affaires Etrangeres (AMAE)*, Vol. 11, Fond Asie, Paris, ff. 296–301 (*AMAE* hereafter).

[5] S.P. Sen, *The French in India, 1763–1816*, 2nd edn, New Delhi, 1971.

[6] See the long letter from Surat dated 6 February 1702, in *Archives Nationales et Coloniales*, Paris, Colonie C(2) 66, f. 272 post.

[7] *AMAE*, Vol. 5, ff. 15–20.

[8] Ibid., Vol. 12, 'Commerce de la Compagnie des Indes', ff. 5–7.

[9] Ibid., Vol. 12, 'Memoire concernant la Compagnie des Indes', written in November 1741, f. 32.

[10] Ibid., ff. 33–33v.

[11] Ibid., f. 43.

[12] Ibid., 'Memoire sur la Compagnie des Indes', 16 September 1749, ff. 117–126v.

[13] A. Sinha, 'French Trade in India in the XVIII Century', paper (unpublished) presented at a seminar in New Delhi on Indo–French Relations, 1990, pp. 39–49, with two graphs.

[14] *AMAE*, 'Madrid, 1774' by Louis de Longiere, ff. 77–73v.

[15] Ibid., f. 74.

[16] Sen, *The French in India*, p. 46.

[17] *AMAE*, 'Mémoire de la Chambre de Commerce des Guyenne', Vol. 5, ff. 239–71v. Interestingly, the *Mémoire* calls for the privatization of Indian commerce, as it would bring better profit than the one earned by the official Company. Also see A. Ray, 'Invasion of Nadir Shah and Origin of French Imperialist Thought as Exemplified by Dupleix', *Proceedings of the Indian History Congress*, 33rd session, 1972, pp. 362–88.

[18] *AMAE*, 'Reflexions sur la Compagnie', Vol. 5, ff. 40–40v; on buying from the foreigners, see ibid., 'Precis du les different Projets de la Compagnie des Indes', by Du Pont, Paris, 29 October 1784, ff. 122–122v.

[19] Ibid., Vol. 13, 'Mémoire sur la Compagnie des Indes', London, 20 November 1755, by M. de Mirep, ff. 27–28.

[20] Ibid., Vol. 13, 'Anonymous Mémoire sur l'Inde', ff. 46–47; also, 'Observations sur le Mémoire concernant la Compagnie des Indes communique au M. de Choiseul', 27 December 1754, ff. 48–49v.

[21] Ibid., Vol. 13, 'Sur la Compagnie des Indes', June 1761', ff. 156–64v; 'Letter of M. Pilty', Paris, 17 July 1761, ff. 161–71v.

[22] For the difference between Bussy's and Dupleix's strategies, see Alfred Martineau, *Bussy et l'Inde Francaises*, Paris, 1935, pp. 444–46.

[23] Sen, *The French in India*, pp. 48–49.

[24] Ibid., pp. 52–53.

[25] Ibid., p. 65.

[26] Ibid., pp. 69–70.

[27] Ibid., p. 71. Law was succeeded at Pondicherry by Bellecombe.

[28] Ibid., p. 73.

[29] N.K. Sinha, *The Economic History of Bengal*, 3 vols, Calcutta, 1981, Vol. I, pp. 35–51, especially pp. 44–45.

[30] Sen, *The French in India*, pp. 112–24.

[31] Ibid., pp. 124–25.

[32] Ibid., pp. 132–33.

[33] Ibid., pp. 125–26.

[34] Ibid., p. 141.

[35] Ibid., pp. 125–26.

[36] Ibid., pp. 140–41.

[37] Ibid., pp. 154–72.

[38] Ibid., pp. 174–79.

[39] Ibid., p. 178.

[40] *AMAE*, Vol. 7, 'Reflexion sur les Evenements', May 1781, ff. 338–44.

[41] Ibid., Vol.7, 'Mémoire sur l'Inde', ff. 272–85.

[42] Ibid., ff. 294–294v.

[43] Ibid., f. 301v.

[44] Ibid., f. 308; the author laments that Tipu Sultan had forgotten that he could get the throne only due to French help, a view that is different from the account given by Hasan (*History of Tipu Sultan*, pp. 78–79).

137

[45] Ibid., f. 317.

[46] Ibid., f. 328.

[47] Ibid., f. 328v.

[48] Ibid., Vol. 11, 'Mémoire concernant de l'etat present', f. 63.

[49] Ibid., see the table of imports of France from India between 1725 and 1782, showing parallel commerce of the private merchants (Vol. 11, ff. 15v–16), in which the data of China trade are also given.

[50] Hasan, *History of Tipu Sultan*, pp. 115–16.

[51] *AMAE*, Vol. 11, 'Consideration sur l'Inde', 1793, f. 109.

[52] Ibid., Letter to the Director, ff. 119v–120v.

[53] Ibid., 'Mémoire', 13 Brumiere l'an 5, f. 123.

[54] Sen, *The French in India*, pp. 273–76.

[55] Ibid., pp. 283–84.

[56] Ibid., p. 291.

[57] Ibid.

[58] Ibid., p. 295.

[59] Ibid., p. 315.

[60] Ibid.

[61] Hasan, *History of Tipu Sultan*, p. 112.

[62] Sen, *The French in India*, p. 324.

[63] Ibid., p. 392.

[64] Hasan, *History of Tipu Sultan*, p. 114 post.

[65] Ibid., p. 115.

[66] Sen, *The French in India*, p. 401.

[67] Ibid., p. 406.

[68] Ibid., p. 408.

[69] Ibid., p. 418. See also a letter by Conway from Pondicherry on 20 July 1788, in which he describes the absolute power of the English and the frightful character of Tipu Sultan 'whose policy would harm the interests of the King', *AMAE*, Vol. 19, ff. 181–86.

[70] Sen, *The French in India*, pp. 430–31.

[71] Hasan, *History of Tipu Sultan*, p. 114.

[72] Sen, *The French in India*, pp. 493–98.

[73] Ibid., pp. 497–98.

[74] Ibid., p. 501.

[75] Ibid., p. 516.

[76] French documents relating to this embassy are translated by Suman Venkatesh, *The Correspondence of the French during the Reign of Hyder Ali and Tipu Sultan, 1788 to 1789*, Vol. III, Bangalore, 1998. The very revealing brief to his envoys is translated in the present volume by Professor Iqbal Husain.

[77] Sen, *The French in India*, p. 526.

[78] Ibid.

[79] Ibid., pp. 527–28.

[80] *AMAE*, Vol. 19, ff. 260–277v.

[81] Ibid., Vol. 19, 2 December 1790, ff. 280–91.

[82] Ibid., Vol. 19, 'Mémoire', 1791, ff. 389–401.

[83] Ibid., Vol. 11, 'Resume', 1792. ff. 97–100v; also, 'Rapport sur la maniere de faire parvenir promptement de depeche dans l'Inde', 20 January 1793, ff.103–07.

[84] Ibid., 'Considerations sur l'Inde', ff. 109–111v.

[85] Ibid., 'Letter', ff. 119–121v.

[86] Ibid., 'Mémoire to the Director', 13 Brumiere l'an 5, ff. 112–113v. On the title of the French possessions in India see a report by Wallicz, Paris, 17 Messidor l'an 5, ff. 149–50. On peace with England, see a proposal by G. Bonnecane, 5 Messidor l'an 5, ff. 151–66.

[87] Sen, *The French in India*, pp. 442–43.

[88] AMAE, Vol. 20, 'Politique des Indes, rapport: expose de nos relations avec Tipu Sultan', ff. 150–59.

[89] Ibid., ff. 153v–155. Sen and Hasan briefly refer to the letter (Hasan, *History of Tipu Sultan*, pp. 284–85; Sen, *The French in India*, pp. 530–32).

[90] Ibid., f. 154.

[91] Ibid., report of Lescallier, f. 155.

[92] *Archives Nationales et Coloniales* (Paris), Colonie C(2) 304, No. 45. The treaty is not there among the documents of AMAE, as suggested by Hasan (*History of Tipu Sultan*, 284, fn. 2).

[93] AMAE, Vol. 20, 30 Vendome l'an 6, ff. 216–17.

[94] See Aniruddha Ray, 'France in Madagascar, 1642–1674', *Calcutta Historical Journal* (Calcutta University), 1982, Vol. VI, No. 2, pp. 33–63.

[95] Sen, *The French in India*, p. 535.

[96] Ibid.

[97] Ibid., p. 548.

[98] Ibid., p. 594 post.

[99] See Aniruddha Ray, *The Rebel Nawab: The Revolt of Vizir Ali Khan of Oudh in 1799*, Calcutta, 1991.

[100] Ibid., pp. 193–200.

[101] F. Charles Roux, *L' Angleterre et l'expedition Francaisses en Egypt*, Cairo, 1925, 2 vols.

[102] For a full discussion in English, see Sen, *The French in India*, pp. 555–59, which is a summary of Charles Roux's brilliant thesis.

[103] AMAE, Vol. 11, 'Mémoire sur l'Inde presente au Premier Consul le 5 Prairial an 9 par pierre Dubuc', ff. 270–273v.

[104] Hasan, *History of Tipu Sultan*, pp. 327–28, on the basis of Kirmani's narrative.

Srirangapatnam Revisited

History as Experience rather than Event

Kate Brittlebank

> When the European seized the kingdom of Tipu Sultan
> And murdered him by deception
> In the year of his martyrdom
> In grief and mourning
> The torch of the firmament said
> 'The light of the sun is withdrawn'[1]

On 4 May 1799 the British captured the island fortress of Srirangapattaña, capital of Mysore, and killed its ruler Tipu Sultan. Two hundred years later it is perhaps opportune to reflect upon how we should approach the study of this significant historical event. The following discussion presents several issues that have arisen during an ongoing research project into Tipu's death and the fall of Srirangapatnam. Historiographical in nature, the paper offers some preliminary thoughts on alternative interpretations and how, as historians, we might attempt to recapture the past.

While the basic outline of what happened in 1799 is undoubtedly well known, it will do no harm to provide a brief summary here. Mysore was a powerful kingdom during the second half of the eighteenth century. Tipu's father, Haidar Ali, had seized power from the ruling Wodeyar dynasty in the early 1760s, and his son had succeeded him on his death from natural causes in 1782. Under Haidar and Tipu, the kingdom fought four wars with the British, the last one culminating in Tipu's death as he defended his capital. Following his death, the victors—the British and their ally, the Nizam of Hyderabad—carved up the kingdom between them, leaving a rump state, on the throne of which they placed a child descendant of the Wodeyars. Purnaiya, who had been Tipu's most senior official, agreed to take over the role of

Diwan, or chief minister, thus becoming regent, and a British resident was installed. The court was moved to the town of Mysore and Arthur Wellesley, later Duke of Wellington, was made military commander of Mysore and Srirangapatnam. The island of Srirangapatnam remained under direct British control. (It was in fact Arthur's brother Richard, Lord Mornington, the incumbent Governor-General, whose aggressive policies had ultimately led to Tipu's fall.)

The fall of Srirangapatnam was a crucial event in the establishment of British power in India, and it is this aspect that has been the focus of most research up to now, with little attention having been paid to the Indian response and how it was interpreted on the subcontinent. The present study, therefore, rather than present a narrative account located within the wider Eurocentric historiography of colonial India, seeks to elucidate Tipu's death, the fall and its aftermath, as experienced by local participants and observers who lacked foresight of later developments. Its methodology is informed by Paul Cohen's prize-winning book on the Yi He Tuan or Boxer Rebellion, *History in Three Keys: The Boxers as Event, Experience and Myth.*[2] This innovative work takes the Boxer Rebellion as a case study to discuss in detail the historian's craft, and to suggest different ways in which the past may be understood or interpreted. In so doing, Cohen presents what he suggests are three equally valid ways of writing about the Boxers:

(i) as event, that is, the narrative account of an historical event within the wider historiography of China, written with hindsight;

(ii) as experience, that is, how it was experienced and understood by the participants in the rebellion, who did not have foresight of later events;

(iii) and finally as myth, that is, symbolic representations produced by later propagandists.

These are all ways, he argues, of 'accessing' the past and of 'knowing' it. They are also ways in which the past 'may be configured or shaped';[3] they are, in a sense, different forms of historical consciousness.

Dividing his book into three sections, Cohen first looks at the 'story' of the Boxers, as told by later historians, who have 'foreknowledge of how things turned out, a wide-angle picture of the entire event, and the goal of *explaining* not only the Boxer phenomenon itself but how it was linked up with prior and subsequent historical developments.' The second, and longest, section probes 'the thought, feelings, and behaviour of the immediate participants [both foreign and Chinese] in different phases of the Boxer experience'. Here he addresses the significance of such issues as drought, mass spirit possession, magic and female pollution, rumour and death. Finally, he examines the notions surrounding the Boxers and Boxerism in twentieth-century China.[4]

One need not replicate Cohen's approach entirely, but it does provide means of locating a study of the fall of Mysore historiographically. Although they are separated by 100 years, as historical events the fall of Srirangapatnam and the Boxer Rebellion have much in common. Both have been heavily mythologized. Both have attached to them—in the West and at home—what Cohen describes as a 'potent, if somewhat contradictory, set of myths'.[5]

The mythologizing of Tipu in the west started well before his death, particularly during the third Anglo–Mysore war (1790–92). After Tipu was killed, the victors attempted to justify their invasion by presenting him as an Islamic tyrant and usurper, the archetypal oriental despot, if you like.[6] The invasion had not been well received by the authorities at home. In addition, popular interest in the event in Britain resulted in the production of several plays, as well as triumphant paintings and, later on, novels, the most famous being Wilkie Collins's *The Moonstone*, published in 1868.[7] In India, on the other hand, Tipu's image has been ambiguous. For some he is the first Indian nationalist; for others, particularly more recently, he is a Muslim persecutor of Hindus.[8] During the nineteenth century he served as inspiration for those Indian Muslims who regarded themselves as involved in *jihad.*[9]

Further, both events have come to be seen as 'watersheds' or 'turning points', the Boxers in the history of the late Qing dynasty,[10] the fall of Srirangapatnam in the rise of British colonial power. As Cohen points out, events can be 'enlarged' by consequences, following or ensuing events can give 'considerable retrospective meaning' to them.[11] This has quite clearly been the case with the fall of Mysore and Tipu's death.

By studying the fall of Srirangapatnam and its aftermath as experience rather than event, however, certain issues can be seen to be significant. One of the most important factors in how participants give meaning to their experience is the cultural framework in which they are operating. In this context, I have analysed elsewhere how local Indians responded to Arthur Wellesley in his role as military commander of Mysore and Srirangapatnam.[12] As noted earlier, following Tipu's death, the British placed on the Mysore throne the boy *raja* of the erstwhile Wodeyar dynasty. In their terminology, then, he was Tipu's successor. However, because of the fluid nature of Indian kingship, the fact that the British retained direct control of Srirangapatnam, and because of certain aspects of his behaviour, it was Arthur Wellesley and not the *raja* who was regarded by the Indians as having inherited Tipu's mantle. It was Wellesley, they believed, who was the ultimate authority in the kingdom, and they acted accordingly. The British interpretation of the structures of power, though, was that Wellesley and Barry Close—who was the British resident at the Mysore court— had separate responsibilities: the former was concerned with military affairs and those relating solely to Srirangapatnam, while the latter dealt with all so-called political issues relating to Mysore, and acted as intermediary between the *raja* and the British, including Wellesley. The fact that, to the Indians, Wellesley rather than the newly-installed *raja* had the more obvious attributes of a king, meant that a fair amount of confusion ensued.

Nor did the Indians at this time necessarily regard the British capture of the kingdom as irreversible. We might now see it as such, but we do so with hindsight, within the narrative of British colonial power. Tipu's envoys, for example, whom he had despatched to the Ottoman Sultan to seek assistance, refused to believe that he had been killed when they were given the news in Basra. And even if he had been killed, they argued, since his sons were alive, they would succeed him.[13] In fact, as we shall see later, the existence of Tipu's sons proved to be something of a problem for the British.

In the south, the years immediately following the fall were particularly turbulent.[14] Company rule was not accepted unopposed. Tipu's death had resulted in a regional power vacuum and some looked to use this to their advantage. Others remained loyal to Tipu's memory, refusing to cooperate with the British.[15] Minor and not so minor rebellions occurred, and conspiracies were suspected everywhere. The loss of the powerful Mysore ruler and his court at Srirangapatnam brought about social disruption and financial disadvantage. Many Muslim military men, for example, found themselves in difficult

143

circumstances, since they refused to take service with the British, and regarded other employment, such as agricultural, as beneath them.[16] Royal patronage was an important commercial stimulus on the sub-continent,[17] and those who had depended on the court for their livelihood suffered financially. The weavers of Bangalore who provided the court with luxury cloth are a good example.[18]

If we return to Cohen's analysis, we find that it is just such an environment that is fertile breeding-ground for rumours. Drawing on the research of Ralph Rosnow, he argues that, 'The creation and passing of rumours occurs when there is an optimal combination of four variables: personal anxiety, general uncertainty, credulity, and "outcome-relevant involvement",' meaning 'an individual's personal stake in whether a rumour's content turns out to be true of false'.[19] Cohen sees the study of rumours and their social locus as important since they can provide symbolic information about 'the collective worries of societies in crisis'.[20] It can clearly be argued that south-Indian society at this time was a society in crisis, and the role of rumours is one area that suggests itself as a promising avenue of research. The existence of Tipu's sons, for example, although they were prisoners of the British, provided material for rumours. In April 1800, Arthur Wellesley started getting reports of someone in the south of Mysore raising recruits by masquerading as one of Tipu's sons. He noted that whoever it was had apparently been well received, as he put it, by 'the disaffected in those parts'.[21]

After Tipu's death, his family, including his eldest son Fath Haidar, as well as several other younger sons and all the women, was transported to the fort of Vellore, a military garrison town in the Carnatic, where they were kept in surroundings befitting their royal status until 1806. In that year, the Vellore Mutiny occurred, in which the sepoys rebelled against certain changes in their uniform, particularly with regard to headgear, which they took as evidence of British intentions to convert them by force to Christianity.[22] Tipu's sons were implicated in the uprising and, following its suppression, the family was moved north, to Calcutta. It has not been properly established how involved the sons actually were, and it is clear that the uniform issue was only one of several factors that led to the mutiny.[23] However, C.A. Bayly, in his book on intelligence networks of the British Raj, has noted that during the preceding months wandering puppeteers had been spreading the news that Tipu's sons were about to regain power, with the assistance of the French. Even after their removal from the south, the sons continued to engage in intrigue. Bayly found evidence of links existing between them and the Burmese court, the Marathas, the Gurkha kingdom of Nepal and possibly the Punjab.[25]

Also linked with the mutiny and other uprisings were wandering *faqirs*, or Muslim holy men, who often acted as messengers and were frequently associated with what Susan Bayly has described as millenarian movements. The warrior holy man, *shahid* or martyr, is a potent figure in south Indian Islam, and cults grew around the memory of Tipu and his family. The wandering *faqirs* were sometimes described as 'associates' of the late Mysore ruler.[26] There is an interesting story relating to the disposal by the Seringapatam Prize Committee, responsible for the distribution of booty, of items of Tipu's clothing from the royal wardrobe. The Committee had originally planned to auction the items off, but Wellesley very quickly recognized the symbolic meaning they would hold for local Indians. He noted that if the public auction were not prevented, the clothing would be bought 'by the discontented Moormen of this place. This will not only be disgraceful, but may be very unpleasant.'[27]

More widely, the decline of the Mughals and the rise of British power brought about a new order on the subcontinent, which for many required adaptation and adjustment. Some saw advantages in allying with the British, others opposed them. Many distrusted them. What had happened to Tipu was well known. The Gurkha kingdom, about fifteen years after the fall, used him as an example of why the British could not be trusted. It is clear the Gurkhas feared that if they entered into a treaty with them they would receive similar treatment. In a letter they noted that should the enemy accept their terms he would serve them as he did Tipu from whom he first 'accepted of an indemnification of 6 crores of Rupees in money and in territory, and [then] wrested from him his whole country'.[28]

If we turn to contemporary accounts of the event, they too reveal a range of responses. Most interesting is how Tipu himself is described and the titles attributed to him. He very quickly came to be perceived, not surprisingly, as an Islamic martyr or *shahid*, killed while fighting the infidel.[29] However he is not always styled thus. Mir Hussein Ali Khan Kirmani, who wrote the most well-known history of Haidar and Tipu, refers to him neither as a *shahid* nor as a *ghazi*, a warrior who fights in defence of Islam. Instead, he reverts to titles awarded to him by the Mughal emperor and which Tipu never used. Kirmani, who had been briefly employed by Tipu and his father, was by this stage a pensioner of the British, which undoubtedly accounts for his decision not to use either such terms, nor the grand royal titles used by Tipu himself.[30]

The adoption and granting of titles played an important role in royal ritual. Titles were significant markers of rank and status, and their use was thus tightly controlled. For Indians, they were loaded with meaning; thus, how Tipu is described in chronicles and accounts is a good indicator of the author's attitude towards him. An undated anonymous account, very probably written for the British, devotes one brief final paragraph to the invasion and Tipu's death. This document gives him no titles or epithets, merely calling him 'Tipu Sultan' ('Sultan' is part of his name, not a title, although he is referred to in some accounts as 'the Sultan').[31] These omissions suggest the author had little or no emotional attachment to his subject as a royal personage.[32]

Another undated account, however, treats Tipu very differently. The author's reverential attitude towards him, and his knowledge of events, suggest that he could have been a loyal subject, or at least someone who did not question the Mysore ruler's legitimacy. He refers to Tipu as 'Hazrat Tipu Sultan Shahid Padshah Ghazi, Lord of Karnatak, the Light of God'.[33] The title Hazrat is similar to 'majesty' or 'lordship' and is commonly applied to Sufi saints, as well as other great men. This would accord with Tipu's transformation into something of a cult figure. The title *Padshah* was that adopted by Tipu and is usually translated as 'king'. The Mughals claimed sole use of the title and Tipu's claim to it was not acknowledged by those outside his realm. The author also refers to him as '*shahanshah*', a title I have not seen attached to Tipu before.[34] Meaning 'king of kings', in India this title was usually only associated with the Mughal emperor.

There is actually an ingenuousness about this account because it too appears to have been written for the British. The final paragraph is full of praise for their just treatment, following Tipu's death, of the princes and the women of the family, as well as their munificence in giving pensions.[35] Unlike Kirmani, though, the author has not felt constrained in displaying his reverence for the late ruler, or presenting him as a warrior fearlessly facing death.

How to describe Tipu was a problem even if you were not writing for the British. This is wonderfully demonstrated in a first sketch of a vast general history of India completed in 1825 by Nur Muhammad and dedicated to the then Nawab of the Carnatic, a dependent of the British.[36] Nur Muhammad had spent some years in London, so we can probably assume that he was someone who had adjusted to the British presence in India. Because the work is a draft it contains deletions, alterations and additions, and the author seems to have struggled against an instinctive desire to refer to Haidar and Tipu in a manner that he perhaps later realized was not judicious. Originally describing Tipu as 'the Sultan', he has then clearly changed his mind and gone back and altered it to just 'Tipu'.[37] However, he does not appear to have had a difficulty with describing Tipu as a martyr, although his style is somewhat critical of the late ruler's actions, presenting him as proud and foolish.[38] The *nawabs* of the Carnatic had not on the whole been friendly with Haidar and Tipu, although towards the end there had been some evidence of cordiality, much to the annoyance of the British.

What these texts do is demonstrate that there was no uniformity of response to what happened at Srirangapatnam and its aftermath. Furthermore, they underline the problematic nature of Tipu's position in the hierarchy of the subcontinent, a hierarchy he had vigorously challenged throughout his reign. And most interestingly, they provide glimpses of Indians attempting to adjust to radical changes in the local status quo. In this context, C.A. Bayly has argued that a self-consciously modern Indian historiography really began with post-Mughal elite groups attempting to adjust to change in the political order during the eighteenth century.[39] The texts referred to here could very well be examples of this process.

It is easy to forget, with the benefit of hindsight, that those who experienced and were affected by the fall of Srirangapatnam and its consequences, would not have understood the events as we do 200 years later. For many people the death of Tipu and the ensuing years brought uncertainty and disruption; while some might have prospered, others suffered dramatic changes in fortune. Such an apparently unstable environment led to anxiety, which in turn allowed the proliferation of rumours, often focusing on Tipu's sons. The contemporary accounts examined here also reflect differing responses, reminding us how the needs of the time invariably shape views of the past. It is of course perfectly valid to situate Tipu's death and the fall of Srirangapatnam within the narrative of the rise of British colonial power. But it

147

is not the only way to write about the events. We can approach instead them as would an ethnographer, who has the task of describing the present and has little concern with either future or past. By doing so we can gain a clearer picture of what was happening on the ground, unobscured by later developments, enabling us to improve our understanding of both the processes of change and responses to colonialism during this turbulent transitional period in the history of Mysore and the south.

Notes and References

[1] Chronogram giving the date of Tipu's death. For the Persian text, see Muhammad Karim, *Sawanihat-i-Mumtaz*, Pt. 1, in S. Muhammad Husayn Nainar, trans., *Sources of the History of the Nawwabs of the Carnatic,* 3, Madras, 1939–50, p. 187.

[2] Paul A. Cohen, *History in Three Keys: The Boxers as Event, Experience and Myth,* New York, 1997. I am grateful to Hakan Friberg for drawing this book to my attention.

[3] Ibid., p. 289.

[4] Ibid., p. xiii.

[5] Ibid., p. xii. In terms of the Boxers, in the west they represented the 'Yellow Peril', and in pre-1920s China they were viewed by intellectuals as backward and superstitious. Later in China a more positive image developed, centred on qualities of patriotism and anti-imperialism.

[6] See my *Tipu Sultan's Search for Legitimacy: Islam and Kingship in a Hindu Domain,* Delhi, 1997, pp. 10–12.

[7] See, for example, S.I. Agha, 'Tipu Sultan: Favourite of the British Playwrights', *India Perspectives,* Oct. 1995, pp. 28–29; Anne Buddle, 'The Tipu Mania: Narrative Sketches of the Conquest of Mysore', in Pauline Rohatgi and Pheroza Godrej, *India: A Pageant of Prints,* Bombay, 1989, pp. 53–70; Richard H. Davis, *Lives of Indian Images,* Princeton, 1997, pp. 153–57, 167–74.

[8] *Tipu Sultan's Search for Legitimacy,* pp. 1–2.

[9] Mujeeb Ashraf, *Muslim Attitudes towards British Rule and Western Culture in India,* Delhi, 1982, pp. 169–70, 217.

[10] Cohen, *Three Keys,* p. 22.

[11] Ibid., pp. 20–22.

[12] 'The White Raja of Srirangapattana: Was Arthur Wellesley Tipu Sultan's True Successor?', *Indo–British Review,* Special Edition on Reconstructing South Indian History, in press.

[13] Mohibbul Hasan, *History of Tipu Sultan,* 2nd edn, Calcutta, 1971, p. 301.

[14] See, for example, P. Chinnian, *The First Struggle for Freedom in South India in 1806: Sporadic Events after the Vellore Mutiny,* Erode, 1983; K. Rajayyan, *South Indian Rebellion: The First War of Independence 1800–1801,* Mysore, 1971.

15 Lt. Col. Gurwood, ed., *Despatches of the Field Marshal The Duke of Wellington During his Various Campaigns in India, Denmark, Portugal, Spain, the Low Countries, and France from 1799 to 1818*, London, 1834, 1, p. 125.

16 Francis Buchanan, *Journey from Madras through the Countries of Mysore, Canara, and Malabar*, 3, London, 1807, pp. 258–59.

17 C.A. Bayly, *Rulers, Townsmen and Bazaars: North Indian Society in the Age of British Expansion, 1770–1870*, Cambridge, 1983, pp. 57–63 and *passim*.

18 Buchanan, *Journey from Madras*, 1, p. 221.

19 Cohen, *Three Keys*, p. 147.

20 Ibid., p. 171.

21 Arthur Wellesley, *The Mysore Letters and Dispatches of the Duke of Wellington 1799–1805*, Bangalore, 1862, p. 54.

22 Susan Bayly, *Saints, Goddesses and Kings: Muslims and Christians in South Indian Society 1700–1870*, Cambridge, 1989, p. 226.

23 For an account of the mutiny, see P. Chinnian, *The Vellore Mutiny 1806 (The First Uprising against the British)*, Madras, 1982.

24 C.A. Bayly, *Empire and Information: Intelligence gathering and social communication in India, 1780–1870*, Cambridge, 1996, p. 209. See also Bayly, *Saints, Goddesses and Kings*, p. 226.

25 Bayly, *Empire and Information*, p. 123.

26 Bayly, *Saints, Goddesses and Kings*, p. 226. See Ghulam 'Abdu'l-Qadir Nazir, *Bahar-i-A'zam Jahi*, in Nainar, *Sources*, 5, p. 132, who reports a miraculous occurrence associated with the tomb of Tipu's step-mother, Bakhshi Begum, at Vellore.

27 Cited in Davis, *Lives of Indian Images*, p. 156. See also *The Asiatic Annual Register*, 2, London, 1801, p. 342, where it is stated that the local Muslims planned to purchase the clothing 'as sacred relics of his pretended prophetic and holy character'. This was a reasonable assumption on the part of the British: the chronicler of the *nawabs* of the Carnatic, for example, refers to the practice of distributing as 'sacred relics', items of clothing once worn by the ruler. *Sawanihat-i-Mumtaz*, Pt. 1, Nainar, *Sources*, 3, p. 16.

28 Cited in Bayly, *Empire and Information*, p. 111.

29 See my 'Islamic Responses to the Fall of Srirangapattana and the Death of Tipu Sultan (1799)', in Howard Brasted and Asim Roy (eds), *Islam in History and Politics: South Asian Perspectives*, New Delhi, in press.

30 Meer Hussein Ali Khan Kirmani, *The History of the Reign of Tipu Sultan Being a Continuation of the Neshani Hyduri*, translated by W. Miles, New Delhi, 1980; first published, 1844. Kirmani's history was completed in 1801.

31 'A short historical account of Seringapatan and its Rajahs, their contests with Haidar 'Ali and Tipu Sultan of Mysore, and the final annexation of the district to the English territory, from AH 1144–1214 (AD 1731–1800)', OIOC Pers. MS, Ethé 529.

32 That these accounts are written in Persian is no guarantee, naturally, that the author was a Muslim. Persian was the language of diplomacy and the court, as well as high literature, for both Hindus and Muslims. It continued

to be the language of government for the British until the third decade of the nineteenth century.

33 'Account of Seringapatan, and the contest of its rajahs, with Haidar 'Alikhan and Tipu Sultan, down to the latter Sultan's death, AH 1213 (AD 1799), and the annexation of the territory by the English', OIOC Pers. MS, Ethé 531, f. 60b.

34 Ibid., f. 114b.

35 Ibid.

36 *Siraj al-Tawarikh*, OIOC Pers. MS, Ethé 3009.

37 Ibid., 2, f. 110a and *passim*. The author appears to have had more difficulty with how to refer to Tipu than he had with Haidar, whom he usually refers to as Nawab Haidar 'Ali Khan Bahadur. However, see f. 102b, where he first refers to him as 'the Bahadur' but then changes his mind and replaces it with 'the Naik'.

38 Ibid., ff. 111b, 113b, 114a.

39 Bayly, *Empire and Information*, p. 84.

Appendix:
The Calendar of Tippoo Sultan

Translation by William Kirkpatrick

Before I could proceed in the translation of the following letters,[1] it was necessary that I should acquire some insight into the construction of the Calendar instituted by Tippoo Sultan, and always employed by him, excepting in his correspondence with persons not subjected to his authority, when he condescended to use the common Mahommedan reckoning. Till I could attain this knowledge, it would neither be possible for me to rectify the confusion in the arrangement of the manuscript, occasioned by the accident noticed in the Preface, nor to convert the *Sultan's* dates into the corresponding English dates. Of the necessity of the first of these operations, or the classing of the letters in the order of time, there could be no doubt, since this was absolutely necessary to the right understanding of many of them; while the utility of others, in an historical view, depended, in some measure, on the degree of accuracy with which the dates of the original might be reduced to our chronology.

When, however, I came to examine the means I possessed for this purpose, I found that they were much more scanty than I had supposed them to be: nor have I been so fortunate as to supply the deficiency, by such enquiries as it has been in my power to make in this country. No doubt, the requisite information might have been obtained from India; but the fact is, that it was not until very lately that I discovered the want of any. As it is, I trust that I have, at least, made such an approximation to the truth (if I have not actually arrived at it), as will sufficiently answer the main ends in view.

I have no means of ascertaining with precision, at what period of his reign Tippoo Sultan introduced his first innovation in the Calendar; but there is good reason to believe, that it was about a year after his accession to the *Musnud*. The earliest document in my possession, dated according to his new Calendar, is an edict, or regulation, of the 15th *Jaafury* of the year Uzl (or thirty-eighth of the cycle hereafter explained), corresponding, as I reckon, to the 10th of June 1784: but another, issued about six months anterior to this, or in January 1784, shows that the reformed Calendar was not in use at the latter period, since the edict in question bears no other date than the Mahommedan one of *Zilhijjeh*, A.H. 1197.[2] From these data it may be inferred, that the new Calendar was established some time between January and June 1784.

There is no doubt, that this Calendar was founded on the reckoning i. common use in *Mysore*, which was that of the Malabar cycle of sixty years. To the years composing this cycle, the *Sultan* gave new names; as he did to the months of the year. But though he took the Hindoo computation for his ground-work, he would not appear to have adhered strictly to it, since disagreements between the two reckonings sometimes occur. Thus the 14th *Tulooey* (or ninth month of Tippoo Sultan's year), which was the *Sultan's* birth-day, did not coincide with the 14th, but with the 17th of *Margaiser* or *Ughun* (ninth month of the Hindoo year). The cause of this discrepancy may probably be traced in the following division of the year, according to the *Sultan's* first regulation of it.

Order of the Month	Name	No. of Days	Corresponding with the Hindoo Month and Zodiacal Sign
1st	*Ahmedy*	29	Choiter .... Aries
2nd	*Behary*	30	Bysak .... Taurus
3rd	*Jaafury*	30	Joister (Jait)..................... Gemini
4th	*Daraey*	29	Asar ....Cancer
5th	*Hashimy*	29	Sawan or Srawun .... Leo
6th	*Wasaaey*	30	Bhadon or Bhader .... Virgo
7th	*Zuburjudy*	29	Asin ....Libra
8th	*Hydery*	30	Kartic ....Scorpio
9th	*Tulooey*	29	Margaiser or Ughun ...... Sagittarius
10th	*Yoosufy*	30	Poos .... Capricornus
11th	*Eezidy*	29	Magh .... Aquarius
12th	*Byazy*	30	Phagun .... Pisces

Though the foregoing names are not absolutely unmeaning, yet they would not appear to have had any appropriate signification attached to them; with the exception of the first, called by one of the names of Mahommed, and of the eighth, or *Hydery,* which might possibly have been so denominated in honour of the *Sultan's* father, as *Tulooey* might likewise have been, in allusion to its being the month in which the *Sultan* himself *arose,* or was born. Whether *Behary* had any reference to the spring, in which season it always occurred, is uncertain. Of the whole of these months it is, however, to be observed, that the initial letter of each denotes its place in the Calendar, according to the well-known notation called or *Ubjud,* which assigned a certain numerical power to every letter in the albhabet.[3] There being no single letter to express either 11, or 12, the two first letters of *Eezidy* and *Byazy,* added together, denote the place of each, respectively, in the order of months, viz. 1+10=11; 2+10=12.

I cannot state positively, whether or not these months invariably consisted of the same number of days; but, as far as the documents in *my* possession enable me to judge, it would not appear that any fluctuation took place in this respect. It is here, however, proper to notice, that in the Appendix to Colonel Beatson's book, a memorandum of the *Sultan's* appears (respecting the battle of Suddasir), according to which the month of *Razy* would seem to have consisted of thirty, whereas my table assigns to it only twenty-nine days.[4] I have not the means, at present, of consulting the original document; but it occurs to me as being possible, that the *Sultan* may have written *Sulkh,* or, 'the last day', and that the translator may have supposed the thirtieth to be meant. If this should not be the case, it will not be easy to reconcile the disagreement in question.

The names given to the years of the cycle were formed also on the principle of the *Ubjud* notation, with the exception of the two first years, which were denominated *Ahd* (one or unity), and *Ahmed* (Mahommed), in honour of God and the Prophet; and implying that the latter was the *second,* as the Almighty was the *first* object of veneration. The rest of the names, though like those of the months, not entirely destitute of meaning, had no specific import. They merely denoted the order of each year in the cycle, which was found by adding together the numerical powers of the several letters composing the name, the amount being the number of the year. Thus *Uzl* (the name of the year with which the following correspondence commences) is equivalent to 38 (1+7+30); and denotes that the year, so called, is the thirty-eighth of the cycle (corresponding to AD 1784–85.)

But this arrangement was, after some time, superseded by another; the *Sultan* having, as there is reason to believe, made a second reform of the Calendar, in the forty-first year of the cycle (or AD 1787–88). The latter alteration, however, would not appear to have extended further than to the substitution of new names to the months and years, in the place of those first assigned to them. These new names possessed the same property as the old; namely, that of severally indicating the number of the year, and the order of the month, by virtue of their numerical power. The notation, however, now used was different from the *Ubjud*, and has been called by some *Ubtus* (an unmeaning word, formed by a combination of the first four letters of the alphabet[5]); but is, by the *Sultan* himself, in one of the letters of the present collection, denominated (if there be no error in the manuscrip) *Zur*, and derived by him, but I do not distinctly understand *how*, from the *Koran*. The difference between the two schemes consists in this: in the *Ubjud*, the numerical powers of the letters depend on the order of the latter; in *Ubtus*, or *Zur*, they depend on the order of the letters of the alphabet:[6]

a	1	z	60
b	2	t	70
t	3	z	80
s	4	'a	90
j	5	gh	100
h	6	f	200
kh	7	q	300
d	8	k	400
z	9	l	500
r	10	m	600
z	20	n	700
s	30	w	800
sh	40	h	900
s	50	y	1000

If, as there is reason to think, and as I shall presently endeav-our to show, the new era invented by the *Sultan*, and which he sometimes called the era of Mahommed, and sometimes the *Mow-loody*, or era of the birth (i.e. of Mahommed), was introduced at the same time with the change in the names of the years and months, just described; his motive for the latter innovation was not, perhaps, entirely capricious, but may be safely referred, in some measure, to his zeal for the glory of his religion. As the new epoch was, no doubt, designed to do honour to the Prophet whom he seems to have thought degraded by the designation given to that in common use,[7] so, probably, were the new names of the years and months, which, instead of being formed upon a vulgar or profane practice, were now constituted upon a principle, sanctified, as it would seem, by the word of the law. Be this, however, as it may, there are good grounds for believing, that the new era, and the second regulation respecting the names of the years and months, took place together, and that the use of both commenced with the forty-first year of the Malabar cycle.

It happens unfortunately, that one of the chasms in the following correspondence occurs at that very period; there not being a single letter of the forty-first year in the collection, nor any document whatever, of that date, among the papers in my possession. But though we are, by this means, deprived of any direct or positive proof on the subject, yet there are not wanting circumstances that afford, what will probably be deemed a sufficient presumption in favour of the opinion I have offered.

1st. In a letter to his diplomatic agents at *Dehli*, dated in *Hydery* (or eighth month) of the fortieth year (*Dullo*), the *Sultan* enumerated the names of the years and months, according to the second or new arrangement, which he had then probably determined on, but which he certainly did not carry into effect during the remainder of the fortieth year, as abundantly appears from existing documents. The letter here referred to is manifestly imperfect; otherwise we might have learnt from it, why the arrangement in question was announced so long before the period of its actual adoption. Possibly the great distance of *Dehli* may have suggested the expediency of an anticipated communication.

2d. It is established by a variety of documents, that both the new nomenclature and the new era were in use in the forty-second year of the cycle, which was accordingly called *Sara*; whereas, under the preceding arrangement, it would have been named *Kubk*.

3d. It is improbable, that the *Sultan*, after announcing the new nomenclature, so early as *Hydery* of the fortieth year, should have delayed the introduction of it till the forty-second year, or *Jara*: it is, therefore, most likely, that it commenced with the forty-first year, which, in this case, would be called *Sha*, while, according to the former rule it would be *Ma*.

4th. In a letter, dated the 29th *Eezidy* (eleventh month) of *Dullo*, or the fortieth year, the *Sultan* directs an enquiry to be instituted among the learned men in different parts of his dominions, for the purpose of ascertaining, with exactness, the respective dates of the birth, mission, and flight of the Prophet. An explanation of the cause of the *Higera*, or flight, is also required by this letter. This investigation seems to have been preparatory to the establishment of the epoch under consideration.

5th. But the most unequivocal of the *Mowloody* era having been established in the forty-first year, is furnished by a decree, or regulation, of the year *Rasikh*, or forty-eighth of the cycle (corresponding to the 1209th year of the *Higera*), to which a seal is affixed, bearing the date 1215.[8] Now as this date could not be meant for the *Higera*, it must, of necessity, have been intended to denote the year of Mahommed. The 1215th year of Mahommed coincided with the forty-first of the cycle: and as we know that the *Mowloody* era was not in use during the fortieth of the cycle (or *Dullo*), it necessarily follows, that the seal in question was engraved in the *first* year of the institution of that epoch.

I will add here the few remaining observations that I have to make on the subject of the *Mowloody* era, and then return to the consideration of the Calendar.

As this era was not adopted till after the time to which the letters in the present volume reach [November 1793], it was not absolutely necessary to my immediate purpose, to have offered any explanation of it: but being upon the subject of the *Sultan's* Calendar, I thought it right to state what I knew, respecting so prominent an article of it. Even in the later documents, wherein it pretty constantly occurs, it is of little or no use in fixing the date of any letter, regulation, or transaction; since it is generally, if not invariably, accompanied by the year of the cycle. The first time that I meet with it is in an edict of the year *Sard*, or forty-second of the cycle (and 1216 of Mahommed). It is continually employed, however, in the *Sultan's* Memoir of his own reign, where it is applied even to events which took place many years before its actual introduction. Thus, among other instances, Hyder Ali

Khan is said to have died on Saturday, the 3d of *Zakiry* 'of the year of Mahommed 1209'. But of these Memoirs it is to be observed, that they bear internal evidence of having been composed subsequently to the peace of *Seringapatam*, in 1792.

The term *Mowloody*, strictly considered, is certainly not applicable to the era in question; according to which there would appear to have been no more than an interval of thirteen years between the birth and flight of Mahommed. It has been conjectured, that, instead of the birth, this era was, in fact, reckoned from the mission of Mahommed, or the period when he first announced himself as the messenger of God: and this notion receives some countenance, from the tenor of the enquiry spoken of above, which strongly implies a dislike of the term *Higera*, and an intention to sink the event it alludes to, in a reference to one of a more dignified and memorable kind. But, even in this view of the matter, it is difficult to account for the new era being called *Mowloody*, rather than *Nuboowet;* unless it be supposed, that the *birth* was put as a metonymy for the regeneration of the Prophet, which might be reckoned from the commencement of his mission.[9]

I now resume my account of the Calendar, which was interrupted by this digression concerning the *Mowloody* era.

The names of the months, according to the second and latest arrangement, became as follows:

1st month *Ahmedy*, being the same as in the former scheme.

2d. .... *Behary* —do—

3rd. .... *Tuky*

4th. .... *Sumry*

5th .... *Jaafury*, being the third month of the former scheme.

6th .... *Hydery*, being the eighth —do—

7th .... *Khusrowy*

8th .... *Deeny*

9th .... *Zakiry*

10th ...... *Rehmany*

11th ...... *Razy*

12th ...... *Rubbany*

The eleventh and twelfth months are here indicated, as in the former scheme, by the first two letters of their respective names, (*ra*) being 10+1; and *r(u)b*, 10+2.

Although I could present the reader with a table, exhibiting the names of every year in the cycle, according to both the schemes which have been described, yet it would answer no useful purpose, that will not be equally accomplished by the following abridgement, including only the years of Tippoo Sultan's reign.

Year of the Cycle	Name according to the First Scheme	Name according to the Second Scheme	Corresponding with AD
36	Jebal	Rub-taz	1782–3
37	Zuky	Sukh..........	1783–4
38	Uzl	Sukha	1784–5
39	Jullo	Duraz	1785–6
40	Dullo	Busd	1786–7
41	Ma	Sha	1787–8
42	Kubk	Sara	1788–9
43	Jum	Surab	1789–90
44	Jam	Sheta	1790–1
45	Adam	Zuburjud	1791–2
46	Wuly	Sehr	1792–3
47	Waly	Sahir	1793–4
48	Kaukub..........	Rasikh	1794–5
49	Kuwakib	Shad	1795–6
50	Yum	Hiraset	1796–7
51	Duwam	Saz	1797–8
52	Ilumd	Shadab	1798–9
53	Hamid	Barish	1799

It is worthy of remark, that the name of the last of these years, or *Barish*, signifying *rain*, was changed by the *Sultan*, only a short time before his death, to *Bashir*;[10] which meaning *joyful*, or *auspicious*, he thought a word of better omen than the other. But it did not prove such to him; for on the last day of *Ahmedy* (first month) of that very year, he lost his life, and the sovereignty of *Mysore* passed away from the *Khodadad Sircar*,[11] to the hands of those, towards whom he ever cherished the most deep and irreconcileable hatred; paralleled, perhaps, only by that borne, in ancient times, by Hannibal against the Romans.

It will be seen, by the table of months inserted earlier, that the *Sultan's* year, though considered by him as solar, consisted of no more than 354 days. In order, therefore, to correct this reckoning, and to approximate it to the true solar time, he occasionally added a *thirteenth* month to the year. I say, *occasionally:* because I have not been able to discover (if, as is probable, there existed) any fixed rule for determining either the return of the leap year, or the period of such year, at which the intercalary or supplementary month was to be introduced. It is stated in some of my notes, collected at *Seringapatam,* that every third year was considered as embolismal, and that the supplementary month was always inserted, according to one account, after the tenth, and, according to another, after the eleventh month. But each of these statements is clearly proved to be wrong by a variety of authentic documents, showing that the thirty-ninth, forty-fourth, forty-seventh, forty-ninth and fifty-second of the cycle were leap years. On what year, between thirty-nine and forty-four, leap year fell is not known, owing to the want of documents for that period: but whether we suppose it to have been the forty-first or forty-second year, it will be equally manifest, that the embolismal year did not uniformly occur every third year. The same thing is shown by the fact of the forty-seventh and forty-ninth years having both been leap years. It is a known rule that to make the solar and lunar years accord, *seven* returns of the intercalary, or supplementary month, are required in the course of *nineteen* years. Now from the thirty-fifth to the fifty-third year of the cycle (both inclusive) is a period of nineteen years, in the course of which seven leap years occur, (*viz.* five which are clearly ascertained, and two which have been assumed). But, notwithstanding this apparent conformity, the two reckonings do not coincide, when, according to this rule, they might be expected to do so. The reason of this disagreement, no doubt, is, that though the months established by Tippoo were ordinarily called *lunar,* they were not strictly so; six of the twelve months of the year having consisted of thirty, and the other six of twenty-nine days each: the common year, therefore, comprising 354 days, was, in fact, neither *lunar* nor *solar.*

The documents abundantly prove, that the intercalary, or supplementary month, called by the *Sultan Zaid* (as *zaid Ahmedy, zaid*

159

Behary, &c., according to the month *before*[12] which it was inserted) was not added at any fixed or regulated period of the year, but, apparently, according to his fancy: at least I have not met with any clue to the principle (if principle there was) on which it was arranged. All that is certain is, that in the thirty-ninth year the *Zaid,* or adscititious month, was *Ahmedy;* in the forty-fourth year, *Sumry;* in the forty-seventh year, *Behary;* in the forty-ninth year, *Hydery;* and the fifty-second year, *Jaafury:* by which unquestionable facts it appears, that in no one instance, in so many years, did it happen to fall either on the tenth or eleventh month.

But although so much uncertainly prevails on this article, yet being apprised, as we are, that the first day of the fifty-third year coincided with the 6th April 1799, and knowing, also, both the names of the leap-years, and of the supplementary months which occurred between that time and the forty-fourth year, inclusive, we are fortunately enabled to convert the *Sultan*'s dates, during that period, with sufficient accuracy into our own. It is after passing, in a retrogade progression, the forty-fourth year, that the principal difficulty commences; since there are, at present, no means of ascertaining in what year, between that and the thirty-ninth, the leap-year occurred, or at what period of such year the intercalary month was added.

In this difficulty I could only arrive at the fortieth and thirty-ninth years (so essential to my immediate purpose, on account of the principal portion of the following letters belonging to those years) by assuming, at a venture, one of the intervening years, between forty-four and thirty-nine, as the leap-year. I therefore fixed upon *Sara,* or the forty-second year, by which means something like system and regularity is made to appear in the recurrence of the embolism; which, by this distribution, would seem to have returned (as far as our materials enable us to judge) alternately, every third and every second year: that is to say, in the thirty-ninth, forty-second, forty-fourth, forty-seventh, forty-ninth, and fifty-second. With regard to the supplementary month of the assumed leap-year, I was obliged to resort to the same expedient; and, accordingly, fixed on the third month, or *Tuky.* By this means, each of the first six months of the year (though not in regular succession) will appear to have served as the intercalary months, three of them being months of thirty days, and the three others months of twenty-nine days. Hence the leap years, thirty-nine, forty-four, and fifty-two, are made to contain 383 days; and the leap-

Appendix

years, forty-two, forty-seven, and forty-nine, each 384 days.[13]

Having constructed my table of corresponding dates in the best manner I could, with the imperfect materials in my possession, I was, fortunately, enabled to verify or correct the same, by means of a practice occasionally observed by the *Sultan*, of giving the day of the week along with the day of the month. An instance of this kind occurs in Letter CCCIV, which led to the discovery of an error I had committed, in converting the 18th of *Jaafury* of the year *Dullo* into our reckoning. I had made it agree with the 20th *June*, which fell on a Tuesday; while the 18th of *Jaafury* being expressly stated to have been a Wednesday, must, of course, have coincided with the 21st June 1786. The detection of this mistake necessarily led to an alteration of the whole series of my dates for the two years comprised in the present volume,[14] every one of which it became requisite to advance *one* day. This correction leaves scarcely any doubt of the perfect accuracy of the dates as now adjusted. The only point in which any mistake can have occurred, is in the number of days assigned to *extra Ahmedy* of the year *Jullo:* for though it is known, that regular *Ahmedy* consisted of twenty-nine days, it is not *certain*, (however probable) that the extra, or supplementary month, always had the same number of days as the regular month of the like name.

This is all that it has been in my power to do, with a view to the attainment of the accuracy so desirable on the present occasion. I trust I have not fallen into any material error. For the rest, I rely on the indulgence of the reader.

Notes and References

[1] [This note, 'Remarks Explanatory of the Kalendar of Tippoo Sultan', is placed immediately after the Preface to William Kirkpatrick's *Select Letters of Tippoo Sultan to Various Public Functionaries*, London, 1911. It is reproduced here with some spellings, such as that of 'calendar' ('kalendar' in Kirkpatrick), modernized—editor.]

[2] Hyder Ali died on the 1st of Mohurrem of this year.

[3] The nonsense verse (after the first word of which this notation is called) as well as the numerical power assigned severally to the letters composing it, may be seen in Richardson's dictionary, under the word *abjud.*

[4] [It will be seen that there is no month named *Razy* in Kirkpatrick's own table above, but from the table of months under a new nomenclature introduced later on, the name *Razy* was substituted for *Eezidy*, the eleventh month—editor.]

5 The Persian letter *pe* being excluded from this scheme, as well as from the *Ubjud*. The Persian letters, *gaf, che* and *zhe*, are in like manner, omitted in both.

6 [The following table presents the numerical values given to letters in Tipu Sultan in a different style than in Kirkpatrick's original table, since, unlike him we have not reproduced the Arabic letters. The arrangement of the alphabet being given, there should be no difficulty in identifying the Arabic letter corresponding to the English in the table—editor.]

7 *Higera* signifies flight. See the *Sultan's* letter [referred to in the main text below].

8 It is usual in India to insert in the seal the year in which it is engraved.

9 [There is no doubt that Tipu Sultan had calculated from the presumed year of birth of the Prophet. His Mauludi era was a solar era, so that if Haidar Ali died in the Mauludi era 1209, its epoch must have lain in AD 573. Tipu, then, must have thought either AD 573 or 574 (depending on whether he allowed his era a 'zero' year) to have been the year of the Prophet's birth—editor.]

10 *Bashir*, consisting of the same letters as *Barish*, has the same numerical power, both words standing for fifty-three.

11 i.e. 'the State or Government by God', which was one of the terms by which the *Sultan* designated his government. The *Ahmedy Sircar* was another. In some places he calls the *Hydery Sircar*, and in others the *Usud-Ilhye*; the former of which might refer to his father's name: but it might, also, like that of *Usud-Ilhye*, allude to *Ali*, one of whose apellations was *Hyder*.

12 The extra, or supplementary month, always preceded the regular month of the same name, for what reason does not appear. Its natural place one would suppose to have been *after* not *before*, the month whose name it took.

13 According to this arrangement, it is evident that, though the *Sultan's* year was in general eleven days shorter than the common year in use with us, yet, owing to the frequent recurrence of his intercalary month (making his leap-year 383, or 384 days) his reckoning must, in a series of years have gained considerably upon ours; apparently no less than at the rate of three days in five years.

14 [The volume, of course, is Kirkpatrick's *Select Letters of Tippoo Sultan*, from which this Appendix is taken—editor.]

Contributors

KATE BRITTLEBANK, Associate Professor, Manash University, Australia.

NIKHILES GUHA, Reader, Department of History, Kalyani University, Nadia, West Bengal.

IQBAL HUSAIN, Professor of History (retired), Aligarh Muslim University, Aligarh.

I.G. KHAN, Reader in History, Aligarh Muslim University, Aligarh.

JEAN-MARIE LAFONT, Senior Fellow CSH, French Embassy, New Delhi.

ANIRUDDHA RAY, Professor of History, Calcutta University, Kolkata.

Index

Index

Index